The Hidden Gift in Divorce

*How to Find Hope, Healing
And Spiritual Growth
When Your Marriage Ends*

Booklocker.com, Inc.
2002

The Hidden Gift in Divorce

*How to Find Hope, Healing
And Spiritual Growth
When Your Marriage Ends*

Mark C. Brown, Ph.D.

To All Our Guides

And so long as you haven't experienced
This: to die and so to grow,
You are only a troubled guest
On the dark earth.

Goethe

Contents

Acknowledgments

As much as writing a book requires incredible individual effort, there is just no completing the task without the help of others. With this clearly in mind, I would like to express my heartfelt gratitude to my friends Jan Assini, Alan Bachers, Jim Brown, and Elizabeth Colebrook for their contributions all along the way.

I owe special thanks to my San Francisco connection, book midwife Caroline Pincus, for her excellent editing, and for her extraordinary combination of warmth and enthusiasm, and personal and professional encouragement, guidance and affirmation. She was a treat to work with.

To Cindy Brown, my wife and original "in-house" editor, I offer my highest appreciation for her faith in this project, her intelligent and insightful observations and suggestions all during its unfoldment, and for her nurturance during the unavoidable dark times.

Finally, I wish to thank my clients whose stories helped shape this work. In all cases cited herein, I have changed identifying information to protect privacy.

Introduction

I once asked a client whom I had helped through an unwanted divorce how she felt about herself now that it was over. She said that in spite of all she had been through, she believed that she was a better person for the experience. I thought so, too.

What we had both seen in her was a profound shift from a life of feeling dependent, self-rejecting and self-disregarding, which seemed to be justified by her husband's decision to leave, to one of self-support and self-affirmation for the first time. She had accomplished this despite the early belief that being divorced was an unmistakable sign of personal failure.

Her path to this new place of growth and deliverance traversed all of the feelings we normally struggle with including rejection, shame, fear and anger. She had risen above all of these to become something special in her own eyes. Significantly, her next man reflected this enhanced self-image. Her ability to change astounded her and filled her with a sense of awe and gratitude about life, love and relationships she had never before imagined. No mere casualty was she.

By the time I faced my own divorce a short while later, I had been a psychotherapist for nearly twenty years. Ironically, it seemed that none of the work I had done with others prepared me for what I was about to go through. In spite of my experience in helping others, I was a fledgling perched on the edge of a very high nest, about to be shoved out into the ethers.

Like most of my divorcing clients, my feelings were intensely mixed. Twenty-two years of marriage, most of it good, weighed heavily against change, and I did not want to hurt anybody. At the same time, I was waking up each day with the feeling that I was dying. The image that kept coming to me was of a tiny man being pressed down under successive petal-shaped layers of concrete, one folding on top of the next like a flower poised to bloom, but capable at the same time of closing with a crushing finality. The challenge was to use all of my strength to force it open, or be entombed forever. All that motivated me in the direction of leaving was an intuition that said I needed to go because I did not belong there anymore.

During this time I never remembered feeling worse. I had seen a six-year-old son through open-heart surgery, and I thought nothing would ever match that experience. I was wrong. With choosing divorce I was violating everything I believed in about love and marriage. I was marching against the beliefs that guided me with clients who were considering divorce. As a conventionally trained marital therapist, it was my job to save marriages, and now I was performing the execution myself. I was quite aware of the existing data about divorce outcome, and I had used this information to discourage clients from pursuing a marital split. My position had always been that divorce was a social ill.

While struggling with my decision to leave, I realized that the people whom I most admired had all been through the divorce experience. This discovery amazed me, partly because I simply never had thought such a thing before then; partly because a forever-kind-of-marriage had always been what I considered success; but most importantly because I began to understand how much these people had grown. They just seemed to have learned something I did not know yet, and they seemed steadier, more mature, and in an inexplicable way, more advanced because of it.

One of the people who helped me most was a Unity minister who herself had been divorced twice. She once said that two failed marriages is a prerequisite for a Unity minister, and probably half-jokingly revealed a truth about necessary change and growth if one is to be a healer of others on a similar journey.

By the time I sought a therapist of my own, it was clear to me that he would had to have been through the experience of divorce himself, because I intuited that the knowledge he would have gained therein would be crucial to my own healing and growth. I knew by then that while to some people separation from the marital state is a disaster, it can also send many people to a whole new place of awareness not available to the uninitiated, and I wanted to speak with someone who knew the language. I sensed that there was much for me to gain as a therapist if I could do this right. Without fully comprehending what it meant, I told him I wanted to become more than a therapist; I wanted to become a healer. Divorce gave me that opportunity.

What subsequently occurred was a most unexpected development. There was a fundamental change in the way I looked at things, the most prominent being, of course, how I viewed the demise of a long-term marriage.

Like most people, I had always thought of divorce as a bad thing, an unfortunate development, something to be avoided, a failure to be ashamed of. To my thinking, the best of us had solid marriages. We were the rock, the foundation. We knew the secret of happiness and contentment. We held the high ground. I was quickly learning otherwise. I was able to see the positive side of this change process from the perspective of people such as my client who had been left by another and did a wonderful job of moving forward, and increasingly from my own perspective as one who needed to grow but did not know that this is what was motivating him.

As a result, what I know now is that there is a way of looking at marriage and divorce that does not require that either state be superior or inferior to the other. There is no use in an endless debate regarding goodness or badness, as no overriding value rests solely with one or the other. Without a doubt, we can do better than to waste time and energy fighting a moral civil war over something that is so common, necessary, and in many instances unavoidable.

It is clear to me that there is every reason for us to become more openly accepting and supportive of the process of divorce. A marriage in which growth has ended is in need of a resolution, just as a physical body in which there is no hope for a return to health is in need of release.

For many of us, this death can be the first step toward a resurrection, a transformation in how we look at life, love, and happiness. We just have to shift from an emphasis of keeping marriages alive at any cost to one in which the healing and growth of the individuals in the marriage are the main focus. When this is true, everyone benefits, whether the marriage continues or not.

Divorce need not be looked at negatively. Done appropriately, divorce can lead to personal growth, not loss. From the right perspective, it is a process of reaching for more rather than settling for less.

As it currently stands, the process of separation and divorce is one of the two or three most difficult experiences that human beings go through. This is true both for the person who initiates the process and for the one who wants to hold to the marital status quo. Realistically speaking, there is probably no way divorce can be anything but difficult because of our natural reactions to change and loss.

What may be possible, however, is to reduce the difficulty of the divorce experience so that those who are involved might encounter only the suffering that is truly necessary as a part of normal grief. There would be great value in such attenuation, not only in terms of lessening the pain, but also in terms of restricting the various kinds of damage incurred in divorce as it is presently practiced.

The courts to some extent have already recognized the reasonableness of making divorce less onerous, as the no-fault divorce, prescribed mediation and court-ordered parenting classes for divorcing parents suggest. These systemic changes represent alterations in what might be thought of as the outer process of ending a marriage. Without question, they have had a useful impact.

However, there has been little change in the inner process of divorce which involves attitude, and which ultimately affects us most. It is only in the inner process that significant changes involving healing and growth can occur. It is therefore with the inner process that this book is concerned.

This book was written with the belief that it will be helpful to everyone, even those who are inclined to remain bitter, or who just want to get on with life as before. We just never know where change is going to lead us. However, it is specifically designed for the person who is ready to trust that his or her separation is a necessary part of a meaningful and positive journey, a spiritual journey, and that he or she will be better for having walked its path.

An early reviewer of the manuscript of this book suggested that my perspective on divorce was too narrowly positive and that I was soft-pedaling the hardship in divorce to make an unrealistic case for the benefits. I believe that he had not had an experience similar to mine, and that he therefore thought my view amounted to opinion rather than knowledge.

There was a time before my divorce that I would have agreed with him regarding anyone who had written this way. However, as difficult as it was, my divorce was an awakening, and an initiation to a level of perception that has grown since that time. The spiritual perspective I am inviting the reader to explore is not something that I was taught; in fact, it was something I resisted, probably as did my critic.

As a psychologist I am aware of the phenomenon of projection, and how an enthusiast on any topic must be careful about universalizing his or her point of view. As a psychotherapist, I am also careful to listen to people in order to determine where they are in their own personal progression before sharing this perspective as a course of treatment. As a writer, however, I do not feel the same professional constraints. Because my awakening to the point of view presented in this book was profound and undeniable, I have a real desire to share it.

Since the time of my awakening I have read and have spoken to many others about similar experiences, whether through divorce or some other life-changing event. I have also seen the changes this perspective has wrought with clients who would otherwise have sunk into bitterness and despair, and have watched them heal and grow instead. Therefore, it would seem a disservice not to provide it as an alternative to the negative perspective that it dispels.

What my critic so helpfully did was to illuminate a contemporary problem. People who have not experienced an awakening to a spiritual view have difficulty believing that the new territory exists, and they will continue to perceive the old as the limit of what is possible despite its being so negative and constricting. Having once lived within the limits of conventional beliefs, people who have had an awakening to the new perspective will acknowledge the old boundaries, but having already seen beyond them, will want to depart the old for the new. However, in trying to do so, they may initially encounter more skeptics than supporters, and may from time-to-time question their own perception. This book is written to provide assistance.

A special note to the reader: because the healing process in divorce is relatively circuitous and timeless, and is different for everyone, I have organized the chapters of this book with something other than a rigid notion of the stages of adjustment to divorce in mind. Nonetheless, I

believe that readers will benefit most by reading the book from
beginning to end before focusing on specific chapters separately, as this
will accentuate the special healing influence that I have built into it.

1
In Search of a Healing Perspective

How could this happen? Why didn't I see it coming? Does love just leave? Will the pain ever end? Will I ever be happy again? Why me? Why us? Why now?

Divorce is difficult: it is hard on our bodies, our minds, our hearts, and our souls. We lose sleep, weight, strength, concentration, judgment, faith, and peace. It can numb our consciousness and blacken our mood. And it can reveal a darker side of us, our mates, our friends, and our life than we might have ever imagined.

Everyone suffers in a divorce. Like death, it is a great equalizer that spares no one. Because our own suffering can make us insensitive to those around us, we may not recognize the pain of our mate, children, family and friends; but it is always there.

At its best divorce is one of those things that we consider bad even when it leads to a better life. This attitude results partly from our fear of endings and loss, and partly because for a long while our suffering seems to outweigh any benefits we might gain.

But there is also something deeper about our aversion to divorce that is part of the cultural heritage we grow up with: in addition to all of the other troubling aspects of ending a marriage, in our society many people still consider divorce a senseless loss and a personal failure. Admit it or not, we unconsciously hold that anything other than being married is second best, which is why we often stay in bad marriages, and why we feel sorry for people who divorce even when we are not so happily married ourselves.

I know that people who divorce are not failures, and that divorce is not the senseless loss it is made out to be, but I also know that just saying so will not eliminate the gnawing suspicion, especially among those who are struggling with a divorce right now. But if we can keep from being defeated by our bad feelings we have a chance to find a healing perspective, a belief that like other natural changes, divorce is a prelude to growth and an important opportunity for gain.

More than most experiences, divorce can open a world of discovery about our selves and our place in life that being forever married can conceal.

This statement is not a therapist's balm to reassure those who have failed; it is a fact. From the right perspective we will see that separation and divorce provide a wealth of learning that is impossible when we are continuously in long-term relationships, even good ones.

The healing perspective is based on an observation that might seem simplistic and overly optimistic, and yet upon deep consideration is a source of understanding that can make a complex life easier to grasp, and provide hope. This observation is that by natural and supernatural design everything in life, including separations and divorces, is meant to advance our growth, and that we not only have the potential to advance, it is our obligation to take every opportunity to do so.

This being the case, we should be able to find within separation and divorce the elements that would assure personal development, and indeed they are there if we can see them. We only have to shift our view from the temporal plane to the spiritual dimension to find them.

The shift is not complicated. Even in our darkest moments, most of us believe that we have been created with a purpose; we have the spiritual sense that each of our lives tells a story. The healing perspective merely involves holding to that belief while we slowly learn how our divorce fits the rest of the theme. If we follow through, we should find that rather than clouding the story divorce helps reveal it in all its complexity: why we are here, what we are to accomplish against what barriers, and how being separated from a committed long-term relationship can help us fulfill our purpose.

I would not be surprised that anyone's first response to this would be skepticism. It is too easy to cite the apparent destructiveness of divorce to counter this idea and to write it off as another New Ageism that hardly reflects the reality of ending a marriage.

I would say in turn that the divorce experiences of many people I have known, including my own, actually prove the point. What is required is the willingness to allow for the possibility that there may be something positive behind the constant high rate of marital endings regardless of our personal fear and the doomsday attitude of our society.

The Journey

To change perspectives, we start with the consideration that everything we go through as human beings is part of a divine plan for our development. We are not here by accident; our lives are filled with meaning and purpose, and it is our work to discover how each of our experiences fits the blueprint. Embracing the age-old concept of life as a spiritual journey is a tremendous aid to seeing that all of our human experiences are necessary - and potentially good.

As with any journey, there are times of effortless flow, getting tired, resting, feeling lost, retracing steps, becoming discouraged, but mostly forward movement. This is the heart and soul of the journey in which heart represents the lighter, more expansive and simple spiritual side of us and soul represents the heavier, more compressed and complex human side.

In daily living, things of the heart are illuminated by love, which includes the love we have for each other and the love life has for us. In contrast, things of the soul are found in the shadows of life, and generally include the requirements of physical and psychological survival. At their extremes, the heart floats above life's concerns, and the soul sinks deeply into them. The heartfelt activities are those that we want to do, the soulful activities are those that we have to do, like leisure and toil where one restores us and the other slowly uses us up.

On this spiritual journey there is no one path; no one right way for everyone to go. All the paths are unique, combining heart and soul in particular ways that reflect the variety of Creation and allow each of us some sense of control by way of free will as to how we will look at our choices and what we will do with them. Uniqueness and free will underscore the importance of us as individuals in the journey of life. None of us actually shares our path with anyone else. We may walk parallel with each other for varying distances, but in fact we come into and go out of life alone, which implies being essentially solitary for the whole journey.

In regard to marriage, this is not bad or sad, nor should it be scary. Everyone will agree that part of the work of growing up is to become an individual. But when we wed in our youth, and then follow one marriage quickly with another, going from one dependent relationship, the family, to another, the marriage, we lessen our chances of ever getting to know "us" apart from others.

This is not to say that there is anything wrong with wanting a continuous sense of belonging; among other things our attachments help us feel grounded and safe. But if we look closely we will see that we tend to identify our selves mainly in association with others. In fact, blending is considered ideal: losing our self in another is our image of the highest love.

But our journeys need balance. This is true of all aspects of life. When we are out of balance, something usually gives it away; some consequence such as sickness, boredom, fatigue or resentment results and forces us to think about change.

The same may be true of the natural place for separation as we travel through married life.   For many of us, breaking up may be the interpersonal version of a response to imbalance. The urge to change by one or both of the mates may be a sign that our life is seriously skewed, only we do not think about it in this way because it is so contrary to our cultural ideal, and because our desire to be married is so strong.

But healthy spiritual development demands balance, especially in the area of self and other, and it may only be when we are forced to be truly alone, and we get used to it, that many of us discover that being bonded to someone else is not the only desirable state. We may not be in any shape emotionally to comprehend it as it is happening, but the dissolution of our marriage may truly set us free to grow in ways we may have never imagined.

My Awakening to Growth

I feel certain that life is essentially about spiritual growth, and that unexpected change always has a hand in it. I am also convinced that fundamental growth, where we gain a whole new way of looking at the world, results from unexpected changes that are so powerful that they make us reconsider our beliefs. When our concepts have to evolve to fit our new experiences, we grow.

I did not always think this way, however. For most of my adult life I saw growth as something we tried to accomplish under controlled conditions, where we know what the motives for it are and have a pretty good idea what the outcome will be. I thought of traumatic changes as more likely to hinder growth than encourage it, and I therefore wanted to prevent them. This was especially true of separation and divorce.

Then, when I had been married just over ten years, the near loss of my son to a defective heart started a course of change within me that ultimately involved a divorce, although I had no inkling of it at the time.

As frequently happens, once the emergency with my son was over and he was safe, I went into an emotional tailspin. Sleeping fitfully over the next several months, I had several lucid dreams. Two powerful ones came in quick succession and seemed related, although I could not understand just how. No matter: they made perfect sense ten years later when I was in the process of separation.

In the first of them, I was in the bow of a sleek powerboat with my father confidently at the helm. We were relaxed and happy. He drove the boat across a lake that was funneled into a white channel, which began to go upward into a brilliant sky. The channel narrowed sharply to a terminus where we crashed, sending me tumbling over the bow, down through the air to the soft earth of a tropical bog. I lay there shocked, and before long a search party headed by my then-wife snaked through the undergrowth and found me.

The meaning of the dream seemed clear. Like others who needed to believe that their family history was better than it was, I had distorted the facts of an unhappy childhood into a survivable fiction. In truth, my life had not been relaxed and happy, and I was particularly disappointed in my relationship with my father.

I thought that the dream showed that I was finally being rescued after having felt abandoned and lost. I concluded that it was my marriage (rather than surviving the terrifying experience with my own son) that had given me the foundation I needed to safely explore and grieve the past. It seemed reasonable to think that being loved by my wife had helped me make a transition from illusion to truth.

I know that this interpretation fit my belief about love and personal development: someone special comes into a gloomy life and makes it bright. That is what I had counted on. With marriage, life seemed complete, and I was grateful.

But then there was the second dream. In it I was walking alone one night on a dark path away from the city lights, out into the dim isolation of the countryside. The sky was overcast and I could barely see. As I passed a small lake, someone called to me for help. A man was drowning and I was the only one around. I hurriedly waded out to him, by which time he had gone completely under the gray water. I frantically grabbed for his hair, and as I lifted his head I saw that the face was mine. I awoke breathless!

This mysterious dream made no sense, and it troubled me. Although it seemed somehow congruent with my experience with my son, unlike the previous dream, I had no frame of reference for this one. While I could intuit that it was deeply significant, I could not begin to fathom its meaning.

What was I to make of a dark journey in which I save my drowning self? And why would such a dream follow the other so closely? Although I did not understand it, I did not forget it, either.

It is interesting that, when newly separated about ten years later and trying to explain my need to leave, I recalled these dreams to my estranged wife. She said that I had told her about the first one, but not the second. It had never occurred to me that I had kept it to myself, but indeed I had, and I knew then why.

Both of the dreams were about my life's journey, but they told different stories. The first dream I think of as a reflection of the conventional path in life, one that I, like most of us, had thought of as mirroring reality and had wanted to follow. After all, it represented the fairy tale; an emotional rags-to-riches love story that fits our cherished image of falling in love and achieving the marital dream-come-true. The dream seemed to affirm that the life I enjoyed, the core of which was a solid marriage, had been my destiny, and that there was every reason to think that it would continue to unfold in the same direction.

But being rescued in love by another was not going to be the endpoint of my journey after all. The sense of achievement that my marriage had provided would prove as transitory as the boat ride with my father. The fairy tale was going to have to end in order that the rest of the journey could continue.

That was the mysterious meaning of the second dream that I could not have comprehended when the dream first occurred, and why I unconsciously knew to suppress it. With appropriate foreboding, the dream introduced the next phase of my life: an odyssey whose assignment was to leave everything that had provided significance and security, and find and save myself.

That the second dream proved prophetic is obvious: I eventually left a twenty-two year marriage to live alone. That decision initiated a series of important changes that could not have occurred had I tried to maintain life as it had been.

Up From Failure

The spiritual message of my dreams is clear: I was on a journey that was being guided from another dimension and did not know it. But my grasp of that is retrospective; I had no such viewpoint at the time.

I can say, though, that even back then my comfort was being increasingly disturbed by the unhappiness I perceived in the lives of many others around me, which because of my profession occurred all the time. My dream reflected my own deliverance by way of a happy marriage, but what about them? Why would I get to enjoy the ultimate and others would not? I certainly did not feel more deserving than anyone else did, and I apparently did not really control what came my way. So why me and not them?

I was uneasy about what this might mean; that the deciding factors in what we get may well include accident and coincidence. No one would consciously choose to be unhappy, and no divinity would prescribe it. This dissonance made me question my faith, and distrust the refuge I believed I had found by being happily married.

My conflict was rooted in the need to see everyone who wanted it in a happy marriage also, and I was distressed that some apparently deserving souls would have to be without one. This was no mere romantic fancy; I really wanted everyone to share my good fortune. More than I could have imagined, my faith in life depended on it. Lacking the concept of life as a journey, I had no thought that being alone could be a developmentally appropriate place.

When things appeared to be working out for others as I had hoped, my confidence in a Divine plan would get a boost. When they did not, sometimes I would just have to stop thinking about it. Finally, when I joined the ranks of the " less fortunate," the need to understand what was happening to me impelled a search for a healing perspective.

Oddly, although I was a psychologist who often recommended reading material as part of treatment, my healing did not begin with books on divorce or a pursuit of some connection between my past and what was happening now. The divorce literature and psychological theories of the time were not talking to me. None of it provided what I really needed, which was a cosmic-level justification for having caused the hurt that I had, and an explanation for why a marriage that was good for so long would have to end.

The prophetic dream and its strange timing colored all considerations, and I sensed that the answers I was looking for did not exist in conventional thought. Not finding what I needed from the usual social science resources, I was forced to look in another direction. Using the dream as a fulcrum, I consciously began to shift the weight of my focus to the spiritual realm.

It was not a graceful shift; I had never examined that side of me with any impartiality. I had instead shut out sources that contended that most of what occurs in life is out of our conscious control and is in the hands of another power.

Friends who understood the spiritual path were helpful. I was provided with some literature having generally to do with our finding our place in the Grand Design. I began to see that what propelled me was a need to determine who I really was apart from the conventional belief system I had grown up with.

The concept of life being a journey in which we take human form in order to progress spiritually began to have more validity for me; that all of our experiences are grist for the spiritual growth mill, that nothing happens randomly, including separation and divorce. Being a natural skeptic, I did not take too quickly to this belief; I had to find coherence and logic in it first, and slowly I did.

What became obvious upon self-examination was that life had always provided for my best interest, whether it seemed like it at any given moment of change or not. What was also obvious was that I had little influence over the big things that had happened to promote my growth, and that as much as I had liked to feel like a self-made man, I had frequently gotten unanticipated breaks and assistance.

Life began to make sense again, but this time from a wholly new point of view. I found new depth in all aspects of my life: spiritually oriented clients and friends could share themselves more openly with me, and were glad to be able to.

All of this took me farther and farther from my old life, and reconciliation with my former perspective became impossible. Now I had the explanation I needed: I had been called away from it to another path of spiritual growth.

Conscious Living - Faithfully

Like the boat ride in my dream, my introduction to spirituality took an unusual course. But life was never really out of control: I found that my fall was not from grace but into it. If there was a problem at all it was in believing that my marriage was an endpoint, and that it represented my highest development rather than a step toward it. The crash of separation happened just as needed to shatter that illusion so that my life could deepen and I could grow.

I think it is at the point where the recognition finally dawns that our lives are not entirely ours to decide, but that we are being appropriately channeled by unseen guidance, that we cross the threshold from unconscious to conscious living. This means that we really know that the spiritual dimension exists because we sense an interaction with it rather than simply thinking it exists because we have been told so and want to believe it. This is where faith enters and becomes a mainstay of the journey.

However, anyone who is familiar with conscious spirituality knows that it is a challenging path and that faith in it is always being tested. We never get to see where we are being led until after we get there. To me the working definition of faith is the capacity to let go and trust when everything human in us wants to be able to predict and control the outcome. When we let go - faithfully, our perception of the reality of the spiritual dimension together with its challenge allows that faith to strengthen and grow, and we are sustained, time-and-time again.

This brings me back to the concept of life as a purposeful journey. Having faith in life implies holding to the belief that we are on a guided pilgrimage while foundering in many bewildering circumstances, including the transition from falling-in-love, to marriage, to separation and divorce.

We have to keep in mind that journeying implies purposeful movement. When purposeful movement ends, a void occurs in the growth process, and since life abhors a vacuum, change will naturally insinuate itself. Transitioning out of a relationship that no longer sustains our growth reflects this natural design. We may not perceive its value at the time, but faith in the journey can provide the reassurance that the change is happening out of necessity.

There is much I need to learn about faith, but I do know that it is helpful to occasionally have our beliefs thoroughly tested by new personal experience. If our beliefs remain carved in stone, we might have a petrified spirituality, also.

Faith is tested when what we have always come to expect does not happen. What this meant in my case was facing the incongruities I struggled with when comparing my beliefs about marriage and happiness with the direction that my life had taken. If the model implied in the journey holds, and we grow when stretched by life events, the dramatic change in the perspective I maintained about marital loss could only have begun when I faced such loss personally.

Without my suspecting it, my belief system was headed for a change. My own separation was to usher me to a new place of perception where everything fit, even marital break-ups. The same has been true for others I have known.

Overcoming Fear

When I am asked what I think is the common theme in all of our journeys, the development of faith is always the first thing that comes to mind. I believe that growing our faith is at the heart of our work, which means feeling increasingly connected with the Creator and the rest of Creation until we accomplish a complete sense of unity. I am convinced that it is in our nature to accomplish this goal, and that we are provided with built-in motivation for doing it, which is our constant struggle with and our desire to master fear.

As a psychologist, I deal with people's fear everyday; it is one of the chief reasons they seek my help. Until my separation, though, it was not my style to address fear with faith, not even during the period of my son's heart surgery. But with the end of my marriage, when having to face the demise of my image of the happy life and the violation of my values and standards, and having to be on my own, the fear-faith connection became something I could not ignore.

I learned that fear is opposed to faith. It is associated with feeling isolated, abandoned, vulnerable and helpless, where faith helps us feel enfolded, protected and supported. The more we are guided by fear, the weaker our faith; the stronger our faith, the less we fear.

The faith I discovered when at my lowest emotional point has transformed the way I look at life. It has also changed how I serve people who come to me for therapy. When I found a sense of connection with something much larger than me, and was able to see how what occurred in my life was meant to happen, I learned not to fear for myself, and I no longer fear for my clients, either.

Therapy has become a matter of helping clients embrace or strengthen their own sense of the spiritual nature of the journey, if and when they are ready. This assures finding meaning in the divorce experience and it also encourages them to challenge their fear regarding other personal limitations, and thereby to risk growth in unpredictable ways.

Psychologists have long wondered what allows some people to take growthful risks that others avoid. We have generally agreed that there is some sort of readiness factor involved, but no one knows for sure where it comes from. I think one of the best explanations is faith. The more we are inclined to believe that our lives are about something, that things happen for a reason, and that we are meant to benefit from the experience of our journey, the more courageous we are when confronted with difficult situations, like separation and divorce.

Perhaps the best example of this comes from the life of the most courageous person I have known. This was a client whose divorce meant a colossal change in her lifestyle. She had the most to fear of divorcing people I have met, but she also had the strongest faith.

Middle-aged by the time of her separation, she had originally come to see me several years earlier to help one of her children. Having been a lifelong member of the socially insular Amish community, family and religion had circumscribed her life, and her chronic marital unhappiness was something she would ordinarily just have had to bear if the relationship could not be improved.

It is not easy for Amish citizens to seek psychotherapy, especially the men. To his great credit, this woman's husband joined her in my office to try to make improvements, especially in communication and affection. Not much came of it, however; he just could not alter his style to meet her needs. Theirs is a male-dominated culture, and as is true everywhere else, the men have a difficult time giving ground, even if they believe they want to.

Once she decided that marital therapy would not significantly change her relationship with her mate, we began to meet individually and had many remarkable conversations about the path she believed she had to follow if she were to grow and not stagnate.

What happened instead of my client adapting to an unhappy life was that she challenged her heritage and demanded that her needs and desires be considered. Without any encouragement from me, she began to behave more in line with her independent nature and to follow her calling. For example, she began to appear in public without her traditional bonnet; she added a telephone to the home, which was unheard of; she looked for work outside of the home; and she spoke openly about her feelings.

It is nearly impossible for most of us to appreciate her circumstances. The risks she took for standing up to tradition were tremendous considering the real possibility of public sanction and eventual exclusion if she did not bow to convention. Following her heart meant possibly losing everything else.

At stake were the respect and support of her family and friends and the approval of her God as understood by her religion. Along with losing these she faced having to make a life in a foreign culture, for which her eighth-grade Amish education, pre-modern life on the farm, and domestic work history were no preparation.

And there was an additional factor. Because they are a closed culture, Amish usually marry within their own small community, which has led to a high incidence of developmental disabilities among their offspring. Three of my client's children had serious physical and mental handicaps, and needed constant care.

She quickly became a target for gossip, and was visited several times by church elders who admonished her to behave more in line with community expectations. Her church eventually publicly censured her, which in a religiously based community was no minor event.

Undaunted by their attempts to contain her, my client continued to follow her path, saying the whole time that she was sure that she was spiritually guided. Eventually she decided to leave, which meant losing her family, the family farm, her friends and neighbors, her church and her roots, as in that culture, when you decide to leave, you are truly out. She was subsequently shunned, which meant there was no contact with or recognition by anyone from the Amish community, including another daughter and son she had to leave behind.

There is no allowance for divorce in the Amish church. People are married for life. This meant that her husband could not remarry as long as she was alive. This weighed heavily on her, too. Not only was she going to violate the values she had lived with herself, but was in the process sentencing him to a life without another marital partner. Nevertheless, in order to pursue her path in an honest manner, she had to legally dissolve the marital bond so that she could complete her break with her former life.

This woman's separation and divorce presented her with challenges beyond what most of us can imagine. She moved from a lifestyle literally unchanged from the previous century to finding a job, owning a house, and finally learning to drive. During her hardest times, she never spoke a word of disparagement about those who abandoned her and her children. She did not interpret her struggle as with them, but as within herself in terms of doing what was right for her regardless of the cost.

Although apprehensive, at no time did she seriously doubt that her journey was right. Her reward has been immense. Having begun her path of separation and divorce with only faith to go on and visions of hardship awaiting her, she says that she has found more happiness, joy and peace than she ever thought possible. She works, cares for her children, and fashions artistic birdhouses in her spare time. What is best, she notes, is that her growth has affirmed her faith.

Most of our stories are not quite so dramatic, but in their own way they are no less heroic. There are many instances of people taking on their divorce challenges with a trusting heart and little else to go on, and who benefit substantially as a result.

One story is that of a woman who, after more than twenty years of marriage, decided that she had to leave. After meeting with her and her husband individually and together, I remember telling her husband that I did not know where she was going, but it appeared she was not coming back.

What is interesting is that she did not know where she was going, either, or exactly why. She was not happy at home, but things were not terrible. Her husband was a decent man who had begged her on his knees to stay. She remembers that while she was preparing to load a truck with her part of the household furnishings, the older of her two children, a college freshman, tearfully inquired if she thought that what she was doing was really necessary. My client could only answer that she believed it was.

This was a person who had not finished her own college education, who had a job that paid little, and who was leaving a materially comfortable life. Her by-then angry husband was not inclined to help her in any way, and even child support was withheld temporarily. She had been plagued for years with depression and agoraphobia, which she had just recently overcome, so susceptibility to being overwhelmed by pessimism and fear was still a possibility. En route she encountered a real estate saleswoman who advised strongly that she desist, that she knew the world and that my client would never make it on her own.

Still she moved on, never complaining, and continuing to profess her belief in the mysterious guidance that directed her. She found a small house where she lived with her difficult adolescent son, completed college over the next two years, and improved her work circumstances and income to a more livable level. In the process, her fear diminished and her faith grew. When I later told her that I thought she had made a heroic journey, she felt surprise. She said that she had not thought of it that way, but as something she knew she had to do if she were to grow.

She was given an unexpected affirmation when her daughter remarked several years later that she not only understood then why her mother had to leave, but that given the growth that had occurred, she could not imagine her mother having remained in that marriage.

There are other stories of people choosing the same paths of faith when it was their mate who left unexpectedly. None of the stories, however, is substantially different in terms of hardships faced. What they all have in common is that the people involved expressed the belief that the changes were guided, and contributed to their growth.

I recall working with a man whose wife informed him that she believed it was necessary that she leave, that while her affection for him had remained genuine, she no longer loved him as she thought a wife should, and felt stagnant there. Having met with her, I thought her decision was sincere, and I told him so.

The man was emotionally unprepared for and devastated by his wife's departure. He had been satisfied with what they had, and himself had no inclination to change. He wanted to be angry, but he believed that her need to go was heartfelt, and right if she truly believed it was. He loved and respected her enough not to try to stand in her way, although at times he considered doing whatever was necessary to keep her around.

His work was to continuously apply the faith he already had that the change process would prove valuable to his own growth as well as hers. He remained true to this idea, and adapted to his new life with greater ease than would have been possible otherwise. He would have preferred not to have gone through this ordeal, but he knew in his heart that both of them were better off as a result. His was a heroic journey, too.

Truly spiritual people always do better with change. Those newer to spiritual guidance may be trepidatious about separation, but they are still inclined to go with the flow. The more spiritually advanced are even eager to see what awaits them with change. And because from experience they have no question that they are being guided, those who are most intimately familiar with the spiritual nature of the journey tend to move with the most grace.

Until we have made the journey ourselves, we just cannot really appreciate what having a sense of the eternal in daily life can mean. How wonderful to think, feel and behave as if everything is meant to assist us in our spiritual development, and to be able to let go of our need for control. This is the road to inner peace.

Spiritual Guidance

Like the others, I never expected my marriage to end. Even as the separation unfolded I found the whole idea of not being with my wife unimaginable. At no time had I thought of anything but that we would always be together. And although I had voluntarily initiated the separation, it seemed more like someone else had actually engineered it. I also never anticipated the spiritual awakening it would bring.

But it is obviously significant that I did not tell my wife about the second dream. The message it contained was of an individual journey that by the fact of my having kept it private was in effect already underway. The shared aspect of our path was ending. I might even say that the first dream was a cover, the surface sleight-of-hand that hides the more important work that is going on below.

At the time it arrived, the second dream could not have openly guided me. For one thing, it had come while the marriage was good. We had weathered the near loss of a child and all of the financial and other hardships that go with multiple hospitalizations. My mood may have been down, but everything else was looking up. There was no hint of what was to come.

More importantly, it had no relevance for me because of my unevolved spiritual consciousness. I loved Nature; I marveled at the stars and clouds; I thought of life as a miracle, but I denied the possibility of a spiritual dimension, much less that we could have any substantive interaction with it. I could explain much of people's spiritual beliefs away with psychological theory, and as a trained professional I was pretty certain about my grasp of the truth.

Besides my lack of readiness, the dream had no logical context from which an interpretation could be suspected since it was not remotely associated in time with the events it foretold (and which I could never imagine anyway). Furthermore, I latched onto the preferred image of the first dream: a heartwarming and romantic reflection of the life I had been living. Nothing strange about the unconscious brain replaying reality. Besides, the other was dismal and filled with images no one likes, such as isolation and danger. Who would want to pay attention to a dream that is so dark and depressing?

I have indicated that in hindsight the dream's timing was in fact perfect. It initiated an undercurrent of new possibility at just the right time when, because of my son's surgery and its aftermath, my emotional vulnerability was great.

I had been afraid of love because I feared losing what I would become attached to. The fear of his dying made me want to run, but his need of me made me stay. There was no escape. The conflict between these needs kept me riveted in place while tearing me up from within. The reward for hanging-in and facing my worst fear when I wanted to do anything but was a loosening of the defenses that had held my spirituality in check. A spiritual healing had taken place: love had overcome fear. Heart and soul had clashed and growth resulted.

Spiritual guidance is complex. In guiding dreams, for example, we can discern some of the meaning immediately; but some is hard to fathom because it has meaning only in the context of future time. I believe that in part we are provided with things that we understand immediately so that we will be more likely to take a dream seriously and to remember it, and acknowledge the significance of its unknown aspects while it incubates and we mature.

Because I did not forget the dream, I have to assume that it etched itself embryonically into the walls of my subconscious, and once embedded it quietly and incrementally prepared me for change in a way that I did not perceive and therefore could not reject.

Thus, from the perspective of my spiritual development, while my conventional grounding had allowed me to find meaning in my first dream, it would take another level of perception for me to understand the second. Life gave me the time necessary to gain that perceptiveness and then laid the changes out in a way where, like connecting the dots, I could not help but make the association between the dream and the later events it had predicted.

The consideration of timing itself lent weight to an argument for the existence of the spiritual dimension and suggested that it had an investment in me individually. When what was so mysterious and unforgettable eventually played itself out in its own perfect time, with a message that I could only appreciate later, I had to acknowledge the existence of a larger context for my life than I had known.

Important things were in motion in the spirit zone without my having any sense of them. Attention was being paid to my life. A plan was underway.

To me, the complexity, timing, and accuracy of my dream were convincing evidence of Divine Providence in everything, including something as awful as divorce. And if the mysteries of the purposefulness of past experiences could be so clearly revealed, I know that those that I do not understand in today's will eventually be revealed, also.

Easing Suffering

This infusion of a belief in meaning and purpose makes all of life more acceptable. We all have experienced apparently meaningless suffering, the kind that can cause feelings of helplessness and hopelessness, enough of which can lead to desperate acts. The suffering of separation and divorce is of this kind. Spiritual awareness will not take all suffering away, but believing that what we go through has meaning that we will understand at some time can reduce it.

With separation, for example, when from fear of failure and loss we try to hold onto what is no longer appropriate for us, faith in the journey and the inevitability of growth can overcome our grip on the status quo.

Fear of change breeds resistance to it, which prevents movement and in turn hinders healing and growth, forming a vicious cycle. Letting go is painful, but until we let go our emotional wounds cannot heal.

Much of our suffering comes from our desire for security, order and predictability in life, which a marriage provides. Faith provides a context for our suffering and a reason for letting go when a marriage ends and our desires are frustrated.

I worked with a client whose husband had been involved with a lover for two years, and who had been living on his own for several months. My client knew of the affair, and knew the marriage was probably over. She liked the comfort of their lifestyle and feared being alone, and so was afraid of facing change. Because of this she had not told even her closest kin, sensing that talking about it would add the weight of reality to the process and tip the scale in favor of separation for real.

Her husband had often traveled on his job, so she allowed that to explain his absence. She was trying to forestall the inevitable even after it was actually well underway. She was afraid of letting go: of him, their lifestyle, her status, the house, and the sense of order, predictability and security they combined to provide.

When we first met she wanted nothing more than to be angry, and to in some spiteful way get back at him. She really had the normal sense of entitlement we all tend to develop with a lengthy marriage. She was willing, however, to hear another approach to the matter.

With support and the understanding that she was avoiding the inevitable, she informed her family, and then some others that her husband had left her. Once she had, the healing process began, and she did some excellent work. Ironically, because her husband had already removed himself from her life in a substantial way, she had already begun managing daily life alone. She had not really held off change; she had tried to circumvent the fear of change through the illusion of order and control.

When she released the energy she had invested in maintaining the status quo, and faced life courageously as it presented itself to her, she was able to begin to discover security that was not dependent on the marriage. She began to realize that she did not need him to feel secure after all. This discovery would have remained outside her grasp if she continued to struggle against the flow of her life. She had genuine sadness, but she steadily gained confidence in herself and trust in the path that her life was following. Had she remained stuck, this treasure could not have been hers.

Another client, whose divorce hearing was near, felt the tingling feeling of fear that often comes at the end. Her husband promised anything if she would reconsider. Her lawyer hinted that a temporary stay would help her financial position in the divorce. A new relationship she had enjoyed had abruptly ended. She felt tempted, but did not think it was right to agree to a postponement unless she really wanted to reconcile. In spite of this, the fear lingered.

She had a dream in which she was being pursued by a dark gray energy, like a wind that she could see. The image had multiple meanings, but we surmised an immediately relevant one had to do with the fear of change she had expressed. Just as the energy was about to collide with her from behind, she intuited what to do. She merely bent over at the waist, and it flew by her. In other words, her guidance was to resist the impulse to run or to turn and fight. She was not to try to have control over the force, but to get out of the way.

Significantly, while the darkness pursued her, she arrived at a door which, when she opened it, revealed her luminously transfigured self, kneeling in prayer. She needed only to remain on her path of letting go to embrace that image.

I worked with this client for many months after her divorce. Her spiritual growth was remarkable. Having moved in faith during the hard times, she found applying it once the load has been lightened much easier to do.

She now looks for the meaning in everything, and she feels more secure than ever. This has allowed her to do significant healing of wounds suffered at the hands of a father who had sexually abused her many times over many years, and the betrayal of a mother who did not try to stop him. Had she not followed her inner guidance to exit the financial security of her marriage, it is doubtful this healing would have taken place.

A third client seemed to have the longest road to healing of all. Having married a man she knew to be an alcoholic and drug abuser, she should not have been surprised when his addictions worsened and became so intolerable that she had to ask him to leave.

During the entire first year of this separation, he remained completely out of contact with her, and she finally filed for divorce to gain closure. She did well with her feelings during this time by using the same process of denial that she employed to convince herself that his substance abuse would not hinder their relationship in the first place.

When I first saw her one-year later, just after the divorce was final, she was in an extreme state. All of the feelings of loss and abandonment she had denied were pouring forth. She was hurt and bitter, and angry to the point of having thoughts of shooting him for the pain he had caused and burning down the dream house they had built and now had to sell. There was no spiritual lightness here; life had for her become all soul.

This was no time for me to point out that she had set herself up for it in the first place when she fell in love with such a compromised man. Instead I talked with her about a larger framework for viewing her situation; a spiritual framework from which she could begin to gain a sense that what she was going through might have some meaning, which was for her like hearing a foreign language.

What was so awful for this woman, and the reason she wanted to kill her ex-husband, is that she felt that her life had ended with his departure. As limited as life with him had been, it had supplied the only sense of connection she had. Her belief was that there was nothing for her in life beyond that paltry love experience and its material trappings.

This client's healing work began with a discussion of the limits of her perspective on life, a non-judgmental observation of the darkness of her own feelings and motives, and an invitation to open herself to some new light as a palliative for her pain.

She began to understand that her rage and feelings of entitlement to satisfaction arose from her lack of a spiritual foundation regarding what her being in life was really about, and that his leaving had only brought this to the surface, not caused it. Without a spiritual foundation there could be no hope of finding meaning in her experiences, so of course she teetered on the verge of annihilation. Could her life have been only about trying to fashion an intimacy with a drug and alcohol addicted mate? She was stuck with believing so.

Rather than continuing to rail against this man's limitations and wallow in her sense of loss, she began to seek a healing perspective. And soon her life began to change. She could appreciate her marital ending as a necessary conveyance to growth, not as the death sentence she had unconsciously concluded it was, and probably wished to pass on to her ex-husband.

Transcendence

As a therapist I teach that in order to grow we have to move through a progression of relationships, all of which have to change, and most of which eventually have to end, including our relationship with life itself. We progress past early childhood friendships and first-loves; we graduate from families; we change jobs and communities and leave friends and neighbors behind; and parents and others die. In each instance, we have to encounter life without the support those relationships provided, which by design is essential to our growth.

Not all of our relationship transitions result in a sense of loss, of course, but some, such as leaving or losing family and best friends, cause immense distress. And although we may have others around to comfort us at those times, there is always a private side to such loss that we have to handle alone.

When we have a choice we usually prefer change that comes without a price. Few of us want to experience pain, and many of us are only grudgingly grateful for new advantages if loss is part of the equation. But if we are open-minded about the relationship between what we have suffered and how we have progressed, we will acknowledge that we can have gratitude for this sequence of events where loss results in gain.

Acknowledging this design should reassure us that divorce will prove as important to our growth as was the marriage it ended. In the logic of the change process, each one is a progression from a previous state.

Discovering how this is true is the work of the journey we are on, and as unlikely as it might sound at the moment, the discovery will eventually be made. For now it is only important that we allow for the possibility that this difficult ending is in essence no different than many others that also hurt, only pain and bias cloud our perception of its value.

To see divorce as part of a natural progression is consistent with the rest of our nature where going forward often requires a timely, if scary, release of what we have been holding onto. A wonderful illustration of this principle comes from early childhood. In order to walk, we all had to let go of the hand that steadied us. We may have been nervous at that moment, but we were urged on by an incomprehensible inner drive to get to our feet and move.

The separation that followed helped to end dependency and led to other unimaginable possibilities for our continued growth. Without a successful separation, our sense of self and our belief in our ability to master other new challenges would have been impaired. Would anyone distrust the wisdom of this design? And yet the cost was to relinquish all of the safety and security the previous phase offered.

Like learning to walk without aid, divorce has a natural place in our adult development. Even when only one of the partners wants to go, it is clear that the other is being guided by the same unconscious drive to greater emotional independence and mobility. We have to learn to trust the idea that, just as when a child is driven inexplicably from hands and knees to his feet, our adult growth has its own perfect timing, and it is usually just a matter of having faith in letting go.

Of course, letting go of a marriage is never an easy matter. Since we have been encouraged by our culture to become one with our marriage partner, many marital relationships are quite emotionally dependent, meaning that the individuals lean too heavily on their spouses in order to feel sustained. Whether we admit it or not, most of us have tremendous fear about being completely apart from our mates, and not only because we love them.

So many times a client's expressed decision to leave an unhappy marriage magnifies his or her emotional dependency, so that even in cases where love had abandoned the marriage years before, the tendency to hold onto the familiar is strong. (I always wonder what will happen at the brink of change when complaints collide with reality. At the moment of truth, backpedaling is common.)

Almost no one I have spoken to has been completely sure a divorce is what he or she wanted. Most would prefer to try to make the marriage work again. We tend to rally around our commitments, and to dig for reasons to justify staying. Before it is over, we will have asked ourselves, our mates, our friends, our therapists, and God, time-and-time-again, "Is this parting really necessary?"

In a sense such obsessive self-evaluation honors the value of marriage and commitment, and it assures that the timing for letting go is right. It also reflects how hard it is to face being apart from the interpersonal context that had defined us. But when we are ready and it is time to move to the next level of our spiritual development, letting go is inevitable.

The growth accomplished by everyone I have described is not merely change: it is transcendence. This means each has moved significantly beyond the perspective about life and their place in it that he or she had lived by, and that the marriage he or she was in represented.

Think of the change in perspective achieved by the former Amish woman whose tiny subculture believed that the ways of the larger society could only hurt one's relationship with God. Separation and divorce challenged every aspect of her world- view, and for having maintained her faith in the journey, her spirituality expanded to embrace what she had been raised to fear.

Consider the faith of the man who decided not to stand in his wife's path although his heart was breaking, and his anger pushed for expression just as his upbringing had taught it should. Or the woman, who despite her desire to hold on as her husband moved off in another relationship, moved on herself.

Reflect on the healing for the woman who had been so badly failed by parents who abused her body and her trust, and how she followed her path to letting go of what she could well have thought her financial due. And think of the progression of a psychologist who held to the traditional view of his upbringing and his profession as he followed the lead of his dream.

There are many other stories, all of them with the same theme of movement from a narrow to a larger understanding of their purpose in being here. What everyone of their authors shares is a belief that they were doing right in approaching their challenges as they did, regardless of what they might have thought in the past, or what others around them said as they pursued their goals.

The heart of the journey was the love and new level of awareness they gained for having stood up to the limited view; the soul of the journey was the hard work and suffering that accompanied the decision to do things differently.

Yes, everyone suffers in divorce. As we advance we accept pain as unavoidable and necessary to growth. Faith helps with the bad feelings we may have for hurting others as we change, or that come from being hurt ourselves as others change. The next chapter talks about these feelings in depth.

Reflections

Sit quietly, breathe slowly, and relax your mind.

Silently read the following phrases:

- My path has changed. I am entering a new phase of my journey. I am being led as part of a plan for me.

- The purpose of this change is growth. The growth I will experience from this change will be made clear to me in time.

- I will make the most of this growth experience. I will be a better person as a result.

- I have nothing to be ashamed of. Other good people have been through this experience, also. I am as worthy as anyone is.

- Everyone suffers in life. The suffering I am experiencing now will eventually pass as other suffering in my life has passed.

- Each path in life is special. My path is special, too. I have complete faith in it.

Now, repeat the phrases, paying close attention to the calmness that comes to you as you consider each one intently.

If you are in a place to do so, read each phrase aloud, and repeat it several times.

Think of people you know and like who have also been through this experience.   Write their names and something about them that you admire.

Recall other difficult passages in your life and how you have changed and grown from them. Write briefly about these, too.

2
Seeing Things Differently

For some people, setting up housekeeping after separation is an adventure. For me it was an ordeal.

I had taken almost nothing with me when I left the marital home. After living awhile without things like pots and eating utensils, a pillow for my sleeping bag, or a hose to wash the car, I made a list and went to the local K-Mart, only to find that I had to leave without purchasing anything because I felt sick with anxiety.

This happened a second time, also. All I was trying to do was to purchase a few essentials, but my reaction to replacing some of what I had left behind was so negative that it nearly overpowered my need for articles that would make life even minimally convenient.

Obviously I could not face buying things that symbolized a permanent separation from my marriage. What blocked my path was guilt. Regardless of being completely justified in my intended purchases, deep within I felt undeserving.

This chapter is about guilt and its counterpart, anger, their roles in inhibiting fundamental change, and how we can use the separation experience to heal them.

The healing I have in mind is not the traditional recovery experience that we anticipate after divorce: it does not simply come with the passage of time, a change of relationship circumstances such as finding a new mate, or trying to suppress feeling guilty or angry. What I found is that none of these remedies is truly healing. Guilt and anger have deeper roots. Until this deeper healing happens, were separation to come again, the feelings would be there again, too.

To me, genuine healing involves getting to a place where guilt and anger are no longer major influences in our life. In fact, healing from the perspective of the spiritual journey implies eventually moving past having to experience them at all.

This is an ideal of course; but such improvement only seems unrealistic because our upbringing recognizes guilt and anger as the appropriate responses to a failed marriage when they are not. If we can only imagine that they ultimately hinder rather than abet our spiritual growth, we will have accomplished an essential part of our healing work.

Separation and divorce are excellent circumstances for such work because they generate guilt and anger in high intensity. Also, the pain involved can motivate us to try to see things differently if we believe that by doing so we may ease our suffering.

The path that offers us the best chance to end the suffering that guilt and anger cause begins with an enlightened understanding of them. The vital first step in this is realizing that guilt and anger arise and come forward to be healed, not as guides for our behavior.

This is not to say that they provide no useful information; they do let us know that something is wrong and that we need to pay attention to what it is. Beyond that, however, angry and guilty reactions mostly cause us to harm others or ourselves. Clearly we want to be led by higher forms of guidance.

The work of growing spiritually requires trying to move creatively beyond our normal way of perceiving things while at the same time our human side continues to automatically follow existing patterns. As if to make sure that fundamental change is anything but easy, we have been designed with a complex psychophysiological defensive system to prevent our seeing life differently than we were raised to, even if by doing so it works to our disadvantage in the long run. The battle for fundamental change, then, is essentially that between being able to make autonomous choices and having to live according to programmed reactions, of which guilt and anger are elements.

Our Brain and the Biological Opposition to Change

Understanding our most basic defenses against autonomous choice and spiritual healing begins with envisioning our development in a strictly biological sense. Since there is no true separation between our minds and our bodies, as much as we might assume that they are solely productions of our minds, our thinking and emotions have a base in our physiology. Therefore, we have to know what is going on with us physically at the time of change in order to take full advantage of our situation and grow.

Like the brains of animals everywhere, our essential brain has its own survival as its chief concern. As the central regulating device in our body, everything the brain does serves to maintain the balance and order that assure its continued functioning. If it fails at this, the rest of our body fails also, which is why there is a kind of mutual survival pact between the body and the brain in which the body subjugates itself to the brain's demands.

The brain's currency is energy, and it monitors energy use very closely. Change takes energy. If all systems are functioning efficiently and there is a surplus of energy, some novel experimentation might be allowed. However, anything that requires the brain to release high amounts of energy, such as fundamental change, is perceived as threatening and is discouraged.

The brain does a superb job in maintaining balance and order; however, it does not differentiate between healthy and harmful demands for energy. In most instances it will reflexively try to stop any excessive energy use and return to the status quo. Even thinking about a major change will set off alarms and recruit its conservative defenses.

For example, anyone who has dieted or tried to stop smoking knows how much effort is involved. We might think that because these are healthy choices the brain would support change. Instead, it resists change through such devices as cravings and hunger, pleasurable images and memories, and an inner urge to believe that giving-in "just this once" will do no harm.

Likewise, people who have run marathons are well familiar with the phenomenon called 'hitting the wall" in which the brain begins to utter enticements to stop such as, "You know, you really don't have to do this. Why don't you just go and sit on that curb and find something cool to drink."

The same is true when considering the change of separation. Even when it is obvious to both mates that a marriage is no longer viable, alluring memories, romantic images, nostalgia and sentimentalism, and other inducements, no matter how exaggerated or distorted, encourage us to hold on and try again. And when these do not work we also encounter the prohibitive emotions of guilt and anger.

This is our essential brain at work instinctively repairing the breach in the dam that allows energy to escape. And it is all done without need of our conscious input. That is the way a homeostatic monitoring device is meant to work: we do not have to pay attention; it pays attention for us and automatically makes the corrections necessary to put things right back where they were.

How Our Psyche Defends Against Change

Feelings such as guilt and anger are a natural part of our human repertoire. However, their place, timing, and intensity are not programmed before birth. Our brain does not innately dictate that we respond with those particular feelings at a particular time; it only wants to maintain physiological harmony, and it will use what is in storage in its programming to do so.

What is actually expressed emotionally is the province of our psychology, which has itself been programmed by our upbringing, and joins the brain in the effort to maintain status quo by enforcing the programmed limits of acceptable thought and behavior. Our psychology is firmly wedded to our biology and any thought or action that is significantly different from established cultural boundaries will set off an alarm in the brain. Thus, the system through which our beliefs are maintained is that very same one that regulates heartbeat and breathing.

We experience guilt and anger, then, because we have certain expectations built into our thinking through enculturation. Values and traditions are from infancy seared into the unconscious to form the belief system we accept as reality. Our beliefs produce our expectations, and in large measure determine the boundaries of how we think and feel about what is right and wrong, good and bad, and possible and impossible in life.

Through repetition and reinforcement over many years, these expectations become a predisposition: a filter made up of our biases, prejudices, and preconceptions, and the basis from which we judge our behavior and that of others. Guilt is our reaction to believing we have violated our values, especially if it hurts others; anger is our reaction to thinking that someone else violated them, especially if it hurts us.

Once programmed with a belief system, the brain uses its energy conservancy function to inhibit change in that belief system. It does this by restricting perception; that is, by filtering out information that contradicts our own beliefs. In a sense, it allows us to perceive only what we have learned to think is real: we mainly see what we have been conditioned to believe is there.

What really brought this concept home to me was reading about an experiment with newborn kittens from the same litter that were divided into two groups. One group was raised in a room with vertical stripes on the walls, and the other with horizontal stripes.

Later, when the vertical-stripe group was placed in a room with horizontally shaped furnishings, they kept bumping into these things. They could not perceive what was literally right in front of them. The same thing happened with the horizontal-stripe group when placed in a room with vertical shapes.

We grow up believing that we know reality, and in all innocence think our way is the only way. We tend to reject any new perception that threatens our belief even as, like the kittens, we bump repeatedly into it.

Our Culture and Social Barriers to Change

The common beliefs and values of our social group will insulate us from new information and support us in denying or distorting what we feel or think that threatens consensual reality. Growing up in the same culture, we all share a set of cognitive and emotional reactions with our fellows, and as we interact, ours reaffirm theirs and vice versa. Our shared values and traditions orient and direct us, and provide us with a sense of certainty and reassurance when we face unfamiliar situations.

Together we may form institutions that mirror our beliefs and successfully keep everything either vertical or horizontal, depending on our needs. With the strength of numbers it is easier to believe that we possess the truth, and having achieved this we may behave in the most ungenerous ways toward "non-believing" others, thus keeping the threat they represent at a safe psychological distance.

An example of this from my own life was my religious upbringing, which taught that ours was the true religion, and that while we would enter heaven, others would go to a lesser place because they were not baptized. I had a continuous religious education until I reached college. There I found that I admired a man who, as it turned out, was of another religion. I had to consciously reconsider and break through my prejudices to allow that he was as good as I was, even though he was a religious "outsider." That change in thinking was not easy, but being in a new environment away from the direct influence of my religious group helped immensely.

The defense against new perception has a social manifestation, also. When we challenge our own beliefs, we simultaneously threaten the integrity of the mindset of our social group. The general reaction is anger, with the additional threat of social rejection; the internal reaction is guilt. The very hint of social disapproval can be enough to move most of us back toward our shared beliefs.

Perhaps the best known example of this in our century was the "McCarthy Era" during which prominent people who were suspected of un-American thinking were publicly vilified by Senator Joseph McCarthy. Their persecution included loss of jobs and worse. Television was used to make the spectacle widespread so that, like an execution on the Town Square, the potential horror of being a judged a threat to our traditional way of thinking was displayed in millions of living rooms everyday.

Of course, the experience of my client for challenging the precepts of her Amish community is also an example. I know of others in her community that succumbed to the fear of public sanction and exclusion with which she had struggled prior to deciding to leave.

There are also back-up systems to our main social defenses against fundamental change that permit us to act-out our need for feeling different and having autonomous control, but do not threaten belief systems or engender personal guilt or social anger. One is to allow minor, non-threatening changes to occur that fulfill our need to feel that we are doing something different. These might include such things as changing jobs, residences, neighborhoods, churches, political parties, wardrobes, hairstyles, or interior décor.

These changes can provide pleasurable, temporary gratification, as well as distraction from the need for more substantive change, without actually threatening the existing order. Just a new hairstyle or wardrobe can give a sense of uniqueness and creative self-expression, and moving from an "old' neighborhood to a "new" one can provide a sense of forward movement without engendering substantial guilt or anger. These changes might cause someone some inconvenience, but all of it is socially anticipated and allowable. There is no fundamental threat, and therefore, no real upset.

We may even act in rebellious ways that bend the rules as long as we do not threaten the status quo. We have seen this in each teenage generation in terms of dress and attitude. We now see it increasingly with mid-lifers whose desire for a sense of autonomy leads to such acts as buying noisy and ostentatious motor cycles, sporting designer cigars, and behaving in other uncharacteristic ways.

Because we unconsciously agree that we have the right to do these things, such pseudo-rebellion creates the perception of revolution without actually violating cultural norms or representing a real threat to the boundaries of our beliefs. In fact, it gives the rest of us something to talk about, a chance to live vicariously in a faster lane. Thus, if we allow some minor rule bending, we will avoid major breakage.

The other back-up system is the minutiae of day-by-day life in our very busy, information-deluged, compulsively active society that does not allow time to look up from our involvement to see what is happening to us. This is the "can't-see-the-forest-for-the-trees" defense wherein more and more is continually piled on so that we think we have little choice but to attend to it or be buried, and are thereby able to remain ignorant of the fact that we are living on automatic pilot.

By way of this defense, we can go an entire lifetime without the slightest awareness that we have never questioned the belief system by which we have been guided, much less that there is one. It is just the same as our taking little notice of our heartbeat or breathing simply because they are always reliably there and we have other more important considerations. We tend to pay attention only if something goes wrong, and once righted we go back to living inattentively. We may only feel guilt or anger later as we contemplate death and look back and sense that we have missed something important and we realize it is too late to change.

Anxiety as a Defense against Change

Until the time that we are able to examine our own beliefs from a new perspective we will most likely conclude that any threatening new information is wrong, and that we were foolish, confused and mistaken for considering it. But if we bump into contrary experience often enough and we persist in pushing our perceptual boundaries by examining our old beliefs in light of new information, such as happened when I began to reconsider my religious prejudices, other defenses come into play. Chief among them is anxiety.

When the brain senses threat, it calls for the release of the powerful hormone adrenaline into the bloodstream. This chemical initiates the thousands-of-years' old "fight or flight" defense that helps us to cope with danger by preparing us to either do battle or to beat a fast retreat. This awesome biological program automatically shuts down non-essential functions like digestion and shunts blood to the brain and other major organs.

It also puts the nervous system on high alert: pupils dilate, hearing becomes acute, our muscles tense for action, and we empty our bladder and bowels to lighten the load. We become vigilant and scan the environment for threat. In seconds we are ready for anything.

But adrenaline was originally meant to handle a physical emergency where it could be dissipated in the heat of the moment. In our current world, physical threat has largely been eliminated. Because the brain does not differentiate between physical and psychological threats, that is, between real and imagined emergencies, that automatic response comes into play more often to deal with psychological threat, including fundamental change.

With a persistent psychological scare, such as an impending change to our belief system, adrenaline tends to remain in the bloodstream. When we feel threatened over time, visual and auditory wariness and acute attunement to threat then become habitual, resulting in incessant worry. A vicious cycle is instituted wherein the brain calls for additional adrenaline in response to perpetual worrying as if the worry signals another emergency.

This hypervigilance of anxiety includes rapid, shallow breathing, which helps in acute emergencies, but when it becomes chronic it creates an emotional state rife with feelings of panic and dread, and guilt and anger. In terms of keeping a belief system intact, anxiety works like the static charge around an electrified fence. The closer we get to the wire, the more we feel the threat from the electrical field. Our hair literally stands on end and we feel a prickly sensation all over. The sensation is a warning to back away, which we automatically do. We may never see what the anxiety blocks from view, which, of course, is the point.

Because it can mimic terrifying physical conditions such as heart disease and neurological disorders, the physical manifestation of anxiety can become a crisis all by itself. When it does, it galvanizes our attention and marshals our energy reserves to deal with our fears from a medical perspective, removing our focus from the spiritual to the physical realm. Again, we are effectively steered away from fundamental change.

If we want to begin to function more autonomously, which is necessary for true spiritual healing and growth, we have to do more than just revolt against the prohibitions thrown up by the defenses in our physiological, psychological and social selves, although that may be a start.

Our real work involves coming into contact with and consciously observing the automatic reactions we have to any situation, anger and guilt included, anytime they occur. Simply saying, "This is anger," or "I am feeling guilt," when either of these feelings arise is a strategy that works to bring the true nature of the defenses against change into consciousness.

The stronger a reaction, the more we need to step back and examine it. If we are serious about change, we cannot afford to let any reaction slip by unnoticed or unevaluated any more than we can risk smoking one more cigarette. Each time we do, we give up our autonomy and we reinforce old programming.

Struggling Against Our Defenses

Just as an acute pain in a limb or a sharp headache cause us to pay attention to what is wrong so that we might fix it, guilt also arises to be healed. And a separation is an excellent occasion for healing because guilt is so intense at that time that we cannot ignore it. As a psychotherapist, I have witnessed the guilt that so often follows a decision to divorce bringing many people into my office that ordinarily might not come, their profound suffering often representing their best chance for spiritual healing and growth.

A good example of the two-edged struggle with guilt is that of a thirty-something-year-old man who asked for a session just prior to his final divorce hearing. He and his wife had been in many months before trying to sort out their relationship. Over the period since we had last met he had decided to live apart, and although his wife was reluctant to make that arrangement permanent, they subsequently decided to divorce.

As the final date approached, he suffered the tremendous guilt that many men and women feel who initiate a separation. Complicating this was the fact that he had recently been in another relationship, which he also ended. He feared that these two decisions indicated that he was selfish, that he was insensitive to the feelings and needs of people he had professed to love, and that he had a problem with loyalty and commitment. His self-image and self-esteem were under siege.

The psychological and social constraints on this man's spirit were fairly typical of our culture. His frame of reference for success was that of being happily ensconced in a marital and family context, and now that that particular image was shattered, he believed himself to be a loathsome failure.

Here was a very decent man who assumed that something had to be wrong with him, some character defect because he felt so bad about his decisions. Having met with his wife and him, I knew that their problems were not his doing, or at least not solely his doing. They had both tried to make things better, but there was significant incompatibility that seemed to fester into new wounds even as they attempted to heal the old ones.

If the new love had lasted, at least he could say that he was exchanging one love relationship for another, which would have caused some problems but would not have been so outside of the boundaries of what he believed was healthy and right for a grown man.

Worse yet was that, although he had no current relationship and really did not want another one anytime soon, he was also already talking about how he would probably get into another marriage in the future and fail at that, too. His perceptual filter was so imbued with a belief about the primacy of marriage that it would not allow the possibility of a state other than marriage. He was simply programmed to see himself as either married or a failure; there was no other possible reality. Because of this he felt miserable and hopeless.

His guilt worked well in its function as a defense against change. It was keeping him bound to the expectation that he would become a reliable family man, or else. In fact, this defense was so evolved that it manipulated time so that it borrowed assumed failure and guilt from the future and transferred it into the present.

Sadly, the fact of his being highly successful as a single father caring for his daughter did little to make remedy his guilt about being a failure as a family man. The marriage was missing, and that made any other arrangement unacceptable. And the fact that he enjoyed his alone time had no impact on resolving his guilt about abandoning his interpersonal duties. Ironically, both of these unanticipated developments made him feel even guiltier for his success in being separated.

This man wanted and needed to be free, but not just in the negative stereotypical way we tend to think of men who want to escape the committed responsibility of a marriage. His need was the same as anyone's, man or woman, whose upbringing interfered with autonomous thinking and decision making. In order to heal fundamentally he had to see the yoke that his early conditioning and his belief system had become for him. In a sense he seemed destined to be a prisoner of prescribed love, and it was important that he understood that his guilt resulted not from his being a bad man, but because he was now finally balking at this program.

We could say that his letting go of both relationships, one after the other, was a sign of hope. Without being aware of it he was behaving in accordance with his inner guidance, and against great odds was attempting to free his spirit; now he just had to grasp the spiritual motives behind his self-encounter and self-rescue. He had to find that he was more than he had ever thought he was, and that his separation was meant to be his conveyance to a new level of awareness, freedom and joy.

We worked to awaken his consciousness to the effects of his social conditioning, and to the fact that his guilt was designed to prevent a shift out of a life of obligation to one of autonomous choice. Far more important than being able to effect a fulfilling marriage was his need to escape the deceptive limits of his perception of what was right and possible in his life.

I have to think that my client's social upbringing regarding the place of marriage may well have precluded his having one successful marriage. It challenged him instead to resist the confining nature of the requirement to be a steadfast provider in a traditional family setting.

It may be that his marriage never really had a chance because he subconsciously chose someone with whom there would be enough conflict to force an escape. Of course, he would then have to encounter guilt, but as we have seen, this would set up his awakening and his release. By struggling to get free, he was championing his integrity, not abandoning it.

Perhaps a new relationship will work for him when he no longer feels compelled to be married and responsible. At that point it would more likely be an independent decision. He would know that there were options.

Another example of someone struggling with restrictive programming was a woman who had been married to an abusive man who continued to menace her during the separation. She was a successful professional who had a position of high status and authority, who now was terrified to leave my office after our evening meetings. She had not loved her husband for many years, and yet, as the final hearing approached, she became unsure of herself, and was tortured by images of giving in to his admonitions and returning to him. And then she would look at me and ask me if she were sick.

In spite of dreadful physical and verbal abuse, she wondered if she had a right to make him unhappy. Her own happiness seemed shaded by some deep feeling of being unworthy, and perhaps by the fear that true happiness was not to be hers.

Our work was twofold. One aspect had always to do with holding up her resolve against the eroding force of his manipulations on her self-confidence. He was a master salesman, and he instinctively used his considerable skill against her untested strength.

The other aspect was helping her discover that her ambivalence had nothing to do with what she actually wanted, but was a manifestation of a negative belief system she had been bequeathed about herself and love. Fear was part of the glue that bound her, but guilt was a more powerful ingredient. While she needed no convincing that her husband did not care for her, she really was not sure she deserved better.

Her challenge was incredible. Prior to meeting him she had been abducted and raped. While married to him, he had left her to live with another woman. Her own family seemed unsupportive of her decision to leave even though they knew the marital history. She had very little faith that she would get through the ordeal and be able to make it one her own. She did not trust herself, and she did not trust life.

She had to find a justification to be free of him and to have faith in an uncertain future. It helped her greatly to think that she was being guided by an inner desire to heal, and that her decision to leave was growth-oriented.

Her best hope was to awaken to how she had been indoctrinated with negative expectations that were reinforced by her marital experiences, and to see that these were now held in place by guilt, and then to counter it with a larger perspective that included her actual personal accomplishments. As she looked past her perceptual defenses, it became apparent to her that she could expect more than her beliefs suggested. She saw that although the road had been extremely difficult, she had done well in so many ways, and with encouragement she began to anticipate continued success.

This woman's growth in self-love, faith and courage was remarkable. She got her divorce and has since married a man who is gentle and sweet to her and her children. She has risen above her limited view of herself and life. Her guilt proved to be one more hurdle to overcome on her path to greater awareness, freedom, and happiness.

A final example of the power of guilt to maintain the status quo was a man who came to talk about how he had separated from his wife so that he could be near a woman who he loved. He had been separated in his home as it was, with no sexual contact between his wife and him after several years of a bland relationship. He had known his new love for many years as a friend, and had watched the relationship unfold into something more.

However, after describing a deep connection in the new relationship, he told me that when he was apart from his lover, he could imagine a life with his wife only. He did not mean by this that she was that special to him and that he was having serious second thoughts. He meant that his mind would literally only project images of his wife, not his new love.

He told me that he had spent the previous weekend at his wife's house because he had felt guilty about hurting her and about choosing his desire to leave over her desire that he stay. He felt obligated, duty bound and responsible. It was apparent that he wanted to get out and that guilt barred his way.

I decided to continue to meet with him apart from his wife since he showed no abiding interest in trying to improve that relationship. He was able to spend quality time with his new love, but he was plagued by a sense that he was wrong for not sacrificing himself for the sake of the marriage. His wife and their mutual friends agreed, which made him feel guiltier still.

He brought his new love to a session one day, and indeed they seemed to have found something good. It was no wonder that he wanted to hold on. And yet there were the undermining effects of his guilt.

Here is a wonderful illustration of the role of guilt in defending the status quo. His brain automatically filtered out thoughts of his lover in favor of images of his wife. It distorted his memories of the lack of passion at home and filled his thinking with considerations of duty and sacrifice. The social arm of the home defense, his friends, reinforced his guilt by, in effect, shunning him for his behavior.

His fight was to open his perception to allow the new possibility in. As we might now suspect, nothing in his established life encouraged this. The feedback he received when he spoke of or spent time with his new love helped to maintain the breach in his defenses, but the battle raged.

Again we have an opportunity to see how our conservative human nature will attempt to prohibit a major change in the way we experience life even when the change is good. This man lived a stagnant life at home. He and his wife spent their evenings in different rooms watching television, and they slept in different beds. She was apparently satisfied with his physical presence, but he craved more and he believed life had sent an invitation to him.

Now he wanted to grow in the direction of love, but he first had to awaken to the internal programming that was preventing it. Healing meant that he had to be able to see things differently or he was not going to be able to find higher love. Guilt tried to stop him.

Anger as Resistance to Change

From the "seeing things differently" perspective, anger is an automatic response to the threat to the perceptual status quo posed by a mate who begins to look at life from a fundamentally new viewpoint.

The main difference between anger and guilt is in the form they take, which is dependent on whether we are the perpetrator or the victim of change. Guilt might ask: "How can you do this to her?" Anger might ask: "How can you do this to me?" When the rift continues, guilt will say: "You can't do that to her! Who do you think you are?" And anger will warn: "You can't do this to me! You have no right." In a sense, the closer we get to irremediable change, the more guilt and anger blend into accusation and intimidation (one is just more inner directed while the other comes from without), and begin to counter the threat of change with threats if change persists.

Anger's role is to repel any threatening intrusions into our belief system, and to restore the offending mate's perceptions of life to their original form. The mind uses its learned sense of what is honorable and right to justify an angry reaction. At our angriest we are most sure that our sense of what is right is pure, and that we should be upset because the rules have been broken.

On a perceptual level, our feelings reflect the belief that the way we had perceived reality is correct and that the perception should be protected. When we say, "You can't do that to me," we are also saying,

"You can't look at things that way, period," as if in shocked disbelief that anyone would even try. We perceive our attacks on the offender as counterattacks rather than preemptive strikes because our beliefs are under assault and we are on the defensive.

We are using socially sanctioned desperate measures to bring the offender back into harmony. Much the same as a minister trying to save lost souls, we may even feel a sense of obligation to force a return, believing that he or she must be mentally impaired to violate societal expectations as they have. And we may feel a sense of personal failure if we cannot.

To that end, the use of denigration, insult, and threat seem justified; whatever levels of anger or intimidation that are needed to accomplish the task. Encouragement and a lack of censure by our family and friends for such tactics affirm our perceptions.

I remember working with a woman who told her husband that she loved him dearly and did not want a divorce. When he replied that he was leaving anyway, she coldly said, "Then I will destroy you," and she meant it. She was able to shift from one emotional state to another in an instant. Our brain will do whatever is necessary to block change.

I know that this woman eventually settled into a stable new life; however, her anger slowed her adjustment significantly. More than healing, she wanted to maintain that she had been wronged, and because she was not getting affirmation for her position, she did not remain in therapy long enough to do the inner work that healing involved. In driving her out of therapy, her anger defended against the threat that an effective therapy would pose to her embedded view.

We might want to think of such a reaction as just "good old pride," but I am inclined to consider all entrenched behavior that prevents growth as more connected to our defenses against fundamental change than simply a temporary display of vanity and conceit.

Some clients have wondered why they felt anger about a spouse's leaving when they were fully aware that both of them were better for the decision. The answer is that, while we might consciously acknowledge the benefits of the change, our unconscious defenses are working to protect our underlying belief system. The defenses are automatic: even when we know that they are serving no rational purpose and are interfering with proper change, we still have to work to get them under conscious control. When this happens we are provided with an excellent opportunity to heal and grow without having to actually become seriously involved in guilt or anger. The separation experience draws the defenses out into the open where they can be seen for what they are, and autonomous control can be instituted.

The Guiding Light of Imagination

I have related several stories here of people's struggles to perceive possibilities for themselves beyond their current marriages, and of their success in overcoming the barriers to seeing things differently. Not everyone is successful, however. I have worked with many people who were truly unhappy in their marital lives, but as much as they might have talked about wanting to leave, they just were not able envision a life different from the one they had.

When I think about describing the difference between the successful and unsuccessful groups, one of the things that spring to mind is Plato's Allegory of the Cave. As I recall the Greek philosopher's fable, the cave's human inhabitants were chained to a log with a fire at their backs and a bare rock wall in front of them. All they were able to perceive beyond the darkness were their own shadows cast onto the wall by the firelight, and over time they came to accept the shadow world as the limit of possibility.

One day one of the cave dwellers had an inspiration. He began to imagine that there was more to life than he had been led to believe, and by simply turning his gaze rearward, his inspiration was rewarded with a panoramic view of a broad, lush, light-filled plain that stretched from the cave opening to a far horizon. He was ecstatic at his discovery.

However, when he tried to tell the others about what he had seen, he was immediately set upon and killed. Clearly, no one else wanted to deal with the threat his inspiration represented to the group's fundamental beliefs. And after the execution, anyone who might have been inclined to imagine an alternative to the shadow reality must have thought seriously about keeping his eyes forward.

I have to think that one of the important variables defining the group that decides to move on from an unhappy marriage, whether they initiate a separation or have to deal with one reactively, is imagination. When it comes to fundamental change, courage and desire, while essential, are not necessarily enough.

We also benefit from the belief that there is something else waiting "out there" for us, from inspired autonomous thinking that counters the weightiness of our social conditioning and releases our creativity from its grasp. As we shall see, this inspiration does not even have to have a recognizable form; if we are open to change, even an indistinct concept or an intuition will often do.

Without inspiration, we tend to hold tight to what we have because, as unrewarding as it might be, at least it seems real. We may suspect that our inspiration is a sham, and we may be reluctant to follow our imaginings for fear that we will find ourselves going nowhere, and will regret it. Of course, when we choose to remain in a lifeless marriage we are also going nowhere; but the programmed play is to prefer the known to the unknown.

People who are ambivalent about being in their marriages are some of the saddest clients I have counseled. Theirs is the worst of worlds. They experience a strong inclination to leave that they feel they cannot trust, but that never leaves, and an equally powerful motive to stay.

Such individuals feel as imprisoned by their unhappy marriages as protected by them, and they resent being there no matter how good the other aspects of their lives are. We may recognize them as the couples who sit in icy silence in each other's company in a restaurant or in the car next to ours, or as the people who openly bicker and battle about everything with no regard for whom might be around to hear them. Their "something is better than nothing" philosophy is merely another defense against autonomous choice.

One of these ambivalent people was a woman who had actually begun the divorce process early one year only to come to speak with me later in the same year because she felt paralyzed by her mixed feelings and had not moved forward with it. She literally looked as if she was in a chronic state of shock, and she needed end the internal stalemate and find a resolution.

I acknowledged her plight and waited for her to relate what she thought was behind her indecision. She said that she was as unhappy at home as ever, and she described the meals and other domestic activities she and her husband continued to share in unavoidable silence. "But," she said, "at least I feel safe."

To me this statement reflected her very traditional ethnic upbringing that taught women to tolerate their marriages for the material comfort and protection there. It also demonstrated an inability to see beyond the unconscious fear she felt about the comparative financial uncertainty of the unknown.

I waited a few moments to allow the significance of that statement to fill her consciousness, and then asked her to describe the safety she thought her marriage provided. Answering that question was the beginning of her release from her fears.

When she mentally pictured her material comfort and associated it with the misery-surcharge that came with it, she saw the safety she had been referring to as a shackle that bound her to a predictably unhappy future. As soon as she began to imagine that, she had a backdrop against which she began to imagine freedom and other possibilities that might follow if she could simply act on faith that she would be able to take care of herself financially.

By the simple technique of looking clearly and honestly at what she actually had and would have in the future if she remained "safe," my client freed her creative energy to inspire herself in a positive way. And however unformed her imaginings might be, they suddenly seemed better than what she knew awaited her without them. She could imagine herself a pioneer, a trailblazer, a pilgrim leaving the unhappy known for the happy unknown. With this recognition she smiled genuinely, which released the mask-like rigidity in her face for the first time that evening.

Individuals who cannot imagine a new life are also the ones most likely to remain emotionally bound to past mates long after the marriage has been terminated by a divorce. They just cannot seem to shift to the new reality. When I listen to them speak of a former mate, I often sense an undercurrent of hostility or a tone of wistful sentimentalism that have been undiluted by time or even the presence of a new marriage.

One of these was a woman who years after her high school sweetheart had left her and been engaged to another, usurped his fiancee's place of managing the funeral when the man suddenly died, as if their divorce had never occurred. A life with this man was all she had ever imagined for herself, and she had not let go of that image even after they had been apart for a long time. Therefore, in her mind it seemed natural rather than presumptuous to run the show at his death.

Another was a woman who many years after their divorce kept a book her ex-husband had written displayed prominently on her coffee table. He had become a minor celebrity, and she continued to try to maintain some of the reflected radiance for herself by pointing to it when people came to visit. She had not yet developed her own sparkle.

A third was a person who, despite a long-term relationship with a new love, kept collages of photos from earlier times on various walls at home. In spite of a several year relationship with a new man, and experiences of their own, she said she kept the photos because they reminded her of the best times of her life.

All of these people were captives of lives in which the light of old images substituted for the flame of fresh inspiration. Each of them seemed able only to acknowledge the life that they had imagined they would always have.

True, none of them had planned that their marriages would end, but this is the case for most people who divorce. Only when each of them could admit that things had in fact not been as good as they imagined would they be free to imagine something better. Barring that, they would still have to let go of worn images in order to find new ones.

Spiritual Assistance and Change

Because of our conservative nature, we tend to fall back on familiar ways of coping when we are stressed. The greater we are stressed, the more conservative we tend to become.

Inspiration is not a reliable survival behavior. This is why emergency services such as fire departments drill as often as they do: during a crisis, practiced fundamentals are more predictable than imaginativeness. Just when we need them most, inspiration can vanish and imagination can dissolve into useless fantasy.

Separation is the kind of crisis that brings out our conservative side and subverts our creative energy to fight change. At this time many of us imagine being different, but we find that our inspiration dissolves in fear and that the best we can accomplish is an imaginary satisfaction of our desire to grow. We might even become part of the vast market for romance novels and other adventure stories, relying on the writer's creativity to help us cope with our unhappiness when our own creativity has failed.

With so much poised against change, by what channel do we receive the inspiration we need to animate growth? I have no doubt that in my case I received what I needed from the spiritual realm. With my conservative upbringing and beliefs, the move to separate could only have come through an act of grace.

The concepts of inspiration and grace fit my own story well. A year before I left (and prior to any time I had consciously contemplated leaving), while on a "dream" vacation, my wife and I had what I thought of as an unnecessary disagreement about our itinerary. As she walked away, I blatantly said to myself that we should "just get it over with" and divorce.

This completely uncharacteristic thought was met with instant opposition: I had sobering visions of trying to explain that decision to our families and friends and thoughts about the harm that it would cause. I sensed in a flash all that I would have to go through, and in the end I was struck with a profound sense of the impossible.

I had no idea where the urge came from, but the thought left as quickly as it arose. By the time I had walked back to the hotel room I just wanted to get things back to normal. However, as it turned out, this had been no passing fancy, but a premonition, a brief image of something important in the offing. And as is the case with all such threatening images, because it would not be permitted to remain conscious, it took the path that premonitions take and went underground to begin its work of change without my awareness.

Things were quiet for several months, and then by mid-winter I began to feel openly irritated and fatigued by my marriage. Still, the thought of leaving did not take form until one night the next spring.

As I sat alone on our porch, a very strange but very compelling image materialized in the dark sky in front of me. At best I might describe it as daybreak, a fissure on the very early morning horizon where threads of deep red appear in advance of the sunrise.

But it was more than a visual image. Somehow it intimated another level of reality awaiting me, a way of "knowing" life that was beyond what I had been living, and was available if I could only believe in it and get there. I felt a very real longing for it, whatever it was, and at the same moment I was afraid that I might find my way to it. I am sure I sensed both the grand possibility that I have since realized and the stirring of all of the defenses that would be thrown up to block my way, and the struggle that awaited me.

This experience may sound bizarre, but it seemed rational and meaningful at the time. I believe that this peculiar image and its message were the very inspiration I needed to begin to consciously formulate plans for moving on. I am grateful that it arrived in the form it did. As imbued by traditional images of marriage and family as my thinking had been, something unusual had to inveigle my imagination and coax my will to action.

If I were going to be consciously invited on a spiritual journey, I would want the announcement to be wrapped in mystery. Still, I am amazed that I recognized it for what it was because I had never had a similar visual experience in the past. I must have been ready because I did not hesitate to accept it, and I did risk telling anyone about it who might disapprove and discourage it, which at the time meant just about everyone I knew.

All of this fits with the idea of fundamental change as a creative act; one through which we begin to look at reality from a perspective other than the usual and normal; one that expands our ability to perceive life.

The realm of Spirit fits perfectly, too, although perceiving how this could be might require stretching our conventional religious boundaries a bit. All that means is that we keep in mind that the things of the spirit are based on love, which promotes freedom, encourages expansion, and remains flexible to accept the guidance that comes from within. If guilt or anger arise, we have only to know that it is our defenses against spiritual growth coming into play.

Doing the Everyday Work of Change

Ultimately, healing guilt and anger requires discovering the hand of God in our journey. But while taking a spiritual perspective sets the stage for fundamental change, it does not protect us from the hard work of seeing things differently. We have learned how much is aligned against healing and growth, and we are destined to have to grapple hands-on with our biological, psychological, and cultural heritage to become free of their controlling effects.

From everything I have read about the human aspect of the spiritual journey, and from what I have seen through many years of observation, I have to conclude that no one gets a free pass to understanding. Every human being has to work bottom-up through similar stages from unknowing to knowing, which in a divorce usually means many months of toil. We all have to walk the walk.

From a psychological perspective, a large part of healing guilt and anger involves changing our thinking about rights, responsibility, and entitlements in marital relationships. In this regard, it is vital that we conceive marriage to be a voluntary state from beginning to end, so that it does not remove individual autonomy or the right to free choice. We have to allow the unassailable truth that if a person wants to leave a marriage, he or she has every right to go. We have to feel sovereignty over ourselves, and that we are accountable only for our own behavior.

This may seem selfish and extreme, especially where children are involved (which I will discuss later), but if our choices are to be truly autonomous, our first rule must be that no one is entitled to anyone else's life. This means that no one but the individual making the decision can say whether or not a marriage is worthwhile, or when an ending should occur. And since none of us can know what someone else's healing and growth requires, it is not our place to judge them.

I believe that self-direction and self-ownership are so important to individual healing and growth that even if a mate acts only on a heartfelt hunch that a separation is needed, he or she is right to follow that feeling, and experiment with change. The other mate has the right to choose whether or not to tolerate this disruption, but not to attempt to stop it or even to comment on it negatively.

Again this may seem extreme, and in my experience few people actually act on mere hunches. But everyone needs to feel as unrestricted as possible in autonomously deciding as much of his or her life as is realistic. This assures that free will and personal responsibility will be kept at the forefront of human behavior, which to me is an essential consideration for our spiritual progression.

Guilt and anger are encouraged by the belief that once married, one mate has a proprietary claim on the other. Guilt comes when we believe that we owe our spouses more than we owe ourselves, or that his or her desires or interests are more important than our own. Anger results from thinking that our interests and desires supersede a mate's interests and desires, and that he or she owes us compensation for disrupting our lives by wanting to go.

Guilt and anger usually indicate that the relationship has been a dependent one; that the basis of the marriage has been need and obligation as much as love; and that there is probably a kind of unspoken mutual protection contract that is being violated. They tend to imply that the person leaving is in a superior position, and that the one being left is being harmed. This suggests something other than what was supposed to be a healthy, balanced relationship between equals.

Interestingly, guilt falls to the one who first arrives at the place of initiating the split, even if there has been discontent on both persons' parts. The person who acts first is held accountable for the hurt and unhappiness that may have actually been a part of the relationship for years.

I have seen people jockey for the victim's place so as to avoid the presumed responsibility for the break-up, leaving the guilt for having officially called it quits to the other. Sometimes this is unconscious, but often it is planned, such as when someone leaves and then just sits until the other has to file, or makes life at home miserable until the other exits, thus making him or her the ostensible initiator when the truth is otherwise. Ironically, the "guilty" person is frequently the partner who had the courage and love to do the hard work of officially starting the separation for both.

With guilt, the real conflict is not between the marital partners; it is an inner one involving low feelings of personal worth, an underdeveloped concept of self-ownership, and an unrealistic sense of obligation on one's part and entitlement on the other's. Unless we are being enormously unfair, feelings of guilt are a clue that we need to begin to consciously value ourselves in a higher way, and if we feel an unrealistic urge to take care of the other, to encourage initiative and growth on his or her part. In a relationship between independent individuals, assuming that a separation is done legally and equably, each partner is responsible for himself or herself.

Too often a guilty person prevents a just outcome for himself or herself because of the mistaken belief that love means self-sacrifice, and that he or she has not been loving and is therefore not deserving of equity. A reevaluation from a spiritual growth perspective would reveal that true affection is never based on guilt. Love involves giving freely and has nothing to do with the fear of disappointing others.

With anger, the conflict is an internal one also, its pivotal issue being the belief that we are owed the continued presence and support of our mate. We get frustrated and angry when we are deprived of what we think we need, what we desire, and what we believe we have coming to us. And we can easily use the marital vows to cement the claim. After all, they promised to share everything and to always be here.

Disappointment at having to give up that to which we are accustomed is natural, and is what typically lights our fuse. Having to face life without a mate is scary, as is a reduction in material lifestyle, and an increase in other responsibilities, such as producing personal income and managing unassisted child care.

Therefore, if we look closely we will discover that almost always these feelings are at least somewhat self-serving and self-centered. Therefore, while we may want to angrily judge our mate, we have to first be honest about our motives. Automatic anger tends to blind us to reason, fairness, respect, and compassion. Losing these, we have lost our way on the spiritual path.

Holding Tight to the New Perspective

In my own life and in my association with clients who have taken a healing path, I have found that the greatest aid to maintaining a growth perspective is to honor everyone as worthy of our love, and to regard each other's paths as equally unique and important. It is narcissistic to believe that another person was created for our convenience or that we were created for theirs and that they will be lost without us. We are special, but not that special.

While it is true that we have a purpose in each other's lives, those purposes are always secondary to our own purposes in being here. We need to share, but true sharing can only happen if we are separate beings who can reach across the chasm of individuality and give from a place of free will.

To my thinking as a therapist, anger is harder to heal than guilt, and it is potentially more destructive. At its root, guilt may emanate from a misguided sense of compassion.

Many of the clients I see express regret at their mate's suffering and would do most anything to make it go away. They often have an urge to return to the marriage in order to stop the suffering. This is a misperception of their role in a mate's life, but it also suggests that the mate being left remains a concern. Truly self-centered people do not feel guilty because they lack compassion.

By contrast, anger has no discernible relationship with compassion, except perhaps as a form of feeling sorry for oneself and being self-protective. If we step back and examine our motives when we are angry, we will see that nothing more than self-concern and the wish that the other mate also feels hurt for leaving us are what mainly generate this emotion.

Anger can cause us to fail to honor a mate's right to free choice, which we know is essential to spiritual growth, and to fail to recognize his or her suffering, which kills our compassion. Here we might tragically lose sight of the humanity of the other, which in turn clouds our own, and benefits the best interests of no one. This can then lead to becoming very demanding in our requirements that a mate return or pay compensation, sometimes in an extreme way.

Anger also often results in aggression or at least passive-aggressive behavior. It is more likely that it is when we are angry that we will do something unthinking and unhealthy such as involving our children, parents, in-laws, and friends in the marital fray as a means of punishing a mate or anyone who seems sympathetic to the mate.

I have to say that I rarely see guilty people clean-out bank accounts, or hold up divorce proceedings, or refuse fair settlements, or drag things out so as to prevent a mate from getting away. These are behaviors associated with anger. More often, I have had to caution guilty people against inappropriately giving their rights, goods and freedom away in an effort to pacify a mate, and assuage their own pain. And when I caution angry people, it is more often to be fair.

It is hard to imagine that if an angry individual stepped back and looked at the effects of his or her behavior, he or she would not feel chastened. And yet anger has a way of justifying itself, so that many are not chastened, or at least not right away.

Changing any of this is challenging, even with good support. I have had clients leave therapy because I affirmed their right to separate before they could sustain it within themselves. I have also had clients leave my office because I would not endorse their feeling of entitlement to punish their departing mates. The guilty continued to sabotage their own lives because they felt undeserving, and the angry continued to sabotage the lives of their mates for the opposite reason.

I have had fair success with angry clients when I could reach them early in the separation, before their anger crystallized into bitterness, but not always. Some angry people have a pathological degree of narcissism. They want what they want when they want it, and they are sure they deserve it and that they are right in becoming rageful when their expectations are unmet.

People who want to remain angry either only talk to people who agree with them or they keep their own counsel. Once they quit therapy because they have not been affirmed, they rarely return. If they had been in treatment with their mate and the mate still decides to leave, therapy usually ends, too.

Narcissistic persons tend to not look to themselves for fault or responsibility; instead they project it out onto others. This means that sometimes therapists are held responsible for the divorce, especially if they endorse autonomy and free choice. Interestingly, narcissists are usually partnered with self-effacing, dependent mates who readily assume responsibility for the anger, believing they caused it.

Anger is lower on the developmental hierarchy than guilt is. Anger is essentially instinctual, which means that it comes from an ancient place within our physiology that assured individual survival through aggressive domination of competitors. It is much harder to control hard-wired instinctual reactions than it is a socially conditioned reaction such as guilt. That is why it is important to get on top of anger right away before it has a chance to tap the deep reservoir of survival-driven emotional energy that can send us out of control.

It is also more difficult to vanquish an out-of-bounds sense of deserving than it is to instill a sense of worth when minimal self-regard has been beaten down or has never existed. The law of possession is part of this: it is usually harder to take something away once it is established than it is to put something in that has not been there.

No matter how we attempt to frame it, the former feels like losing. On the other hand, the latter feels like an undeserved windfall that we have not earned whose ownership is precarious. One seems natural and right; the other seems unnatural and uncomfortable. Moreover, our defensive system will keep whatever is familiar in place and reject anything foreign.

Healing guilt and anger requires persistence; change of the kind we want involves many, many repetitions of catching ourselves in the old pattern and trying on a new one. Breaking a habit is largely a matter of vigilant self-observation, the self-discipline to step back from impulses rather than reacting to them, and the honesty to never justify negative behavior when we do act out.

My therapeutic approach is to coach clients to stay quiet, non-judgmental, centered and calm in the presence of anger and guilt. From here I recommend:

- Staying with our feelings without acting on them, as this naturally counteracts our programmed, automatic reactions and will weaken their power over us. Instead of a flood of adrenaline-driven physical and emotional activity swamping us, we can remain rational and in this way put our new thinking to work. To be able to not react to threat with guilt or anger is self-reinforcing; we feel grown up and in control. A new perspective on emotion is crystallized as we discover that what used to overwhelm us is powerless and harmless in itself if only we do not allow ourselves to become caught-up in it. If we practice deliberately not responding as usual, with time we will see a change in our standard thinking and behavior. The key is paying conscious attention to what had always been reflexive, and having the committed intention to be different.

- Keeping a journal. Writing what we think and feel can help release tension just as effectively as talking does. It also provides a chance to gain some distance from our feelings because they are in print in front of us, and distance is essential in getting a new perspective.

We can use a journal to counter our bad feelings with self-affirmations, thereby creating an inner support system while practicing being positive. This is especially useful when guilt and anger are at their peak and we feel we have not done such a good job managing them. A journal also provides an opportunity to look back over our previous entries and see how we have progressed, which is beneficial in times of doubt.

- Go outdoors as often as possible. Nature is a wonderful healer when we are struggling with emotions. When my struggle with guilt was at it worst I found being next to moving water relaxing and cleansing. Sometimes, while walking a favorite beach, I would talk aloud into the waves and wind about my distress and my desire for relief, which seemed to lessen the burden. I always recommend walks, hiking, bike rides and other outdoor exercise to help release negative energy.

As we encounter success in undoing our defenses, we should expect powerful counterattacks by guilt and anger to dishearten us and reverse our gains. This can happen in unexpected, improbable, and frankly unbelievable ways.

A shocking instance for me was a conference with a lawyer who, in our only meeting, categorized me as "one of those selfish men" who use-up and then dump their wives to pursue a mid-life adventure. He confidently predicted that I would be wandering alone in a mall in five years, and would regret my decision. By then, of course, the damage would be done; it would be too late to correct anything.

Now, where did this come from? This man was recommended by a close friend, and yet I could not have felt more deviously set up by an adversary. The encounter stunned me and sent me reeling backward, giving the defenses against change time to regain a foothold.

My guilt overwhelmed my belief in the correctness of my decision to leave. Feeling defeated, I returned home, which in retrospect seemed unfair to my wife and children because I did not think that I belonged there. Therefore, I was faced with starting the whole leaving process over again, which had been so emotionally draining for all of us that I was not sure I could. Fortunately, the progress that had already been made was real, and the final exit occurred soon after, allowing the healing to begin.

I have seen many similar unanticipated reversals in therapy, so often in fact that I now predict them for clients who are on paths of fundamental change. However, I now see these events as aspects of the healing process.

I said before that from the perspective of the spiritual journey everything we go through is meant to foster growth, and these incidents are no exception. Life tests our resolve and each time we prevail, we grow. In addition, every time guilt and anger come to us we have another chance to heal them.

For me, having to make that final stand broke the grip guilt had on me once and for all. From that point on all that I had to face were occasional squalls and skirmishes. As I deliberately persisted on my course of change, the irrational defenses gave way to conscious control. They had to. It is in the design.

Shame and Embarrassment

I have not talked specifically about shame and embarrassment, which also accompany separation and divorce. I see these as our reaction to anticipated public censure for failing certain social expectations; they have been described as the social expression of our basic defensive system.

Because we live in a culture that sees being married as a high point in our adult development, divorce has to be regarded by contrast as a low point. Marriage is still thought of as the beginning of living happily ever after. Divorce lies in the other direction. Being a modern, liberal and relatively enlightened society has had little impact on this so far.

No one likes to fail, and it is worse when the failure is public. Societal reactions to marital failure are not kind, so we usually do everything we can to avoid public failure, and to avoid public exposure when we believe we have failed.

Healing shame and embarrassment, then, requires an approach essentially similar to healing guilt and anger; the work is the same. We need a commitment to seeing things differently, an understanding of our feelings and society's reactions as defenses against fundamental change, a strategy of calm, centered awareness, and the larger view of life as a spiritual journey.

An awareness-based and faith-centered repetitive practice really does make perfect. Still, fundamental change is slow because we have to overcome inertia. We cannot expect to step from one path onto an entirely new one without adjustment, part of which is getting used to what is new, and also letting go of what is old.

A final note. Some writers on separation and divorce categorize participants according to who is leaving and who is left. While the experiences in those relative positions are different in some ways, from the perspective I have used it does not matter whether we are the leaver or the left. Both are entrees to spiritual healing and growth because the feelings associated with them open us to our fundamental belief system, which is necessary to transcending its influence. Both, therefore, give us an opportunity to heal and grow by way of seeing things differently. It is just that we enter from slightly different ports. I do not know why some of us are in one position, and some in the other, but in terms of the work we are here to do, I do not think of one as worse than the other, just different.

Reflections

Sit quietly, breathe slowly, and relax your mind.

Silently read the following:

- I wish to see things differently.

- The dark emotions that I feel are normal. They are here to be healed, not judged.

- I will not let guilt influence my decisions. I choose to do what is best.

- I will not allow anger to guide my behavior. I will do what is right.

- Fear is natural at times of awakening and change. I choose to move forward now even though fear is my temporary companion.

- Nostalgia has its place, but I prefer the reality of today.

- My life is mine to decide. I will follow my own inspiration.

Now, repeat the phrases, again paying attention to the feelings that come as you consider each one.

Write each of them as before.

Read each phrase aloud if you can do so privately.

Close your eyes and think of things you have done out of guilt or anger. Write them down.

Now think of how you might have acted differently.

Finally, imagine yourself trusting your path and being free from guilt or anger. Feel the lightness. Carry this feeling with you throughout the day.

3
Love Affairs

I remember the look of dawning recognition and relief on a young woman's face when I suggested that the three-year love affair she had been in was not sinful, as she had feared, but was her attempt to find spiritual healing after many years in a very unhappy marriage. She had just related her view that everything in life was part of a guided spiritual process, and although she dearly loved her lover and said that she had grown significantly as a result of their relationship, she did not see her love affair as fitting that concept. Our conversation provided the link she needed to connect the love she felt with the rest of her spiritual beliefs.

She had married a man several years her senior with whom she had begun a relationship when she was in her late teens. He had mistreated her from the beginning, but theirs was one of those unconscious relationships that once started simply goes on-and-on and results in marriage because the couple finally decides that it is either that or break-up. She had stretched their engagement out as long as she could because she sensed that things would not improve, but habit and convenience, family and social pressure, and her fear of change and of being on her own prevailed over her intuition.

Her lover was also a married man, and from her description of things, it seemed that he was never going to be truly available. But in my mind his replacing her husband as a mate was not the point of their relationship; rather, it was meant to initiate her process of healing and growth. If nothing else, the conflict between her guilt and her desire finally brought her to my office where she could begin to see her life from a new perspective. The energy of the love affair was the first step to change.

I also recall a woman who came to see me after she found love letters from another woman to her husband from an affair he said ended ten years earlier. She had no idea that an affair had happened, and probably never would have except that he had saved the letters in a small box in the closet.

Now ten years later she felt as if the affair had just begun. Why had he saved the letters? Their discovery hurt her deeply and jeopardized the marriage.

Having met at length with him, I believe his saving the letters had to do with their marriage not having really progressed over the years. The letters symbolized the strong love he had once felt, and his holding onto them kept the energy of love alive where it would otherwise have been absent. Now revealed, it began to have an overt influence in his life. Although it had happened long before, it too was the first step to change.

Can we even imagine ever believing that an extramarital affair could be a worthy event? For most of us the very idea would seem absurd. People whose mates have been unfaithful suffer tremendously, and many families and homes have disintegrated in the aftermath. Part of my work over the years has been to help pick up the pieces in the wake of love affairs, and I have great compassion for people who have experienced that kind of misery.

As a psychologist, I am also aware of the consensual perspective in our culture that a love affair usually indicates some kind of character defect. Most therapists immediately look to the person having an affair for an interpretation in terms of an emotional problem, and most publications on the topic suggest that people who are unfaithful to their vows are immature or regressive. It is hard to argue with the validity of this point of view knowing the extent to which human beings can behave selfishly, impulsively and superficially.

And yet, in light of our attempt to see things differently, I suggest that we not categorically dishonor love affairs as a sign only of limitation because of the pain they bring. The concept of the spiritual journey can assist us with this. Because love affairs can open us to needed change, I think that it is reasonable that we begin to see them as a potential aid to spiritual progression, not merely a hindrance. Moreover, I believe that it is vital to our spiritual progression that we do so, and I am certain from the results of therapy done from this perspective that it will ultimately lessen suffering.

Like any other encounter on the journey that forces us to become more open emotionally and to reexamine our beliefs, I believe that the unanticipated entry of a foreign love into married life has the capacity to advance us. I have arrived at this view as a result of having witnessed the contribution extramarital love can make to an individual's growth if looked at from a larger perspective than only the interests of marital stability and the avoidance of grief.

In anticipation of an immediate impulse to reject this idea, I suggest that we think again about our hidden defenses against fundamental change. Because love affairs cause immense pain, pose a severe threat to the stability of married and family life, violate our cultural norms, and frequently contribute to divorce, there always is a strong automatic reaction against them. In view of these negative feelings, just allowing for the possibility that extramarital love might have a positive effect is a start in a growthful direction.

Considering a New Point of View

Extramarital love has been with us as long as we have had marriage; in fact, love affairs have such a lengthy association with the institution of marriage that I have come to think of them as marriage's shadow. While this image might initially reflect only the sinister image we have of love affairs, such as a wolf shadowing a flock or death shadowing life, to me it simply describes their ubiquitous nature: they are just always there. Given their ubiquity, and their implication in so many divorces, they - and our assumptions about them - deserve our scrutiny here.

Considering their constancy, it seems a shame that we understand and handle them so poorly; that we are still so baffled when they enter our lives; and that we just do not seem to know what to do with them. A few cultures openly allow for them; a few more turn a blind eye. However, the usual approach is to roundly condemn them, to exact severe punishments from those who participate in them, and to do everything we can to try to prevent their recurrence.

But in spite of our general preference for monogamy, our vows to be faithful, and our efforts to perfect our relationships with our mates, we have accomplished little that is truly helpful in preventing affairs from happening. We might wisely begin to wonder if there is an explanation for this beyond the usual ones having to do with our sinful human tendencies or our wayward biological natures, neither of which has done us much good. I suggest we begin looking for reasons in the possibility that the persistent presence of love affairs may indicate that they have a necessary place in our lives.

Most of the people I have known who were involved in love affairs felt real love, not simply lust and infatuation. They may deny this under hostile interrogation, or to protect a spouse's feelings or save a marriage, and as a group we may want to distort the honest emotion to keep our unsavory image of love affairs alive.

Nevertheless, I would argue that from a spiritual perspective, any relationship in which the participants share love has value. To argue otherwise would seem the worst of travesties since we consider finding and sharing love our highest achievement as human beings, an act or ability that separates the healthiest and most fortunate of us from all others.

And if this is true, does it really make sense to continue to believe that love that leads to marriage is good, and love that contributes to a divorce is not? I see this as manipulating the truth for convenience sake. We have no business manipulating love merely because it complicates our lives, and in the interest of healing and growth, I suggest we instead try to deal differently with the complications.

Further, it seems to me, a change of perspective about love affairs may reduce our suffering. I am not suggesting that we can simply banish the pain any time soon. But it seems logical that if we can allow that an affair might have a useful place, and if we can affirm all love as good, our attitude toward everyone involved in a love affair, including ourselves, will change for the better, and suffering will be reduced.

As it now stands, in cultures where emotional fidelity and sexual exclusivity imply goodness, an affair is considered about the worst thing that can happen. Its psychological effect is devastating. And even if a marriage survives an affair, for most of us things are never the same afterward.

Thus, when an affair is revealed, the drama at home is intense. The aggrieved spouse is usually considered a victim, and feels entitled to sympathy at least and to some form of retribution if preferred, including violence, which we tend to tacitly if not openly justify in our own minds.

If an affair becomes public knowledge, both spouses usually suffer shame and embarrassment. For a long time the couple might be thought of primarily in terms of the scandal, and they often feel that they will forever be the topic of gossip and speculation.

Even if an affair remains an individual's secret, he or she is usually wracked with guilt and self-loathing. On top of this internal punishment there is the incessant dread of eventually being found out.

Reconciling in our culture's present moral atmosphere usually requires that the married "perpetrator" admit to wrongdoing, selfishness, and even insanity; that he or she feels remorse and begs forgiveness; and promises to be faithful in the future. It also usually requires having to allow the lover to become a target of abuse and contempt by the "injured" parties.

Having witnessed this scenario on many occasions, I can only say that none of it fosters healing and growth. What I have seen is that all the people affected by a love affair suffer and that everyone is deserving of compassion. The individuals who have sought my help because of love affairs were mainly ordinary, decent people who were trying to do right by everyone, and who were terribly stuck.

In my experience, to describe people in affairs as deceitful, selfish, weak or immoral is so far from the truth that I can hardly acknowledge it. I suspect that it is our fear of unexpected and uncontrollable emotional involvement that makes us think there is something different about married people who fall in love outside of the marriage.

In truth, we are all more alike than different. It is simply naive to assume that once we enter the married state we are no longer subject to the forces of change. We are on a journey of growth after all, and it would appear contrary to our interests to look for an excuse to remain closed to it.

How Love Affairs Can Promote Growth

When I think of love affairs, images of many people I have worked with over the years come to mind, and I consider how their or their spouses' extramarital experiences added to their lives even as they complicated them. This brings to mind the earlier description of the heart and soul of life and how it applies here.

The heart of a love affair is the lightness, joy, release, hope and optimism that enter a person's life for being in love, especially if the marriage has become stale. The soul is all of the anguish, inconvenience, confusion, and potential loss that being in love can cause when a person is already married. Falling in love is the easy part; the hard work is living with all the difficulty that accompanies it.

Having worked with so many people, I have formed a loose system of classifying love affairs that is based on some of the distinct features that set a few of them apart, including how each fosters growth. To be sure, these are after-the-fact categorizations in that they do not in any way guide my work; nor do I think they diminish or dehumanize the divorce experience. In fact, I think they do the opposite in that they help promote a sense of shared identity and compassion because we are likely to see something of ourselves or people we care about in one or another of them.

I should add that while this book is about divorce, the affairs I will discuss do not necessarily lead there. Some of them may improve faltering marriages, and some may support the continuation of marriages that otherwise might be finished or doomed.

The Parallel Life

The first type is love affairs that continue consistently or intermittently for many years, with the marital partner never knowing about it. In this instance, a clandestine love remains isolated from everyone, allowing a possibly lifelong extramarital relationship. This can amount to a parallel life that differs from the marriage only in its invisibility.

An outsider might never know which relationship is the real love. We may assume that the visible relationship is the important one because it is public; but that could be wrong, as there are many reasons that the unmarried couple would want their privacy that have nothing to do with it being a lesser love.

The stories of these affairs may never come to light, but they sometimes surface when a secret lover dies, as happened recently with Charles Kuralt, a celebrated television journalist whose second family was revealed soon after his death. If we find out about them at all, it is usually because of a child from that union, an unanticipated claim on the estate of the deceased, the presence of a stranger who is seen surreptitiously grieving at the gravesite, or a persistent rumor that ultimately proves true.

When the existence of a parallel life is revealed, everyone is shocked and surprised. We might think that we would notice the signs of a long-term affair, but experience says otherwise. No tell tale clues may ever have registered.

To my knowledge, I have only met one person who might fully qualify for this category. Ironically, we got together on his wife's initiative because he had talked to her about leaving (although he had not revealed his true motivation for wanting to go) and she wanted my help to forestall a separation.

Until he revealed his second life to me in an individual session, I thought we were going to be doing fairly standard marital therapy. He later sent his lover to meet with me also, so I was able to achieve an understanding of what both relationships were like from his and the women's points of view, as well as my own.

The love affair had gone on for almost twenty years by the time we met. Unlike his marriage, he had no children by the second relationship, but their togetherness was relatively uninterrupted and genuine. He had to work hard to see her as regularly as he did, but his desire for her company prevailed and he made it happen.

My interpretation of things was that the stronger emotional bond existed in the second relationship, and that it was there that my client felt most intimate and open. I sensed that he and his wife interacted perfunctorily in their roles with each other, and it seemed to me that she had settled a while ago for just being able to pursue her own interests in lieu of affection.

Everyone was in crisis by the time I entered the picture. He was torn between leaving and staying; his wife did not want to lose what she had; and his lover wished to finally be primary in his life. Unfortunately, I do not know what the outcome of the situation was. He remained undecided too long as to a course of action, and I could not stay involved knowing something that his wife did not. Choosing between lives was not something he seemed ready to do, and as far as I know he may be living a dual life even today.

Nonetheless, I had spent enough time with all of them to be able to draw two important conclusions. One conclusion was that he had married unconsciously, meaning that he did not really know why he married who he did, and that he married before he was ready for intimate sharing. The relationship never grew to accommodate true intimacy, as was evidenced by his secret life, if nothing else. His world at home appeared to be anchored largely by habit, responsibility, and convenience. When he talked about leaving his wife he felt great guilt. He did not want to hurt her or have her lose her lifestyle.

The other conclusion was that the love affair had provided him with an opportunity for intimate sharing that the marriage could not. He clearly felt more comfortable with his lover and he had a more passionate connection with her. From the standpoint of heartfelt affection and communication, it was the real thing.

We might correctly suspect that he had unconsciously placed himself between two relationships so that he could risk opening himself to love in the affair only because he was protected from a complete commitment to it by his loyalty to the marriage. No matter: the emotional bond was real, and the painful struggle I saw him go through convinced me that he was not protected from having to do the hard work that life requires of all of us as the price of our growth.

The conventional view might say that my client's progression in this arrangement was limited by having the second relationship, but it is my view that the affair is what actually made growth possible. I believe that it was largely through the existence of the second relationship that he progressed in his ability to love, even if it was the existence of the marriage that helped him feel safe enough to try letting his deepest feelings out at all.

While he had remained loyal to his wife in terms of keeping the marriage intact, he had apparently gained little in terms of expressing and receiving love in that relationship because it had required so little of him emotionally. Duty and responsibility may have been in the marriage; but love was in the affair, and it stretched him in a way that would probably not have happened otherwise.

I have seen similar arrangements with other people who were engaged in long-term affairs, although none as long as this. I am persuaded that in each instance the love expressed in the extramarital relationships clearly dominated the affection shared at home.

These people remained in their marriages for a variety of reasons including guilt, loyalty, responsibility, fear of material loss, and concerns for consistency in the lives of their children. A few did not think they could afford a divorce, and some had probably correctly predicted that the love affair would not have survived as a marriage, and so would not take a chance on trading what they had for it. Others were in relationships with married people who had similar personal and family concerns and chose to stay. In a way, it appeared that the extramarital relationships were meant to remain just that.

I am not in a position to say that all long-term love affairs promote growth, but I can safely extrapolate from the ones I have seen that many of them can provide an opportunity for the participants to "practice" being loving where that possibility might not normally exist. And while some of us might question the lovers' capacity for committed intimacy in a normal marriage, we have to allow that they demonstrated commitment to the love affairs, many of which outlasted other's marriages, and that this promoted growth. The fact that their love was extra-marital in nature is irrelevant.

The "Forgotten" Affair

The second classification contains the kind of liaisons that I think most of us tend to picture when we think of love affairs. They differ from the first in that they are usually of a shorter duration, they do not involve the same level of personal commitment, and from all outward appearances they seem to have little impact on the life of the participants once they are over.

Because of its apparently superficial nature, an affair of this sort does not seem to have much reason for being; certainly, it is more difficult to affirm its value in fostering growth.   What limits its impact is the overriding intention of the person exiting an affair if it remains secret, and of the spouse if he or she has learned of it, that it not be permitted to disrupt the status quo in any way.

This does not mean that there was no feeling in the affair or regret at having to give it up, or hurt and anger at home if the affair comes to light; but the married couple collaborates to discount and ignore it. So, whether the affair remains unearthed and simply runs out of energy, or ends as the result of an ultimatum from the spouse, or is terminated for other reasons is basically irrelevant. Once the overt drama has run its course, the love affair may seem to disappear without a trace.

It may be hard for some to imagine that people living in a marriage could allow this kind of suppression to happen, but I would estimate that for every marriage that is lost to an affair, one is preserved by such denial. I have had many couples in therapy just long enough to reestablish their emotional equilibrium and relational stability, and once this was accomplished, except for occasional outbursts of bad feelings, no one talked in depth about the relevance of those "forgotten" relationships.

I have also spoken with individuals who have successfully kept their love affairs secret, and were happy just to be able to return to the marriage as it had been without disturbing the mate. In fact, while some have felt ashamed of their unfaithfulness, they also felt at least somewhat redeemed for having borne their guilt without exposing the unsuspecting mate to the suffering and unpredictable changes that the discovery of an affair can cause.

The question is whether a person can really remain unchanged once having been in a love affair. In my experience, the answer is no. I believe that our hearts are designed to respond to the stimulation of love, and therefore it is unlikely that a lover can remain exactly as before. I also believe that love affairs are meant to be disruptive, and that the person involved is always changed even if the marriage seems unaffected.

The best evidence of this is in marriages where denial had reigned and things had seemed to normalize with no significant change, but the seeds of disharmony that led to the affair remained unaltered. These are the people who I see years down the road when new crises arise, or when old unhappiness finally erodes the walls that have contained it.

One such couple had been together for many years. They quarreled incessantly and were rarely peaceful in each other's company. During an early session the woman brought up an affair her husband had had twenty years before, and used it to try to make him feel shameful and look bad in my eyes.

When he and I talked later, he told me that the affair was the best thing that ever happened to him. He said that the only time he felt truly loved and appreciated was in the affair, and that it was only with that woman that he ever felt safe to give himself as completely as he was able. He was transformed when he spoke of her. I sensed that the affair had evoked love unlike anything else in his life had, and that he had grown from it.

That couple stopped seeing me because I could do nothing for them. They seemed committed to remain as unhappily attached as ever. I am glad to at least have had the opportunity to affirm the value of his one real experience in love. That affirmation seemed very important to him. Unfortunately, I am fairly sure that his wife had never experienced a similar degree of love.

Affairs That Benefit Marriages

The third category of love affairs is one in which the marital relationship improves as a consequence of the affair, and the affair ends because of the improvement. In effect, the affair saves the marriage at its own expense. The improvements may occur whether the affair is ever revealed and discussed or not, although they will occur differently if the affair remains secret instead of shared.

The energy that is stimulated by the new love can revitalize a marriage in which creativity is flagging, animating it to where it can begin to generate more creative energy of its own. The new energy can enhance attention, affection, and passion, resulting in a stronger desire to spend time together.

The relationship at home then begins to look attractive and promising again to the unfaithful spouse, and the marriage can now successfully compete with the affair so that the affair naturally fades in significance.

I have witnessed this metamorphosis both with the affairs being revealed and not. When a client has chosen to keep an affair secret and the marriage improves, it is usually because the affair has led that person to do some important individual work that could only occur away from the emotional and physical confinement of the marriage. That individual work then fosters needed change at home.

Ironically, it is often something unanticipated in the marriage that draws unresolved issues into the open that otherwise might never have surfaced, and these lead to the affair. For example, one client who had been abused sexually as a child entered marriage before sufficient healing had been accomplished in regard to individual identity, establishing personal boundaries, and feeling safe enough to open herself to intimacy and commitment, all of which confronted her only once she was married. She felt terrified about losing self-direction and autonomous control and becoming vulnerable.

Because she had not fully entered her marital relationship, she felt unfulfilled. Her husband was not able to get through her defenses to help her feel affirmed, cherished, and safe. A man she worked with became interested in her, and his attention inflamed a passion in her that she had not experienced previously. Each time we talked, she would tell me that she had no idea why the affair was happening. She rated her husband far above her lover, and in fact described her lover as essentially unappealing.

I believe that love was doing its healing work in a mysterious way. She was becoming more-and-more open to the possibility that she was lovable, and that she could safely expose her emotional needs and her sexual desire without risking harm now that she was grown. This had not occurred in her marriage, which makes me think that it just could not. I had met her husband and thought he was the good man she had described him to be. She apparently had to do the work on her own.

When she finally ended the affair, she reentered her marital relationship with a new level of capability for intimate sharing. Her commitment was demonstrated abundantly thereafter. Her husband never knew what had occurred in her private life. He was the unwitting beneficiary of the good work she had done.

I knew another woman who was also confronted by the fear of losing her autonomy. By the time she came to therapy she was thoroughly confused about her marriage, and had even considered leaving it, especially after having become interested in a man she had met quite by accident while on a trip.

In lieu of leaving, she decided to take some time apart, during which she traveled, spent holidays with friends, and worked on her personal healing. Her behavior was anything but ordinary or conventionally acceptable, and yet from an individual healing and growth perspective it was just what she had to do. When she returned to her mate full time, she was finally ready for a commitment. They have done well together.

She had not put her marriage at risk after all, although her behavior had by all conventional standards done exactly that. She chose to keep her extramarital relationship to herself, and although she did not feel good about what she had done, there seemed to be no way around it.

Sometimes it is opening our hearts to someone where there is no commitment that allows us to be able to do it where there is one. Sometimes it takes the excitement of illicit love to break through a barrier to erotic self-expression. Sometimes it can only be an extramarital liaison that provides needed assurance of lovability before we can feel truly lovable at home. And sometimes the pure selfishness of an affair is what is required to open the way to be more fully giving to a mate.

Unlike the "forgotten" affairs, in my experience it is the individual or the couple who deals openly with the affair and searches out the reasons for it who are the ones that will most likely benefit from its positive effects. I have found that where individual healing is not fatal to the marriage, the energy of individual change can initiate a transformation in the marital pair, with the marriage becoming healthier than ever. The love affair allows personal healing, which in turn fills the developmental gaps through which the lover entered, and it leads to a partner who is more capable of loving the other.

Affairs That End Marriages

The final grouping consists of those love affairs that usher in the end of a marriage. What may differentiate these affairs from the others is simply their timing; they happen at the point where someone is preparing for a major change.

Sometimes these affairs are the opening salvo that begins a long process of weakening the defenses against change; sometimes they are the final straws that help break down a moribund marriage that has had little worth; and sometimes they are a shockingly fast-acting agent of transformation. Whatever their point of entry and wherever they ultimately lead, when looked at from the healing and growth point of view, it seems to me that any love affair that contributes to separation was meant to do just that. This is consistent with the concept of the spiritual journey where such disruptive events are meant to move us along, and with my experience that they only happen in marriages where change is needed, although the couple may not be initially aware of it or want to admit it.

When I meet with clients to discuss this type of affair, it is often because they had been taken unawares and are trying to figure out what happened to cause them to become involved with a new love. In most instances, when we look carefully over the tenure of the marital relationship, or we closely examine his or her individual needs, the mystery fades: we are able to determine that there had been at least some indications that things had not been quite right.

For most of these people, the first signs of change usually surfaced in the activities that generally indicate vitality when a marriage is good. Sexual relations had begun to decrease noticeably; conversations had become utilitarian; and special time for each other was lost to other "more practical" concerns with children, work, or social activities. In other words, the behaviors we associate with courting have been neglected, and the bond has weakened.

Often it was only one of the spouses who had felt things wane. Someone may have been changing in ways that the other did not perceive or could not keep up with, and where one of them may have been content with things as they were, the other may have become deeply dissatisfied.

Sometimes sex, conversation, and time together had deteriorated prior to an affair, and then suddenly and mysteriously increased, perhaps lulling a spouse into a false sense of reassurance that things were improving. In hindsight, the "improvement" was a sign of change; the increased courting activity was a result of the energy of the affair and the displaced desire for the new person. This displacement is especially transparent if any new erotic activities were introduced into the bedroom.

And not infrequently we discovered that feelings of guilt for having an affair, and the fear of possibly being found out and losing the marriage, caused a genuine resurgence in efforts to re-engage the mate, or might have motivated a feigned renewal of interest.

The actual finish of a marriage can occur in several variations. A common one is that a mate who is in love with another chooses to leave the marriage without ever disclosing the affair, sometimes departing the relationship in a shroud of mystery. Often the existence of a new love as the reason for going may be suspected by others but never confirmed.

A second variation is that a mutual decision to divorce occurs either right after the affair has come to light, or months later after the affair has been abandoned and great effort has been expended to try to salvage the marriage. In such instances the effects of the affair are, for a variety of reasons, just too great to overcome.

A third variation is that an offended mate chooses to peremptorily leave after having learned of the partner's affair, as if his or her departure was a preordained outcome should an affair occur. Although we might believe otherwise, this variation is unusual: the threat of change and loss usually tends to temper the impulse to go. But feelings of being violated can certainly be great enough to prevail over fear and other barriers.

A fourth variation is where an affair illuminates the chronic mutual dissatisfaction that both of the mates had been feeling about the marriage, and neither spouse blames the other for the affair or the marital decline. In this instance the new love simply provides a convenient reason to finally separate, and the couple takes advantage of it.

The fifth variation is one in which the marriage ends with a spouse secretly or openly pursuing a committed relationship with the lover. This is not entirely different than the other variations, but because leaving a marriage with the new love replacing the old love has special complications, I want to highlight it for later discussion.

Affairs of the Heart

There is actually an additional type of love affair, which does not quite fit into the above categories because it is solely of the heart. Like the others it arises mysteriously, leaving the lovers with all the same questions about how his or her heart got to this place. And like the others it can be a catalyst for change.

In this one, a tangible intimacy with a loved one does not have to develop, in fact, the other person does not even have to be aware of it for the feelings to have a lethal impact on a marital relationship.

We may think of this as romantic fantasy, such as the reverie a romance novel devotee might experience in a favorite story, or the crush a young student might have toward a teacher. But it is neither of these, and we are missing something of significance when we try to diminish it this way. I think of it more as a spiritual relationship, an enthralling connectedness not greatly different than saints have described as their bond with God.

These are true love relationships, in that they are driven by the energy of love and they possess all of the desire, absorption, rapture, painful longing, and even commitment of any physically consummated relationship, and they can grow to dominate a married person's consciousness just as strongly. And like any other love affair that ends a marriage, they do their relentless work of expanding the heart so that the old boundaries cannot hold it, only the process remains concealed from everyone but its bearer.

It would be incorrect to think that this kind of affair is conjured by persons who lack the courage to act on their feelings as happens in an open affair. In my experience, it is just a course to change that is provided for some people whose path does not require acting out their love in a physical way. It provides an alternative for growth of this kind without causing the suffering that might be in store for everyone if it was played out as the lover really wishes it could.

How Affairs Fulfill Their Purpose

Healing takes many forms, and for many married men and women the desire to leave an unhappy marriage is one of them. Sometimes, however, a strong wish to leave is not enough; the thought of actually doing it is so daunting that many people do not have the personal strength to accomplish the change without assistance. I believe that it is in just such a situation that Life provides a new love as a resource to help an individual successfully pull away.

The change proceeds in two phases. First, the new love opens and expands the heart. This is akin to widening the channel of a stream, which has the effect of allowing for a greater flow of love than could have happened before.

Once a heart has been expanded by the new love, the marriage can survive only if the marital relationship can expand to embrace the change, as sometimes happens. However, what often happens is that a marriage will lack the capacity for appropriate growth and not be capable of containing the new love in its expanded volume. The awakened feelings now overflow the marriage, and new growth precludes things being able to stay as they had been.

Second, the extramarital bond is unique. Because the heart's expansion is associated with the lover, it may be impossible to ever share the enhanced feelings of love with the spouse. Once the heart has forged a new union, there may be no going back regardless of intentions. As a heart grows, its proprietor grows also.

Thus, as many clients have so accurately put it, while he or she might continue to feel affection for a husband or wife, they could no longer share as deeply with a mate as with the lover. The spouse's claim was always to the smaller part of his or her heart; the expanded area now belonged to another, and the larger was destined to annex the smaller.

Moreover, the heart can readily overpower the mind, and when it floods the mind with images of the new love, the lover is all that can be thought about. Such obsessive thinking is part of the design of growth.

When an affair arrives to fulfill the purpose of changing a marriage, incessant thoughts about the new love become an irresistible force. Images of the lover intrude into every aspect of the married person's domestic life. The lover may be glimpsed in the bedroom, the kitchen, at a party, a school affair for one of the children, and on vacations. He or she slips into the unconscious, too, and shows up in dreams where no control can be exerted to prevent it. This energy insinuates itself into the very sites where the emotional bond between the mates is rooted and dislodges the marital commitment.

Our defenses against change recognize the danger in this process, and instinctively target the obsession, labeling it as anything but substantive and healthy. We attempt to diminish its worth by calling it infatuation. We try to shame ourselves out of it by saying it is a shallow sexual interest. And we try to delude ourselves as to its ultimate intent by speaking of it as some sort of temporary craziness that will fade with time and a return to sanity.

Nevertheless, as anyone who has tried to talk someone out of a new love knows, explanations, interpretations and warnings are impotent in the presence of a relationship whose time has arrived. It appears that Nature has given love an addictive quality that prohibits easy escape: nothing is more endearing than the new love, and the desire for the lover overrides all arguments against pursuing that path. By compelling increasing involvement, this natural arrangement provides sufficient time for developing an emotional bond strong enough to force a schism at home, assuring that the momentum to change will not be reversed.

The excessive quality of this fixation, and the seeming lack of reasonable restraint and control may seem dismaying, but if we think about it, such excess is necessary to counter the many forces that are aligned to prevent change from occurring. Many people need a Siren song to draw them to advantageous devastation.

If a new love relationship has been circumvented for reasons of fear, distrust, or issues of timing, a sense of yearning for that person and the abbreviated relationship may forever after haunt the marriage. The object of the expanded love does not have to be around to keep the impetus to change alive. After-images of that love and thoughts of what might have been can displace the marital bond just as readily as an actual affair. Affairs of the heart work this way, too.

It is also important to understand that a love affair need not survive long to demonstrate its worth or accomplish its purpose. Just because it does not evolve into a committed relationship is no reason to suspect that it was ill begotten. There is no way to know at the outset where any relationship will end; in fact, most of them do not become marriages. Love affairs may serve only as a path to change, and once that has been accomplished, may disappear. However, from a growth point of view, where they lead is all that is important.

The New Love Takes Over

In situations where marriages have run their course, and where the bond between the lovers is strong and enduring so that it is destined to end the marital relationship, it is inevitable that the new emotional union will challenge the old official union for dominion. Legally the marriage remains primary; but that has no validity from the heart's perspective. The incipient love is the authentic love, and the lovers' bond surpasses the marital bond in importance.

Sooner or later keeping the new love subservient to the old seems morally wrong. This is an odd epiphany because the force of conventional moral thinking is always with the marriage. But when the emotional commitment shifts from the love that was to the love that is, on a spiritual level the new relationship ceases to be only an affair. Love always demands its respected place, and in the heart's view the spouse is now the "other man" or "other woman."

Sometimes the signs of a shift in allegiance are subtle. I remember the time a long-married woman described how over a recent weekend she eschewed attending a major sporting event with her husband so that she could be at home in case her lover called. Her choice was so natural that it took a few beats before the significance of her behavior registered in her awareness. From that point on she was always conscious of who was truly first in her life.

Since from the conventional view love affairs have no honorable place, the lover is an interloper and the love is a travesty. The lovers' perspective is entirely different, of course, and at some point a new accounting of things will have to take place.

This may begin with public attacks against the lover once an affair is revealed. When the new love is tenacious and strong, any assault on the lover is tantamount to throwing down the gauntlet, which finally evokes the only honorable response, which is to defend the new love, regardless of the personal cost or the cost to the marriage.

At this juncture the balance shifts. No more will an angry spouse be allowed to freely belittle the new love, and when he or she realizes this, they know their status in the life of their mate has changed.

When the affair remains secret, the lover feels an inner pressure to promote it to a more respectable stature. The attacks are self-inflicted for not being courageous and honest in honoring what is real.

Once the new love has taken root life at home becomes complicated. This is partly because feelings of love have no regard for marital boundaries. Lovers want to make their joy known and to claim the right to be together openly. Being bound by a moral or legal commitment may stem their overt behavior, but it in no way diminishes their desire for self-expression, and may intensify it by constraining the pressure to the point of explosion.

When the pressure to act authentically asserts itself before an individual feels ready for the next step, he or she gets squeezed between the irresistible press to move forward and the unyielding resistance against letting go. The new love may not yet be compelling enough to risk abandoning a comfortable lifestyle or potent enough to warrant confrontations with a spouse, family and friends.

This situation can go on for months or more. When it does, tension is usually relieved through fantasy resolutions in which mates die by accident or illness, or decide to leave first so that no confrontation is necessary. These drive a further emotional wedge into the commitment, and help keep the impetus to change in force while the individuals gather strength. People may be shocked at their fantasies, but such productions are a natural support in the arduous interval prior to resolving the situation for real.

It is also common for people who fear a confrontation to begin to behave in ways that encourage the partner to quit the marriage. This can include obvious withdrawal of affiliation and affection, verbal taunting and aggressiveness, and even abuse and other hostile acts. Some lovers will disclose the affair to their mates in the hope it will compel them to leave. And sometimes the conflict is resolved only after the bottled-up emotion unconsciously seeps into the marital partner's awareness so that the desire to be elsewhere can no longer be hidden.

Leaving With A New Love

In a culture where divorce is all by itself considered a failure, leaving a marriage in order to be with a new love is thought to be even worse. It is a development that makes almost everyone involved uncomfortable.

I have had the experience of being fooled in marital therapy by men or women who were trying to juggle a lover and a spouse so that they would not lose the marriage while not immediately having to let go of the lover either. I have found it easier, however, to sense the existence of a lover where a spouse is intent on leaving. What I believe gives them away is that they always seem to be in need of confession, as if they are committing a grave sin and can no longer bear its weight on their souls.

In my experience, few people are more in need of affirmation and support than those who choose life with a lover over life with a spouse. While I am aware that some men and women seem impervious to the cultural prejudice against this behavior, most are highly vulnerable. They realize that as soon as the truth gets out that they will become targets for public disdain. In addition, they have to contend with personal feelings of guilt, shame and embarrassment while their intention to leave with a lover remains hidden.

But what is often worse is the feeling many have of weakness and inadequacy for not having enough personal mettle to make the break alone. Sadly for them, as much as the new love may feel completely right in the shadows, leaving a marriage in his or her company can feel completely wrong.

I believe that part of our discomfort about a marital ending where a lover is involved has to do with an unexpressed sense of the inherent unfairness of the situation. Our common belief is that a person who leaves with a new love for support has an advantage over someone who has to go it alone, and when it happens, it seems to indicate that for some reason life favors one person over another.

I sense that we would feel better about a break-up if both spouses had new people to go to. If I am correct about this, it would tend to indicate that our moral indignation is not so much about the love affairs or the marital split, but about one person's having to be alone when the other does not.

In fact, most of the people I have talked to who have left their mates with a new love wish above everything that their spouses also had a new partner as this would assuage their own sense of the unfairness of the situation. And often enough, spouses who have been left wish the same for themselves and are angry that their ex-mate seems to have gotten the better deal.

My perspective about this is that it is our fear of being alone that makes us believe as we do. But if we can begin to think of the primary work of love as creative change, then we might see that there is no unfairness here. We will recognize that what is most important for both spouses is that the marriage ends, not whether they are able to replace the old love with a new one.

We have to think about love as a resource for growth. It is the nature of our journey that we are all supplied with the resources we need to grow. If change is appropriate but the fear of having to face life alone deters a mate from ending a marriage, it would seem to be to both mates' advantage that the exiting person is supplied with a new love when leaving because it makes change possible.

The new love helps in other ways, too. Most people feel ambivalent about ending a marriage. Rarely does a person leave a marriage with all of his or her feelings about the mate resolved. Even in a disastrous one, some affection remains.

Therefore, besides lessening the fear of being alone, having a new companion can counteract the urge to return to an unwanted marriage brought on by sentimentalism or inappropriate feelings of guilt and responsibility. Without the lover's demands that he or she be first, and without the magnetic force of the new love to pull forward, the temptation to return to the familiar may be overpowering.

But there are also disadvantages to the new relationship. Insecurity and vulnerability are always aspects of a recent attachment, and these are intense when the predictable support of the marriage has been lost. For the newly departed there is always the nagging worry that if the marriage failed, how can anyone be sure that the new commitment will prove durable.

There are other issues that people who leave a marriage with a new love have to deal with that involve being judged by the ethical standards by which they had lived their married lives. Because love affairs often involve behavior that we generally consider wrong, some of the judgment is fair.

One of the issues involves having had outside sexual relations that could have placed the mate at health risk. Even where precautions have been taken, there is the question of having carried on two simultaneous sexual relationships without the mate's consent.

Another issue is having deceived a mate when he or she has correctly perceived the existence of an affair. This makes him or her less certain of the accuracy of their perceptions, sometimes to the point of feeling mentally ill and in need of professional care.

There is at least marginal dishonor if the new love is a relative, friend, neighbor or acquaintance, or a boss or subordinate. Even the fact that a lover is smarter or more physically attractive than the mate can be an issue, as it suggests possible superficiality.

Any of these situations complicates healing for all those involved. I think the most difficult of them have to do with having been dishonest. This is such a problem in many ways, especially since I cannot imagine that society's moral position regarding divorce will change anytime soon. The support that is needed by married people who are involved with others will be hard to find, and deceptions will continue.

As much as I cherish full disclosure, having witnessed dreadful reactions to admissions of love affairs, I have to sympathize with clients who have held that there were valid reasons for choosing to keep an affair private. Many have justifiably feared harm from sharing the truth of the love affair, not only to themselves, but to their new love as well.

But anyone who leaves a marriage in order to be with a lover knows that the truth is hard to hide. If an affair existed prior to a separation, when it is eventually revealed, it usually becomes the assumed reason for the break-up, even if those intimately involved know it was not the primary cause of the marital failure. Even after an affair culminates in a new marriage, it is common that one or both of the newlyweds feels embarrassed if someone suspects that the involvement began during the previous marriage.

It is clear to me that most people who find themselves in love affairs do not wish to hurt anyone by them. In fact, their fervent wish is for an easy way to let the past go so that the present could be attended to.

Left for Love

People tend to react in two general ways to the revelation that a mate has a new love and is leaving. One is that the person being left is not particularly disturbed at the news. This might seem odd since we have come to expect people in this situation to be hurt and angry, and we believe that they have a right to.

In fact, when this reaction happens, people are more surprised by their lack of distress than anything else. But when we discuss the matter, they discover that there is no real mystery here; the departure just confirmed what was already sensed, which was that the marriage had lost its meaning, and it was their defenses against change that had prevented their awareness.

In this type of marital relationship, when the truth of the emptiness of the marriage is known for sure, terminating it begins to make a lot of sense. The well-wishing that I spoke of earlier is an appropriate response here since there is no loss of anything important. People are often curious regarding who the new person is and how that relationship came about, and some of them have an issue with the deception that was involved, but that is all.

I have seen individuals in therapy because they were unable to reconcile their belief that they should be more upset by their nonplused behavior. It is an interesting struggle between rational thinking and impulses that they can objectively see for what they are. I have had to dissuade some individuals from trying to get upset because they really thought they should. In such instances our work had not to do so much with adjusting to loss, but with uncovering how they had missed the cues that married life was empty, and why they remained there.

The second reaction is the more common one. It involves being thoroughly overwhelmed at the discovery of the love affair and the impending loss. For most people the affairs and the departure represent a staggering blow. Without any prompting, individuals have compared the trauma and the adjustment process to that of dealing with dying, even if the marriage were an unhappy one. The feeling of disconsolateness often lasts for months, sometimes for years. In the acute phase people struggle with great sadness or anger or both. We have to be aware of the possibility of suicidal thoughts, and sometimes, homicidal fantasies toward mates or their lovers.

There usually are other unpleasant reactions, including physical illness, bewilderment, terror at being abandoned and alone, resentment at the forced life changes, jealousy and envy, and profound grief if the mate was truly liked. Many days it is all a person can do just to get by and to deal with the usual responsibilities. For many people, this is a period of abject emotional survival, with little energy left over for building a new life.

One of the harshest aspects of being left for another love has to do with its impact on self-esteem and self-image. I think of this as the distress of not being chosen. Most of the individuals I have worked with who have been left for another have talked about this aspect of their loss as a tremendous barrier to healing, and readily compare it to the struggles many of us had as children with feeling worthy and finding acceptance.

Looking rearward, the memories of not being chosen stretch from late adolescence all the way back to early childhood. I have heard and read about numerous accounts of grown ups still feeling the sting of having been passed up for proms and homecomings. I personally recall the anxiety of being among the last chosen for neighborhood pick-up baseball games as an older child, and I am sure I will never forget the name of the girl who rebuffed my affection in first grade.

In my experience, it is the combination of the new rejection and unhealed similar feelings from the past that is a prime contributor to the hurt people feel at a mate's betrayal. No one likes rejection, and no one easily forgets it. For many people, part of the exultation of being married was actually relief. Being chosen in love addresses questions about worthiness, and ostensibly ends the worry of never being special enough. No one who believed he or she had escaped the questions and the worry once and for all by being married wants to return to the hated status of being the one who is left out.

The bad feelings that result from being displaced by another are all the more poignant for older individuals who fear that they are more likely to remain alone. It is made worse by the accustomed feelings of attachment that naturally develop for having lived with a person, and is worse yet if a strong attraction to that person continues.

Higher Healing

Healing the hurt of being left for another is complicated. What I have to propose may seem beyond the reasonable grasp of anyone who has been hit by the anguish of an affair revealed. But in the worst of it, if we sense that there is another, higher place to take our grief, we can begin to feel immediate relief.

This has nothing to do with repression; the spiritual path leads through pain not around it. And hiding from suffering is no more healing than immersing ourselves in our misery. Instead, we have to begin to examine our reactions and will ourselves to alter our conventional course of behavior.

Probably the greatest hazard is allowing the feeling of rejection to coalesce into a sense of victimization. Unfortunately, this is a common development out of which may come self-righteousness and bitterness, two powerful opponents to spiritual growth.

Letting go of feeling victimized is some of the hardest work we ever have to do. From the victim position we can justify saying and doing things that we would probably not allow ourselves to do in better moments, things that give us relief for the moment and distract us from the difficult task of moving on.

With victim consciousness also comes a tendency to place all of the responsibility for our problems onto our mate. This is rarely appropriate no matter how complicated our lives have become, but it can feel good, and it again puts off the work of looking within to see how we might have to change.

From a healing and growth standpoint, when we behave in a way that is designed to hurt another it also hurts us. And any time we attempt to relinquish responsibility for our lives it inhibits our spiritual progress. This may sound as if I am unsympathetic to the person who is down, but I have learned the importance of getting a handle on our perspective as quickly as possible before our defenses against healing and growth can take over.

I previously cited the example of the woman in this circumstance who felt every normal urge to become angry and bitter, but who with guidance and support chose to look to her own growth and surprised herself by rapidly overcoming her fear about the changes she had to face. She certainly had to deal with sadness at her loss, but she kept victim consciousness at bay and as a result had that energy available for moving on efficiently.

As difficult as this time might be, if we can keep the spiritual journey in mind, we can successfully counter our negative reactions. As we do, we will discover that this is an opportunity to practice faith that life is unfolding in a purposeful way and that we will eventually find meaning in what is happening to us.

Two thoughts might be healing at this time, both of which relate to the spiritual journey. One is that if the affair is a right path for one mate, then it is right for the other as well. While we might think life has favored the mate who has left with another, experience tells another story. On a journey of healing and growth, the guiding principle is that no one gains anything of real value at the expense of another.

Of course, perceiving this fact requires a perspective beyond the ordinary. Having had the opportunity to counsel many people through this event, I can say with assurance that life unfolds in helpful ways for all of us. If nothing else, each and every experience is an opportunity for new learning, and that is so germane to our forward movement.

The second thought is more of a suggestion, and that is that in all circumstances it pays to be gracious. Once the divorce is over, everyone has some regrets, but these never include regret for having been gracious.

Being gracious reflects our understanding that our lives make sense, that we are here for a reason that will be revealed to us, and that the same is true for our mate. It is an act of faith as well as goodwill, and an attitude that only fosters goodness. It allows us to feel mature and competent, it inspires others, and it can change the atmosphere around us in positive ways. It is our statement of belief in the grand design.

Most of us admire graciousness in those we meet, especially when they are that way in difficult times. I find people who are this way to be heroic. They are the ones that I wish to emulate for their ability to see an alternative attitude.

Loving Unconditionally

Whenever I think of these people, the difference between conditional and unconditional love comes to mind. What most of us accept as love is actually conditional regard, which means being cared for only when we act in a way that pleases the other. To care for a mate only when he or she acts as we want is the hallmark of conditional love.

This is a limited way of giving and receiving love. It is better than not loving at all, but it does little to advance us on our journey. Switching from loving a mate to hating him or her for having chosen to leave indicates a profound need for healing. Once recognized for its lesser quality, anyone who is awake and aware would want to give and receive love of a higher kind. This is most of what we are here to accomplish.

Being left for another provides an excellent and unusual opportunity to practice unconditional love, maybe for the first time. Ironically, the very circumstances that might make us question the existence of love makes this possible. With an open heart and a loving perspective, we can overcome our defenses and again sense the hand of God in our lives. This is a most unusual chance to practice being loving in a manner that befits our spiritual nature. We want to be careful not to lose an opportunity that comes so rarely. Nothing is lost for trying.

Becoming a practitioner of higher love provides a bonus. It is a spiritual maxim that giving and receiving are the same, and that we get back what we give. This means that when we transform our conditional love for another into unconditional love, we end up feeling unconditionally loved ourselves.

One of the most liberating of gifts is to discover that our value does not depend on being chosen by or loved by another. Although most of us want an intimate relationship with someone who wants us, it is possible to feel a deep sense of belonging without a marital relationship providing it.

With a spiritual perspective about the goodness of life, and a daily practice of reaffirming the rightness of our individual path, we can find an exclusive intimacy with the Divine within us and can establish a fulfilling personal bond with all of Creation. These are the most important relationships to be found on the journey, and we do not have to wait for the arrival of another to obtain them.

Reflections

Sit quietly, breathe slowly, and open your mind.

Silently read the following:

- Love in all of its forms is a gift. I am happy for anyone who finds it.

- All forms of love have a necessary place in change and growth.

- Love affairs are difficult for everyone involved and warrant compassion and understanding.

- All love is healing. It expands the heart.

- Loving others and myself unconditionally is the highest love. I choose to love this way.

- Every encounter is an opportunity to open my heart and expand my love.

- I get back what I give. I choose to give love.

- The ultimate goal is Divine intimacy. I do not need a lover to have it. It is entirely personal.

Go over each phrase again and let their meanings settle within. Note how right this feels.

Write each phrase as before, and then speak each one aloud for emphasis.

Visualize situations in which you were not as loving as you could have been, and redo those situations mentally with the new perspective in mind. Note these briefly in your journal.

Promise to always love yourself, especially now when it is so difficult.

4
Separation

From the perspective of the spiritual journey, separation is the passage through which we gain release from a marriage that no longer contributes to our healing and growth. It is a process that allows people to detach from each other in increments that make fundamental change possible. It is also one of those human events that we have to experience first hand to appreciate just how difficult it can be.

When I think about describing the experience, a client comes to mind who I had seen together with her husband a couple of years prior to her panicky phone call asking for an emergency session. I immediately recalled that at their best they had seemed to be always at odds. He was a dominant personality who had been physically intimidating and often verbally abusive and cold, and she was dependent on him. Despite serious problems, they had built a new house and had enjoyed a financially comfortable lifestyle that she was reluctant to give up.

Now she was telling me that she had decided to leave him, but after having actually separated, she became lonely and afraid and wanted to reconcile. To her horror, while he initially resisted the separation, when she approached him about returning, he turned her down. In a short time she had gone from feeling confidently on top of things to feeling hopelessly lost and out-of-control. By the time she phoned me, she had lost twenty pounds and had seen her physician who appropriately prescribed an antidepressant and tranquilizers. She was a self-proclaimed emotional wreck.

Her experience with the early phase of separation is fairly typical. Part of us may well recognize the need for change, but as soon as we begin to act on it in earnest, our fears and other defenses arise to generate serious conflict. In addition to this, more often than not, only one member of the couple is prepared to have the relationship end, which adds to the resistance. Rarely, therefore, does anyone depart from a marriage smoothly.

Nevertheless, because it is the nature of the journey to promote change and growth, the support we need to survive separation is built into the process. This is why most people who face separation are in fact able to go through with it in spite of all the resistance. What I want to do in this chapter is to illuminate how the separation process works in our spiritual development, and to further encourage a healing and growth perspective regarding this passage. The point I wish to share is that, like other aspects of the journey, separation can be hard and sad; but rather than being tragic, it is a rich opportunity for spiritual expansion.

The Subtle Separation ·

Although it formally begins with a move out of the bedroom or home and the announced intention to divorce, separation is a process that does not have a distinct start. Rather, it is usually a lengthy process in which a change in the level of attachment has been in motion without anyone's conscious awareness. This is the subtle separation.

An unplanned emotional disconnection prior to the actual separation is what most of us recall when we examine our separations in retrospect. What has typically occurred is that a growing degree of complacency and habit have at some point displaced spontaneity and conscious interaction, and we have eventually begun to take each other for granted. Expressions of affection and interest that were second nature during the courtship and early years become less frequent, and feelings of entitlement may have replaced appreciation and gratitude for favors and kindness from our partners. Minor disrespect begins to show itself in such behaviors as not listening and expressing criticism instead of affirmation. Lovemaking gets put off, or it has become perfunctory.

As the emotion of a marital relationship cools, partners usually find ways of engaging their interests apart from each other as a means of escaping from discontent. Individual activities that signal a withdrawal can happen at home or away, and might include such things as watching television alone, solitary hours on the Internet, reclusive hobbies in a basement workshop, or avid participation in golf or long distance running. When these activities successfully aid escape, they tend to increase in intensity.

In the unconscious phase of separation, none of these separating activities may have been selected with disconnection in mind. In fact, they might be chosen in an innocent attempt to add interest to a flagging sense of togetherness. And this strategy can work. It is through such unhappiness-driven, isolating activities that relationship energy is re-focused in individual pursuits rather than mutual direction. Spouses who find less-and-less satisfaction with a mate begin to find it on their own, and the attachment balance begins to tip slowly to the negative, opening disenchanted partners to possibilities other than remaining as they have been.

As we become less involved with mates, and increasingly preoccupied with self-concerns, emotional distance naturally grows. Without knowing it we are practicing being alone, and are becoming ever more emotionally independent in the process. This repetition begins to reduce our fear of being apart. The reduction in fear then allows the initial awareness of unhappiness to surface. The first line of defense has begun to give way, after which it is possible to more openly consider the prospect of a marital change.

I have witnessed this subtle separation with many clients, and in retrospect have been able to see its development in my own life. Some of the clearest examples of this unconscious beginning can be seen with those clients whose presenting problems were anxiety attacks that in hindsight obviously signaled an initiation to the phase of subtle separation. Each of them had entered therapy well in advance of being able to acknowledge any marital discontent, much less a desire for change.

I am thinking of three of these clients in particular- all women - who straightforwardly denied marital unhappiness when asked about their marriages as a source of distress. Choosing not to be invasive, I took an indirect route to the deeper problems and worked specifically on the anxiety with breath work and biofeedback. Each client was successful in establishing internal control over fear without using medication, but none of them left therapy having connected their anxiety to problems at home.

I did not hear from any of them for at least two years. When each returned, the immediate subject was the marital relationship. All of them were now able to face their situations and discuss them with candor.

They described problems of long duration that they had sensed were there, but had instinctively avoided because they were not prepared to go where such open recognition would have taken them. In each case separations eventually occurred. Anxiety had been a barrier to awareness, but also a harbinger of the subtle separation.

In my marriage, as close as I can tell, the subtle separation probably began around the time I had an affair of the heart. A new love had surfaced and gone, and I was different afterward without being aware of it, perhaps because that differentness was hidden by my efforts to re-focus on my marriage and channel creative energy in the direction of making things better. I realize now that I was defending against looking truthfully at the marital relationship and admitting my unhappiness. I was not yet ready to see.

Looking back, I realize that the first sense that my marriage had changed was when I noticed that we were quiet in each other's company, and that when we did talk it was not about meaningful things. I observed that while we were on dates and weekend trips, it was no longer us doing the activity that was important, but the activity itself.

I have previously mentioned I had a premonition while on vacation of what was coming a year before leaving my marriage without understanding what it was, and how it went underground to continue its preparatory work. Significantly, I remember no conscious wish to part prior to that instant.

Months later during the holiday season I found that I lacked my usual enthusiasm for decorating the house or in cutting a Christmas tree. Soon after, I went to a movie alone for the first time. I still had no idea what this indicated.

The following spring, the vegetable and flower gardens I had prized went untended, and I began to spend time with a neighbor and his wife in recreational activities. All of this remained innocent and above board, but finally I began to experience thoughts that I could not imagine myself in my marriage in the distant future, and I began to be aware of a desire for change.

The subtle separation is a preliminary or in-between stage prior to becoming fully awake or conscious, and while I was no longer completely unaware of what was happening, I was not quite aware of it, either. More than anything else at that time I remember feeling adrift. I knew that I was not completely in the marriage, but I also could not describe where else I was.

The initial groundwork for leaving had taken its characteristically inconspicuous course, revealing itself only occasionally from the shadows of the unconscious. I know now that this explains why I was so genuinely befuddled when asked when I first noticed that things had gotten bad, when I began to feel a desire to leave, and why I had not been more forthcoming. I actually did not consciously know at the time. Defenses were at work; the marital context was still dominant; fundamental change was happening very subtly; and the intuitive guidance I was receiving was recognized for what it was only after the fact.

The subtle separation can save us from an abrupt awakening, which is too threatening and disorienting to be useful. I have known many people who have been stunned by unexpectedly falling in love, or by a mate falling in love, or by some other means and, having lost their bearings, search frantically for something familiar to ground them again. If it were to happen to us, an abrupt awakening would so distress us that we would most likely be tempted to disregard it, concluding that such precipitate change is not real and not to be trusted.

But when we have tried to make things better and failed, and after endless soul searching conclude that the marriage has become insupportable, we arrive at a marital crossroads where a decision has to be made about the direction our individual paths will take. There is usually nothing but to follow the one that leads away from the marriage. At this point we will take the inaugural step of exiting the marital space. This is the point at which the official separation is ready to begin.

A confusing irony sometimes develops at the point when the prospect of parting becomes real. An unexpected burst of intimacy can emerge when the intense emotion of this moment is shared that temporarily fills the longing for closeness we may have felt for months or years. This powerful emotion in conjunction with the impending fear of the unknown and the grief of an imminent ending may spark an attempt to save the marriage.

In a dying relationship, the high emotion feels as fresh and vital as that which initiated the marriage in the first place; but it is not. The resurrected intimacy cannot last. The intimacy is in reality transitional: it emanates from the need to leave rather than a desire to stay. The optimism is the flaring of a candle just prior to its finally burning out.

The Overt Separation

We enter the conscious phase of separation when we wake up to the need to change. This awakening does not imply that parting is imminent, although it might be. Usually there is further preparation that is necessary to make that climactic moment of release possible. Sometimes both members of a couple awaken to the inevitability of change and process it to a conclusion. Usually, however, one person is ahead of the other in the process, and he or she takes the lead in bringing the relationship to an end.

During the conscious preparatory stage, actions that signal an ending become more purposeful. Additional time is spent apart, but now it is used as time to think, to experiment with being alone, and explore new separate possibilities, such as relationships and new hobbies.

Separating activities now become known to us for what they really are, and increase. Excuses for being apart begin to suggest the truth, for example, that we need time away from the mate in order to "find ourselves." In time even this hedging seems dishonest. It is not unusual that a mate begins to accurately intuit what these are about, too, and if he or she asks, there is less dodging and dissembling, and less need to reassure him or her that nothing is wrong.

Sometimes we will leave abruptly for the express purpose of getting away from a confrontational mate, and we will say so. Overall, there is less and less consideration given to protecting the feelings of the other, or to protecting him or her from discovering the ultimate intention in one's being away. In fact, there may be a dare implied to guess what is going on, and bring the truth to light.

This is also a time when a running inventory of the sources of discontent is kept, and an incessant examination of the state of the marital union is made. Relationship flaws are more readily identified as loyalty and closeness are progressively severed.   We find ourselves increasingly unhappy, which leads to more withdrawal, increasingly direct expressions of dissatisfaction, and less willingness to negotiate and compromise even on minor points.

In effect, we have become prosecutors compiling a case against the marriage, if not the mate.   We may look only to evidence that supports what amounts to a fait accompli, ignoring or giving short notice to that which does not.   We may even list our negative data on a legal pad, both to help give them substance and to provide us with something concrete to refer to when we need it.   Over time, we become single-minded and even obsessed.   Momentum builds, as it must if we are to overcome some final difficult hurdles.

All of this can take place without a statement being made to a mate about what we have in mind.   In a sense, therefore, the process can still be considered unconscious in that a spouse may not have fully awakened to our intentions, and in that we have not expressed them openly and processed them between us in a conscious manner.

It is all a matter of time.   The decision not to nurture the marriage any longer means that there can be no return to the innocence of earlier times. Within weeks tension can build rapidly, and it usually has become clear to us that the relationship has to end, and to our partner that something is terribly wrong.   Soon someone is going to have to relieve the unbearable tension by saying the words that reverse the marriage vows, or by asking the fateful question that will evoke that response.

But that next step is very difficult.   No one wants to have to tell a mate that he or she has decided to leave, and no one wants to ask if leaving is what a mate has in mind after everything indicates that it does. Almost everyone struggles at this juncture, including couples who arrive at the decision mutually.

The distaste for initiating the marital ending is exemplified by the client who told me that she had felt physically ill for a whole year knowing that she had to tell her husband that she wanted to leave. People have said many times that they would find parting easy if they just did not have to speak the words.   Indeed, some have left the home permanently without saying anything about a divorce, thereby placing the responsibility for that deed on the other's shoulders. They know what they want; they just do not want to say it.

When I was close to leaving, I needed help to prepare for my personal confrontation with this moment. I remember asking my neighbors about their divorces. I wanted to hear the stories from admired friends in order to convince myself it could be done. I asked trusted people if they thought what I intended to do had merit. Just prior to telling my wife that I wanted to leave, I met with a very good friend and skilled therapist to talk as we walked the streets of his neighborhood. I knew that my decision was valid; I just wanted to rehearse justifying it because I knew I would have to over and over again in the near future.

I did not sleep that night prior to speaking with my wife, and when the next afternoon arrived, I repeated aloud what I was going to say, and then nervously waited on the front porch for her to come home. I then very straightforwardly proceeded to tell her what I had prepared. It was an improbable, unbelievable and indelible moment that still amazes me if only because of the unimaginable courage it required.

Being on the receiving end is no more pleasant. No one wants to be told that he or she is being left and that a marriage is over. That, too, seems improbable and unbelievable, at least at the time. We may have seen it coming and still been unprepared for the shock of reality.

Interestingly, because it can come on so quickly, both the initiator and the non-initiator may claim surprise at having arrived at this moment, although it is more likely for the person on the receiving end. In my opinion, however, while it is natural that anyone would feel shock at the decision, it is unlikely that something in the marital atmosphere would not in some way have foreshadowed the change. For a complete surprise to occur there would have to have been serious non-communication, blinding preoccupation and inattention, or a significant dismissal of reality. Any of these would itself foretell a possible change.

Also, with our ability to deny what is right in front of us if it is unpleasant, it may require one of us moving out before the discontent is recognized for what it is. And perhaps it is just that, like all momentous changes, when we actually face separation personally it always seems like a surprise.

Speaking the words of parting does not smooth the way to an exit. This is all new, after all, and it is very likely that just a few weeks or months prior to this time there was no thought of separation. Therefore, the shock can send any but the most steadfast of us into a state of paralyzing ambivalence or retreat. Fear at what has been done is immense. The defenses come on strong. And the hurt that is expressed can make even hardened resolve falter. So can anger and threat. Apology, backpedaling, and recanting is common at this time. But by now there really is weight behind the decision, and it is still moving forward.

Even if ambivalent waffling occurs for a time, a knowledgeable person understands that it is part of the prelude to change. This is why promises to try again to work things out, even to undertake marital counseling, eventually fade. There is nothing of substance behind them. The real wish is for the courage and resolve to continue on the path of change.

The first part of the overt separation is one of discovery, but not really one of true healing and growth. For the initiator of change, it is more a period of semi-consciously bulling one's way through tough barriers, using the blunt force of relatively unfocused creative energy in a heads-down assault to get the job done of breaking through. For the non-initiator, this is a time of first adjusting to the shock, and then in a sense one of catching up with the mate in the change process. It is after this all-out offensive that the real work of healing and growth begins, because it is then that both persons can work consciously to clarify what it was that required release from the marital relationship.

For both of members of the couple, up to this time guidance has been provided through an unconscious inner channel. By the same design, there is no closure for having made the initial break. Now that the foundation has been laid essentially for us, the finish work has to be done. This always implies an ever more conscious level of participation in the journey.

The primary task at this point is to unravel the intricate needlework of a life jointly lived. Even where couples are able to mutually agree on every aspect of the marital undoing, we earn completion and release through the often slow and often painstaking process of legally terminating the marriage. Just when we might wish to flee and be free, we are forced to reinvest every part of our already exhausted being for a final push. From the perspective of healing and growth, this passage is priceless.

No preparatory work can make unraveling the details of a married life uncomplicated. Most of the hard work of closure is emotional, but a lot of it also has to do with sorting out physical and material issues. Much like unwinding a battered ball of fragile string, where the beginning is on the outside and the end is actually at the center, and the coils are abraded and worn, we can only achieve closure by working slowly and carefully, revolution by revolution. There is no rushing it, especially emotionally.

The needlework is fragile; too much pull on one end of the string or resistance on the other can cause breakdowns that delay resolution. Healing is additionally complicated if the marriage has children, complex assets or financial liabilities, or if one of the partners refuses to cooperate, which is not unusual in the early part of the passage.

Non-cooperation and other forms of conscious and unconscious sabotage deserve special mention because they are so common, and because they unnecessarily delay healing and closure for everyone. In my experience, the most prevalent of these is the practice of blaming, by which one person attempts to encumber the other with the entire responsibility for the marital problems and the pain of the separation.

Many people might not think of this as a device for hindering movement, but it is clear that the most efficient way to carry a load is to share it equally or just not take it up at all. If someone is fixated on victimhood, the attitude is a barrier against forward movement because creative energy will be expended in self-absolution and making the other pay. This is played out in all sorts of ways.

I should also say that I see blaming from the more traditional perspective of an attempt to manage the pain of separation. People who are in pain try to end it by attacking its source, in the hope that in doing so they will shut it off. This can apply to blaming oneself for one's own pain and for the other person's distress, as well as blaming the other. However, there are other ways of handling pain that do not interfere with healing, which indicates to me that the central motive is not pain management.

If one mate initiates a separation against the other's wishes, and the non-initiator cries foul, the initiator will feel guilty and is likely to believe that all suffering is his or her responsibility. An angry spouse will fuel this belief with his or her own opinions to that effect. The guiltier someone feels, the more he or she questions the goodness or rightness of his or her actions. I can only believe that the outcome is a compromised course of healing. In fact, I have witnessed it many times. The person who is wounded by blaming is emotionally and spiritually hobbled. The person who intends to wound another this way does so to the detriment of his or her own spiritual self.

Both of these people need help to escape the trap of this conventional drama. Here is where the image of the spiritual journey as it is presented in this book can be so effective. With it as a shield an embattled client who feels inordinately blameworthy can fend off the most hurtful blows, whether self- or other-induced, and add reason to the change process. And having it as an alternative to destructive thinking, a self-perceived victim can shift perspectives from antagonism to cooperation.

I have figuratively held the hands of some very strong people who were being crushed under an unfair mass of responsibility for having decided on change. In treating them, I have often found that this was a dynamic of the marriage, too, so that part of the overall healing is to escape that role. People who too-willingly take on blame in one instance will also do so in another. Unless an individual can get out from under a sense of responsibility, in an attempt to buffer the mate's pain, he or she may put off progress, perhaps attempt reconciliation, or give false hope when it is inappropriate to do so. Nothing in this promotes healing and growth, but of course that is the idea.

Truly self-centered people do not take on guilt and responsibility; they see that as the other person's place. What then might this mean about those who try to place blame and responsibility on others? People who project blame and guilt onto others usually feel right about doing so, and easily become further entrenched in self-righteousness in the process.

Like the burden-bearer, this tends to be an aspect of their interpersonal style. While they may claim to be responding to the pain that has been thrust upon them, they are in fact aggressively creating pain for the other person. Energy is directed into fault finding and other diversions from proactive behavior. Therapy has to help them see how this is true. A reversal of perspective is essential to healing and growth.

In instances of blame taking and blame giving, people claim that love is part of the equation. Guilty people believe that they are right to feel bad because they have hurt someone who loves them, and that guilt reflects healthy sensitivity, compassion, and a loving attitude. In truth, their attitudes and behaviors reflect some elements of love in that they do not want their mates to suffer.

But knowing about conditional love, and that the process of fundamental change has its base in our spiritual nature, acts that are born of guilt and that generate self-loathing and inhibit appropriate change cannot truly be love. Love promotes honesty and courage, healing and growth; it does not foster hedging for the sake of temporarily reducing discomfort, or offering unrealistic hope. In my view, it is more harmful and less humane to vacillate than it is to proceed straightforwardly. Drawing things out does not protect anyone; it just lengthens the suffering.

Acts that are derived from anger are also at best expressions of conditional love. One might rationalize them as attempts to save the marriage; as a form of self-protection; or as a means of getting the other to behave responsibly. But love does not support attack in any form; there is no love where behavior is disrespectful or abusive.

Furthermore, laying blame never really makes the pain go away. It seems to be a fact of the human journey that from birth forward pain is an aspect of growth. From a spiritual perspective, the essential pain in a separation is caused by the need for change, not by the people involved. What we require is beyond our ability to contrive. We can reasonably assume that no one leaves a marriage when the loving is good; it is unavoidable and unwanted discontent that underlies the decision to go.

If we are on the path to divorce, separation is not a resting-place the way some use it when they need a break from marital stress. It is a site of significant transition, which means that once we have entered the separation passage we are likely to find little actual repose. Our forced-choice is between voluntarily moving forward as gracefully as we can with the flow, or being swept-up involuntarily and carried helplessly without any sense of participation or control. If we do not want to be separated, it helps if we can admit to ourselves that we are at a place where we face change whether we want it or not, and we should try not to stand in its way.

It is easier to resist blaming our mates or ourselves if we can accept that the difficulty of the passage is essentially the same for both the initiator of the separation and the one who may not want it. Both persons are severely stressed, if in somewhat different ways.

The belief that the initiator is immune from suffering by having chosen the path and the timing is untrue. The whole process often feels as much out of control to the initiator as it does to everyone else. He or she may be farther along in adjusting to the loss at any point compared to the mate and therefore may seem to have an advantage, but overall he or she is usually no better off. Everyone pays a price. No healthy person decides on impulse to undertake such an incredibly hard ordeal, and no one simply walks away without emotional cost.

Living Arrangements

Once the decision to separate has been made, it is almost always in our best interest that one of us departs the marital residence. If we have mutually arrived at the decision to end the marriage and have remained friendly, there may be no rush about this move. But for most of us a certain amount of ill feeling attends a separation, and having to remain in the company of someone we have rejected as a mate, or who has rejected us, quickly becomes emotionally untenable.

We do not really want to be around someone who does not want to be around us, and vice versa. Hostility and aggression are the frequent result of forced companionship. It is also unkind and unfair to try to remain near a person who continues to want us when we no longer want them. It may be convenient for us, but it is unpleasant for our mate, and it may encourage false hope.

Even when financial considerations make moving out a problem, finding some way to accomplish it is wise. Inexpensive rooms can often be found through the classified ads, and moving in temporarily with relatives or friends who have space is a common practice.

Understanding that where we go is a temporary arrangement will help us keep our perspective when we feel we are giving up a great deal in moving out and receiving very little in return.

It is apparently becoming more prevalent that men try to remain in the residence when a woman asks for a separation, where it has been the traditional practice that a man moves first regardless of who initiates the action. The tradition may have had to do simply with the belief that men are supposed to accommodate women, and that the home is the woman's domain; but it may also have to do with the fact that children usually stay in the family residence with their mother. It probably has also been that men are thought to be better able to fend for themselves away from the home, both in terms of financial and physical self-protection.

Whatever the reasons, a man's automatically leaving is not something that a woman can count on anymore. Women are more financially independent than ever, and shared parenting has made the children's being with their father a greater likelihood. And unless there is physical or demonstrable verbal abuse and intimidation, the courts will not require a man to leave.

An additional complication to the matter is that impulsively taking a separate residence has potential legal ramifications in terms of joint claim to the house as an asset. Thus, if a husband refuses to leave, and his mate cannot make him go, she may not be able to just leave instead, even if she believes being apart is necessary. Therefore, a lawyer should be consulted prior to anyone's moving out of the legal residence.

This is not true if the move is meant to be very brief as, for example, when the announcement is first made and the initiator fears an angry confrontation. A short decompression period is not a bad thing to plan for. Discussions soon after can provide reassurance that the residence is safe for a return until other arrangements are made. An agreement should then be made as to who will move, so that there will be no later claim that someone abandoned the house and thereby tacitly gave away his or her right to it.

Remaining in the house when it is reasonable for us to move may be an act of defiance, entitlement, hostile resistance, or other bad will. It may also be a way of trying to hold on to a relationship for as long as we can despite its consequences to others. Therefore, regardless of who initiated the separation, or whether or not we are inconvenienced by the request to leave, we must examine our motives for refusing to leave if it seems appropriate that we go.

If we are trying to hold onto the relationship, we might find it easier to let go if we admit that the process of separation will eventually require that we part company anyway. This inevitability should not be ignored, and it provides a rationale for going when we may not feel emotionally ready to. Healing will begin when we are actually apart and have to face life alone. Separating in a timely and decent manner is acting in the spirit of healing.

Finding a new place is an activity that is usually pursued individually by the one who is leaving. However, sometimes it becomes a joint venture when a separation is mutually agreed upon and amicable. We might go as far as to jointly decorate and furnish the place as if we were both going to be there, too. The good side of this is that the cooperation involved really takes any remaining hostility out of the separation process and keeps it a mutual effort rather than something that is being forced upon someone. The bad side is that this involvement may be a form of dependency, a disguised intrusion into a mate's privacy, a form of control, or a way of maintaining the illusion of togetherness.

The possible negative aspects of such mutuality should be kept in mind when deciding how to approach the search process. It might be better to start our enterprise as single persons right away. We can keep each other informed as to developments in our search if we choose to without fostering undue participation. By doing the work of separation separately, we reinforce in our minds the understanding that we are ending a joint life venture.

Leaving a residence on our own to find a new one may be a once-in-a-lifetime experience. From the perspective of healing and growth, doing this piece of separation work is something we should not avoid, or interfere with for our mates.

Once one of us is out, the separate residences should be seen as protected by the unwritten rules of respect for personal boundaries. Honoring them will help move the separation process along. We will come to appreciate the good effect this has on us, and to enjoy the sense of control over our individual lives that it engenders.

Timing

It has been said that the timing of bad news is never good. If we have decided to end a marriage, we will invariably find that no time is easy for making a move, particularly if a mate is not in accord with our plan. Thus, we often find plausible reasons for putting it off.

Generally speaking, it is better for our mate to know the way we actually feel than to continue living under an illusion. It is also better for us to reveal what is in our hearts than live dishonestly, and to face the outcome instead of live in dread anticipation of it. Having the truth of the relationship out on the table allows all parties to begin the process of adjusting, and is the first step to growth. Nevertheless, we sometimes find that we are just not ready.

Probably the most common reason for delaying the process is a desire to achieve absolute certainty, complete justification, and unfailing confidence before we initiate the venture. The stakes are high and none of us wants to make a decision that we will end up regretting. Just saying the words creates so much grief that we do not want to use them unless we are sure. Once having said them, we do not want to have to take them back and then have to say them again.

With regard to final assurances about the rightness of the decision and our ability to see it through, there is no time prior to making the announcement that we can achieve the kind of certainty we would like; no final piece that completes that puzzle. The process of growth does not unfold that way. Any such searching can become an obsession that keeps us stuck. We achieve certainty and justification only later when we can look back and can see how things have turned out for everyone. We gain confidence for having gone through with the decision on faith alone and survived. In a metaphorical sense, we are paid at the time we finish the work, not in advance. There are no short cuts to the rewards.

Other considerations have more to do with humane concern for others. One of them has to do with the holidays. For example, if Christmas is near we may not wish to spoil the holiday cheer, especially for our children, and we may fear that our families will associate this one with all holidays to come, and will always be unhappy as a result of our act. There are no rational ways to counterbalance this concern, as the holidays, especially Christmas, have become occasions of incredible sentimental importance. Leaving at all will seem bad enough without culpability for holiday angst.

What probably will happen is that the current holiday will be affected; therefore, many of us may want to get past it before we act. After this one, we begin to adjust, so that future holidays are changed but not ruined. Everyone will have to get through the next holiday cycle to make the adjustments, but almost all of us make them, and everything is fine. If holidays had always been good, they will be good again. It is just that they will be different.

The truth is that feelings are going to be hurt regardless of the time of year, and holiday sentimentalism does not actually add to or subtract from the pain. One of the transformations we will want to make is to no longer elevate sentimentalism to the level of real feelings, such as those that attend a marital separation. We may choose to wait through the holidays if we want, but we should do it as a conscious act of kindness, not from fear of violating some important unwritten code. If we feel compelled to go, then we should go. The final word on timing is within each of us, and is a matter of intuition.

How close we have to be to a holiday that it becomes a factor in our decision is a variation on the whole question. For example, is October too close to Christmas to make a move? If we are merely using the holidays as a rationalization for indecision, it will be. It is incumbent upon us that we be as honest as possible. We may still hold off, but we should know the truth of our motivation.

We also have to consider the effect of our own sentimentality on the timing of our move. Do we ourselves wish for the unspoiled image of the family together for just one more Thanksgiving? And if we do this for one holiday, are we going to do it for another, and then another? If we suspect this, we can make an alteration that places truth before fantasy, and honest feelings before sentimentalism. What an excellent opportunity to practice a new way of being.

What also happens when we try to protect family members through the holidays is that the whole thing backfires when we finally make the announcement. We contributed to the illusion that everything was well, and having successfully done that, we now risk really letting people down. So, what have we actually accomplished? They feel that we have set them up, and they have reason to believe it.

There is a great deal of hope and reassurance promoted by allowing holidays as usual. If the marriage had seemed tenuous, this false sense of well being has to prove confusing. We have behaved dishonestly, and our motive of wanting to keep the holiday peace notwithstanding, we may have created more of a problem than existed before.

Perhaps what we should count on is that most of us can handle the truth, regardless of the time of year. How would family members think of themselves or of us once having discovered that we have been withholding in order to protect them from bad feelings? The message we are sending in effect is that we see them as inadequate, which is a far cry from the positive input they need from us at this time.

Whether or not we should keep young children uninformed is a legitimate concern because of the emotional build-up to Christmas. We may have to either share our intentions with them well before December 25th or fairly soon after, which should not be too hard a stretch for us. The adults can just do their best to keep what they know between themselves. Children frequently sense what is happening and will ask about it, in which case we should not choose sentimental considerations over confirming their perceptions, as one is eminently more important than the other. If the truth gets out we can usually salvage the holiday spirit for them with a little extra effort in that direction. It has been done many times.

Other considerations affecting timing might have to do with a mate's or another family member's illness, the imminence of death in an aged parent or grandparent, an upcoming graduation or wedding, a long-planned vacation, a near-term pregnancy, a recent loss of a significant kind, or some other weighty concern. It is sometimes the case that the need to begin the separation process has to be placed on temporary hold for overriding compassionate reasons. As much as possible we want to take the effect of the stress into account in timing an announcement that affects others' lives, especially in regard to someone's health.

Again, people are more capable of handling reality than we might think, regardless of their initial shocked reaction. In the instance of people who are dying, the nearness of death often makes individuals who love us more desirous of sharing than ever, and of wanting to know all that can be known about us. Of course we have to have a realistic sense about their capacity, but people who care about us want to share, and the news of our marital demise can prove to be a subject of memorable intimacy with loved ones that will soon be gone. We may be surprised by the wisdom and nurture they give.

In summary, the revelation of our intention to separate can for the most part be made with safety at any time. In the end it is completely up to those who have the need to go. By this point the emotional disjunction has usually been well established, anyway. If a mate or other people are going to deny that and claim foul, no amount of waiting is going to prevent them from doing so. To say anything but the truth when we are ready works in opposition to our progression, and is probably a distortion intended to salve our own anxiety and to maintain life as it is for as long as possible.

Intimidating Partners

Special attention has to be paid to a separation from mates who have a history of aggression, or who have warned of severe harm to themselves or us if we should ever try to leave. Feeling afraid is almost always an aspect of separation, but in these instances normal fear can be replaced by genuine terror. This may be doubly so when children are involved and we believe they are also at risk.

Some mates just have a dark nature when it comes to intimate relationships. Those who are possessive, jealous, domineering and aggressive may seem to naturally employ threat as a means of achieving control and in the process they darken everyone's life in the home. No matter how much they might apologize after an outburst and seem sincerely bothered by their behavior, they often mean to be frightening. It is their way of holding onto relationships. The apologies only come when the threat has had its effect and homeostasis has been reestablished in the marriage, which means when others have been cowed into doing as they demand.

Being angry, threatening and aggressive is an effective way of keeping intimates around when love and kindness are not a fundamental part of a relationship repertoire. If we make excuses for this kind of behavior, we will enable it. To believe such persons are merely suffering from a lack of love or low self-esteem and to sacrifice ourselves to try to make up for it is to misunderstand the nature of personality. We cannot give people what they do not already possess. When we do see goodness there, we may actually be projecting our own good natures onto theirs, which increases the likelihood that we will forgive them and decide to stay around.

We may also rationalize our decisions because we are so afraid to admit the truth. It is important for us to remember that once we have been sufficiently terrorized we can no longer trust our judgment about such mates or our motives for staying with them. In order to minimize our fear we may unconsciously begin to see the world as they do and to blame ourselves for their anger. We may secretly hope to make whatever changes are necessary in our behavior in order to keep them happy. Our best emotional stuff is lost or misspent as we attempt to avoid our mate's displeasure. Sex and affection can become devices for keeping the peace. We can become enslaved to intimidation without being aware that it has happened. What we are aware of, however, is a vague sense of apprehension even during quiet times. We never know when the bad behavior will show. Ultimately we become depressed from constant wariness and oppression, which precludes our being energetic enough to leave.

One of the immutable facts of life is that we cannot change anyone else. The concept of the conquering power of love is much more complex than to simply mean that by being kind toward another they will become kind toward us also. People who are angry and aggressive by nature cannot change on their own without professional intervention and hard work. People who prey on other's fear do not usually think of themselves as being in need of therapy. Their perspective usually is to think that everyone else is the problem, and that if we would only do as we are told they would not have to get angry. Change requires self-awareness, a willingness to take full responsibility for our behavior, and an investment of time and effort for the purpose of anger control. Even when it finally comes, it is only because of our decision to leave. By then irreparable damage may have occurred.

Very often the people who find themselves in marriages with intimidating mates tend to be emotionally dependent, lacking in self-confidence, and inclined to blame themselves for all of their troubles. When we are this way, a sense of inferiority neutralizes our feelings of entitlement to decent treatment. We will often settle for what we can get in life and try to be satisfied with it. The demeaning nature of the marriage whittles away what self-esteem we may have entered the marriage with, so that we become more beaten-down and dependent over time, and feel less and less deserving. Even when caring others tell us otherwise, we can become so chronically depressed that we cannot imagine a better life for ourselves, and we give up hope.

Some of us spend our entire married lives this way. But for others hope really does seem to spring eternal, and finally fans whatever embers of optimism we may have left into the resolve to change. Sometimes this results from the pride and defiance that tell us we have finally had enough. Sometimes it comes from a desire to protect our children. Sometimes we find a lover or others who treat us well and start us thinking that we deserve better. And sometimes the drive to leave seems to arise inexplicably from no discernible place; we just seem to know that we have to go regardless of the consequences, and the courage to do so arrives at the same time.

At this point some of us are able to simply confront our mates with the fact that we are leaving. We do not spend much time thinking about their possible reaction because it no longer matters. But with some partners this can be truly dangerous. Threats from people who have been physically violent or suicidal have to be taken seriously. For the most part such threats are not acted upon, but bad things do occur often enough to warrant planning ahead.

One of the best methods of minimizing the danger is to engage a mate of this temperament in therapy prior to announcing the desire to leave. An intimation of the possibility of leaving if the anger is not brought under control might help accomplish this, as might a direct request when our mate seems in a responsive frame of mind. If we are at the point where we have decided to leave the marriage, the therapy may be used as a platform for launching our escape. This is a legitimate use of therapy because it allows the possibility that our mate will bond with the therapist and do some needed personal work, and that he or she will be helped to adjust to the change.

Or we may want to employ the therapist's office as the place to make our announcement of intention to leave, using the therapist as a mediator, conciliator and ally for both of us. People usually do not act-out in a therapist's office, and because the therapist is now involved, people are often more reluctant to act out at home. Even when a mate does not join in the therapy, his or her knowing that we are talking to a professional may make for more careful behavior. Priests and ministers may be of similar assistance.

However, if we intuit danger we should prepare for it. This does not mean that we cannot hope to leave. The danger of harm to us is usually greater while in constant close proximity to an angry spouse than in being apart, so getting away is the first step in finding safety. The danger of a mate's suicide cannot be prevented forever. We can provide the resources they need, and then it is up to them.

Women's shelters are excellent resources for protection and advocacy if we feel endangered. Most communities have them. Relatives' homes are also places of safety during a separation, as are those of good friends. Lawyers, the police, and the courts offer protection through direct intervention and injunctions against harassment. And therapists and other counselors can provide essential support through times of fear and doubt. These are proven routes of escape and should be engaged as soon as the desire to end the marriage is clear. Every resource should be used if necessary.

Once begun, the process should be seen through to completion if it is in any way possible. The longer we are apart without having something bad happen, the more likely we are to gain in safety. There is also a momentum factor involved. Going back means having to start all over again, but with less energy.

If we do not take the risk of going, then nothing can ever change. Many people have faced down the threats made to them and moved on to happier lives. Proceeding with a separation under threat is one of the very most trying of experiences, but once successfully done the rewards make it worthwhile.

For reasons that we usually do not know prior to making the change, some of us are destined to have to fight harder for our freedom than seems just. Many of us had abusive parents also, and have had to fight to get them out of our lives, too. And many times it appears that the struggle for freedom will never end.

Why some of us have to pay such dues is a mystery. Its meaning is to be determined after we have rescued ourselves. Those who have found peace know that it is worth whatever price we have to pay. Courage and persistence are staples of this journey, and faith that we can accomplish it is a mainstay.

Children

Marriage is about adults. When a marital relationship is no longer viable, the adults involved need to part or risk a situation that is unhealthy. Therefore, for many adults separation is both unavoidable and necessary. If done well, the parting can be a creative process with a potential for healing that goes well beyond that of the immediate circumstances. It is always difficult, but it is often extremely beneficial.

Although a marriage is not directly about them, children share in the marital fate. A separation is obviously going to affect them. As much as we would like to spare them the pain of a difficult experience, we cannot.

What might reassure us as we take the path of healing and growth is the understanding that something that benefits one person will not occur at the expense of another. This implies that if a marital ending has value for the adults involved, it will have value for the children involved, too. This is a universal law

It will also help to keep in mind that, while there is emotional suffering when a separation occurs, this does not automatically mean that there is trauma and psychological harm. While there is no avoiding pain and suffering, if we do not allow what we are feeling to influence us to act in harmful ways, no damage will be done. It is not the break-up itself that harms our children but the ugly behavior of which we are capable prior to, during and after the separation when our darkest urges surface.

If we can avoid acting on those impulses we will spare our children the damage we fear is inevitable when adults go their separate ways.

Modern children are incredibly attuned to the emotional vibrations of their parents' relationship. The most sensitive of them can pick up on nuances of emotional change we might miss ourselves. They have always paid attention to such things because they are dependent on our care. They know when we are close and when we are distant, although, like us, they may try to close themselves to what they do not wish to see.

Divorce is familiar to our children because it is so prevalent, and therefore they might fear that any discord between their parents could lead to such an outcome in their home, too. Asking parents if they are going to get divorced has happened at some time in almost every family.

On one hand we feel that this kind of sensitivity is unfortunate, in that we would like our children not to have to be concerned with such things as a significant change in the family situation. On the other hand it is adaptive in that it allows children not to be taken completely off guard when things between their parents go seriously wrong. Being able to generally allow for the possibility of divorce is a form of preparation. If they believe that it can happen to them, this thought opens a place in their minds for imagining its eventuality so that they might become less sensitized and less afraid. Being able to do so is part of their survival capability in its contemporary form. With the frequency of divorce in our culture it is actually a good thing that they can.

Children are by nature resilient to the effects of change, provided the changes are not too severe. This is a concept we will want to consider as we begin the undoing of our marriages. We have to be mindful of their needs so that what they have to address at any particular point does not overwhelm them with fear and uncertainty. Mainly we have to help them believe that their lives will remain largely the same, and that they will be provided for. They can then handle much of the rest of what faces them.

If the adults are overcome by the fear of abandonment, are enraged at having to change, are consumed by guilt for their choices, or are lead by feelings of victimization and entitlement, the children's stability will be jeopardized. Someone has to seem to be in charge or the children will perceive that their lives are out of control in a time of incredible peril.

Our strategy has to be an optimistic one that constantly shores up any failing sense of security or stability for our children. To this end we need to keep the worst of our feelings to ourselves, and to talk and listen in an honest and supportive way about their thoughts and feelings. As much as we can, we have to be cooperative with each other in their care. Above all, we must refrain from using them as confidants or allies against the other parent, as a battleground for our continuing fight, or as the spoils in a post-marital war. They have no place as foils in our attempt to reinforce our emotional or financial positions relative to our mates.

In regard to their perceiving that things are bad in the marriage, we have to be careful not to deny what children sense when it is true. Questions from them about the marriage may be gently put off for awhile, but we have to make a decision about confirming their observations at some point so that they do not begin to mistrust us. Therefore, when it is clear to us that a change is coming we should tell them so.

Telling children about a separation is best done simply and straightforwardly, and jointly if at all possible, but separately if we are at serious odds. The atmosphere should be one of sincere feelings and faith, with no blaming or recrimination toward either parent. We can save our anger and guilt for moments with our friends and family if we need to vent. For now the children's need to believe in their parent's goodness and reliability is the foremost concern.

Children frequently express their need for reassurance about the future in questions about what is going to happen to them next. We should listen carefully for this need, and even if we do not specifically hear it, we should always respond as if it were there. Words to the effect that we will always love them and take care of them, and that everything is going to be okay can only be stated too often if in saying them we are trying to reassure ourselves. When we are sure that we will take care of them, they will be sure, too. They will reveal their confidence by letting us know that we do not have to keep reassuring them.

Plans for one of us moving to another place should be shared immediately so that we do not just seem to disappear. It is good if the children can be brought into the process of our finding an apartment or other temporary residence because it reduces the sense of mystery, and gives them a working picture in their minds of where we will be. Ideally this all will be done mainly in a spirit of adventure rather than loss, because in essence it is an adventure for everyone. If they are not included in the relocation, they should be involved in the transition as much as is practical, and introduced to the new space as soon as can be arranged. Their photos and other personal effects can be displayed so that they have some sense of participation, just as at home. Our positive attitude about the change of residence will go a long way in helping their adaptation and comfort in spending time with us.

When one parent is not handling the emotional aspects of the separation very well, it is up to the other to continue to provide optimistic reassurance to the children. This will be enough to encourage acceptance of the change, and will help them deal with the other parent's slower adjustment without being brought down by it. It is possible that at such a time a sensitive child will rally to the defense of a parent that seems to be suffering more, and this cannot be helped. As the better-adjusting one we may feel attacked or rejected in the process. But our optimism, our positive regard for that child, and our compassion for the flagging spirit of our mate, will provide the needed energy until the trouble passes. Reminding ourselves of the value of our journey will help us get through.

It is essential that our relationship with our children is never guided by guilt, nor should we allow ourselves to become subject to manipulation on our children's part because we feel guilty and want their approval, their forgiveness, or their company. We all know parents who try to buy approval, or who attempt to relieve guilt by providing goods or favors. This shifts authority and power to the children, and encourages blackmail and further entitlement, among other things. It can happen almost without our being aware of it, and once it does, the parent-child relationship can be very hard to get back on a proper course.

Children are influenced by instinct more than reason, and may regress to ever more instinctual behavior under these circumstances. Therefore, we can expect them to go for what they can get if allowed to. In the worst of circumstances they are prompted by one or the other of the parents to do just that. This is a development that has to be handled effectively as soon as it appears. If behavior becomes extreme, and children act in an excessively entitled, disrespectful, aggressive manner, they (and the other parent) have to be called on it, and we need to make it clear that our relationship with them will be restricted until that behavior ends. It is better not to have regular contact than to have a relationship of this sort or we risk enabling such actions and expectations. No one feels good when the reason they are together is other than love and good will.

It is our job to do all that we can to keep our fears from making the relationships we have with our children unhealthy. Honesty and courage will guide us in this. If the children will not join us on a positive basis, we can still remain open to them by offering unconditional love, but conditional contact. Usually we just need to wait them out. Eventually their desire to have us in their lives will bring them around.

Visitation arrangements are best decided clearly, perhaps with a lawyer's formalizing input so that there is no confusion. Within this formal arrangement there should be as much flexibility as is tolerable by the adults, which should not be difficult if the children's best interest is central. Boundaries are to be respected so that unannounced dropping-by does not occur unless agreed upon. Parents should also have a general idea where the children will be when with the other, especially if they are going to be traveling, as we do tend to get anxious when our children are not in our immediate control. Return times should be honored for the same reason, and because we all tend to make plans with our children's care in mind. Reasonable telephone contact with them is one way of maintaining the sense of continuity they may need, particularly in the early part of the separation when their anxiety may be high.

When children are not adjusting to the separation, professional therapists can be consulted. They have the needed skills to foster adjustment when it is slow to come. Some children just do not handle change very well, some are more fearful than others, and some feel oppressed by the problems in adjustment that their parents are having. In any event, because professionals can make the whole process smoother and more efficient, there is no reason to hesitate to use them.

Schools also frequently provide individual and group counseling services for children whose parents are separating. This is a valuable resource and should be investigated early in the separation process. It is a good thing to let teachers and guidance counselors know that a major change is underway at home, and to stay in touch with them, as school adjustment is an excellent indication of how children are doing generally.

If at all possible, children should be allowed to remain in their familiar homes and schools, as being in familiar territory makes other change less threatening. If a move has to happen, we have to be prepared for a possible bad reaction. Sometimes it is possible to arrange with a school for an older child to finish a final year, and friends, relatives or former neighbors will often be willing to provide a temporary home for that purpose. In those instances it may be worth having our children away from us, as their social needs supersede our desires to have them around. They are often forever grateful if we can make such arrangements.

In summary, while we do not want to downplay the fear and sadness our children face when we decide to separate, we also cannot let our own fear of confronting their grief interfere with making the changes that we know are needed. Children benefit in the long run when our decision to change is right, and when the separation is managed with sensitivity, maturity, decency and kindness.

If we give ourselves the option of re-deciding our married lives when they are no longer fulfilling, we teach our children that they have control over their lives, too. This increases rather than decreases freedom. It makes it more likely that their choices in relationships will be truly voluntary, which will encourage real intimacy and health.

If we remain in unhappy marriages because we do not wish to disrupt our children's lives, we run the risk that they will blame themselves for our self-sacrifice and unhappiness. This can make them feel guilty for being here and angry with us for putting them in such a hopeless position of responsibility.

When our lives turn out better because of the decision we made to pursue healing and growth rather than remain in an unfulfilling marriage, the influence on our children's lives cannot help but be good. This does not mean that if we are happy they will be automatically happy, too, but at least our move will not be the cause of the struggles they may encounter as they make their own way to personal fulfillment.

One of the unexpected advantages of being a single parent is that the relationships we have with our children are unadulterated by the presence of our mate. This may at times seem a mixed blessing, as we have only our selves to rely on. But because of this we are permitted to engage in a kind of sharing that cannot be experienced in a two-parent household. This makes for hard work, but the payoff in terms of really getting to know our children is worth it. So is the feeling of competence that comes with having done it well.

Reflections

Sit quietly, breathe slowly, and open your mind.

Silently read the following:

- Something important requires my release from the marital bond. I choose to see my separation as an opportunity, not a tragedy.

- In all separations, someone has to take the lead. I acknowledge that it can be as difficult to present the bad news as it is to receive it.

- I may not control the separation process, but I can choose my attitude about it.

- If this separation is about growth, taking or placing blame is senseless. Therefore, I choose neither to place nor to take blame.

- It is not in my best interest to judge or to punish – others or myself.

- Everyone fares better through cooperation. I will neither act selfishly for convenience sake nor interfere with my mate's journey.

- I will respect the new boundaries that separation requires, and expect others to show the same consideration.

Once again, repeat the phrases and attend to how you feel.

Write the phrases in your journal or on a convenient piece of paper.

Read each one aloud to help bring the learning home.

Using the phrases one-by-one to bring things that have already happened to mind, visualize how you might have introduced the growth perspective into your separation through those incidents if only you had another chance. Write briefly about what you discover.

Congratulate yourself for work well done.

5
Seeking Assistance

I have never known anyone who was able to get through a separation without help. It is just too hard. The thought of leaving a mate or of being left by a mate and having to be alone leaves most of us feeling profoundly scared and sad. Furthermore, because of the complexity of ending a modern marriage, there are often moral, legal, and psychological issues to deal with that will require professional assistance. For most of us, then, this is a time of having to appeal to family and friends for personal advice, guidance and emotional support, and of having to consult with experts to help with the special problems that confront us. If nothing else we usually at least want someone available to listen as we talk about our plight.

From the perspective of the journey, all of this connecting with others is potentially good; the various interactions are bound to help us learn about ourselves and life in ways that may never have occurred without the marital separation to induce them. Many of us are forced to go beyond our usual ways of coping, and having exemplary people as resources when we are vulnerable to new learning is a boon to spiritual healing and growth.

However, since these interactions are occurring at a uniquely volatile time, it is exceedingly important to keep the concept of spiritual progress in mind so that we are not harmed when we get caught up in the negative ones. This means being prepared for the defensive reactions from others that are certain to ensue whenever fundamental change is a possibility. On this journey all of our interchanges with others are meant to help us; even disappointments can help by teaching us patience and tolerance, and by instructing us about whom to avoid if we are to remain true to our spiritual path.

If this sounds even faintly like a warning, it is meant to. Separations cause people to behave in extraordinary ways. Not everyone can be expected to be open minded, compassionate and fair. In fact, because the stress of separation tends to bring to the surface the thinking and behavior that are most in need of healing, some of the things people will feel and do may be quite surprising – and distressing.

For most of us this will prove to be a time when, despite our best efforts, we will often find ourselves at our very worst. We have seen, for example, how feeling angry and perceiving ourselves as victims can lead to feeling justified in doing whatever we want to get everything we can. Likewise, we have seen how severe guilt can lead to feeling so unworthy that we believe that we are entitled to nothing at all.

Now, as we engage others for support and guidance because of the separation, we have to anticipate that they will have personal biases and emotional reactions similar to ours, which will have an additive effect on us, also. In fact, it is a spiritual principle that when these emotional states gain the upper hand in any of us, they will tend, in a like-attracts-like manner, to draw people into our lives who will incite us to feel even more as we already do.

Thus, angry people will arrive to inflame our anger; entitled people will show up to affirm our entitlement; and guilt-ridden people will materialize to exacerbate our guilt. All of which is designed to bring these negative states to awareness so that little by little we get tired of them and can then begin to change them.

An excellent example of this principle was the experience I described with the lawyer I consulted who unexpectedly, unprofessionally, and unethically went right after my guilt as if that were his prescribed role in my life, exacerbating it to the point that I briefly ended my separation and returned home. I understood in hindsight that guilt was what I had to heal above every other emotion, and that my path provided the opportunity to encounter it squarely and do the necessary healing work.

Of course, the opposite holds true. When we remain kind, compassionate, and fair, we will tend to attract people to us who will reinforce this positive perspective, and our spiritual progression will speed up as a result.

One of the vital lessons that we are meant to learn on the journey is that we are all independent, autonomous individuals whose job it is to always act responsibly on behalf of our own healing and growth. No one but us is accountable for the outcome of our choices. Therefore, we will want to be sure that we choose to interact with individuals who can help us to move forward spiritually, not hold us back.

This means taking care in these relationships because not all of the people we meet on the journey will have the same sense of spiritual purpose that we do. In fact, many will find the growth perspective as it applies to marriage and divorce unimaginable or threatening since they continue to be guided by the unconscious programming we are working so hard to leave behind.

This does not mean that we are obligated to stop what we are doing and enlighten everyone who does not share our view: our hands are full enough. But we may want to at least discourage negative attitudes and behavior by not engaging in them ourselves, and to curtail interactions with persons whose negativity might impede our spiritual progress.

Appealing to Parents for Aid

When the shock of separation hits, many of us automatically turn to our parents for aid just as we did when we were young. Sometimes this is absolutely the right thing to do; our parents prove to be an excellent resource for appropriate nurturing and guidance, and our connectedness with them is enhanced. But sometimes our experience with them can be discouraging; parents can be invasive, critical, and judgmental, with the result that an emotional break can occur between them and us as severe as the marital separation itself.

We clearly benefit most when parents remain calm and nonjudgmental; when they graciously and unconditionally offer support for everyone involved; and when they provide non-intrusive guidance only after being asked for their point of view. Short of this ideal, it helps if they can at least keep their angst to themselves rather than visiting it on their already emotionally overburdened children.

And the ideal does exist. I remember one couple (mother and stepfather) who handled their daughter's separation beautifully. She had initiated a separation after she learned that her husband was involved with another woman. As is often the case, she was ambivalent about her decision, and went back and forth several times before finally leaving the marriage for good, consulting her mother and stepfather all along the way.

This young woman's parents never criticized her for being indecisive, the way parents can, and they resisted any impulse to peremptorily question her choice, the way parents usually do. Instead, they practiced their faith and patiently waited while she decided on a final course of action. They obviously felt close to their daughter, but because they believed that her life was unfolding in a meaningful way, they were able to remain appropriately detached. Not once were they seriously tempted to intervene nor did they feel that they had to protect her from the consequences of her decision.

This does not mean that they did not have to struggle with the changes themselves. Being sensitive people, they did not like seeing all of the suffering. And because they also liked their son-in-law, they had to contend with having to lose him when the marriage ended.

Certainly the sense of loss could have been worse. But the family-in-law had not become part of the parent's social network, and there were no grandchildren, so that they did not have the dread of possibly losing access to them.

Nonetheless, no loving parents want to see a child's marriage end. It is just that, in this case, out of respect for their child's autonomy, they wisely kept their personal concerns to themselves. This included the mother's concern about how her child rearing practices might have affected her daughter's capacity to be a good mate, or to choose one, or her fear that her own divorce when her daughter was young might have had a deleterious effect on her child's marriage.

I know all of these people, and I can say that their relationship grew as a result of the manner in which this experience was handled. Furthermore, having not only experienced truly healthy parental support, but also having had the opportunity to learn their perspective about her separation and growth, the daughter came through her divorce with much more insight into life than most people her age could hope for.

I offer this example as a sort of model toward which we all can aspire. However, examples of this ideal behavior are fairly rare. In my experience, few parents have the spiritual wherewithal to respond to this crisis from the perspective that this book is offering. In truth, it is difficult for even the most caring parents to keep their feelings appropriately separate and to allow their child to have his or her own unimpeded growth experience.

What I have found more typical is for parents to react from the conditioned perspective that this book is trying to heal, which is that separation and divorce are bad and that they are to be avoided at all costs. Being human, parents are just as capable of negative reactions to divorce as anyone is, and perhaps more so because it is their children who are being hurt, or who are causing hurt, or because the prospect of a divorce in the family is simply so dismaying.

As a result, many of the divorcing people with whom I have worked have had the added challenge of feeling disillusioned by their parent's attitudes and behavior. Their parents just did not know how to provide the nurturance and support my clients wanted. In fact, some of them proved to be quite insensitive and selfish, although I think they usually acted without any intent to be hurtful to their children.

An outstanding example of this unconscious insensitivity was one man's description of his father literally beating his chest, and shouting, "Where did I go wrong?" when told of the separation, thus turning the son's desire for aid into a melodrama in which the father became the center of attention. Devastated, the son silently slipped away.

I also recall an instance in which a client's parents berated her for losing a mate who apparently enhanced their social status. By doing this, they let their child clearly know that she was considered a failure in their eyes, and that her position with them was less favored than that of a non-blood relative. She, too, was devastated.

In an instance similar to this one, although not quite as extreme in terms of rejection, one woman discovered that her parents had maintained an active relationship with her ex-mate without her knowledge or approval, thereby adding feelings of disrespect, disloyalty and betrayal to an already problematic emotional situation.

This violation felt even more profound because her husband had been involved in an affair that had hurt her severely and had contributed to her decision to divorce, and her parents knew it. She did not necessarily want them to side with her against her ex-husband, but to carry on as secretly as they did felt to her like another affair involving people who were supposed to honor her.

I also worked with a man whose parents regularly called and took calls from his ex-wife, during which they discussed his "crazy" behavior for having left her for another. They secretly had her to their home, and surreptitiously visited her when they visited here from out-of-state. He learned of the duplicity when one of them let it slip that they felt sorry for her and were angry with him.

Because his ex-wife had made the divorce difficult, and had attacked his reputation and disrupted his relationship with his children, and because he was a traditional family man who expected family to close ranks around each other, he found their choosing to support her incredibly disheartening. He told them that the marriage had not been happy for many years, and when he found a new love and married her, he had hoped they would share in his joy, but it made no difference.

From a fundamental healing and growth perspective, what these examples illustrate is just how much of a problem it can be for grown children when parents are guided by unconscious programming and defensiveness.

Since they had been family leaders at one time, and they had not grown beyond believing that they know what is best for their children, I have watched unenlightened parents revert to domineering roles that precluded recognizing their child's autonomy. They reacted to the threat their child's separation posed to family integrity with behaviors that were designed to cajole and punish. They also acted as if what is most important is that their own life is being upended by the change, especially when they have meshed their children's lives with their own.

I have known parents to have to deal with guilt or shame when it was their child who initiated the separation. And I have known parents to perceive victimization and abandonment and to be angry where their child was the one being left. And of course, I have known parents to become depressed when they could not adapt to the circumstances.

To prevent change, some parents have presumed to take matters into their hands, confronting their child and his or her mate about their behavior, demanding access to personal information to which they have no right, and requiring that the marital problems be negotiated through them. The invasiveness and sense of entitlement have been worse where children had always remained emotionally dependent, or have become dependent again and have had to ask for financial support or for temporary housing in their home.

For many of us there is often just no way to know how a parent will react to a separation until the crisis arises. I have worked with numerous adults who were so uncertain about how their parents would react to their problems that they hesitated to involve them even though they really wished they could.

For example, I have known clients to wait literally right to the day of the divorce before telling their parents that they had decided to leave a mate, or that the mate had decided to leave them. Some of them simply waited for others to inform their parents rather than tell them personally. And at least one individual even said that she would have to wait until her parents died before getting a divorce.

It might be that some of these individuals had misjudged their parents, and that they would have received the care they desired if they had given their parents a chance. On the other hand, they might have accurately sensed that nothing but problems lay in store if they chose to entrust their parents with their pain and suffering.

Either way, such reluctance to share openly with parents usually reflects a wish not to disappoint or upset them or to risk having to feel ashamed or embarrassed in their eyes. The hesitation is even worse for people going through second or third divorces, all of which illustrates the great power that parents can continue to have in their grown children's lives, especially at times of perceived personal failure.

With the possibility of such unfortunate parental reactions in mind, I caution my clients who want to approach their parents that overall it is not wise to assume that the romantic ideal of family constancy in a crisis will necessarily hold true. I ask them to recall as best they can what their parent's responses have been to crises in general, and to their children's problems in particular, as this is often the best predictor of the future.

I then encourage them to remember that on the spiritual journey it is each person's responsibility as an independent adult to maintain appropriate boundaries. This means being sure that parental rights of access end somewhere outside of one's personal and marital space. It also implies not taking responsibility for a parent's emotional struggle as a result of the separation, as this is a chance for him or her to grow, too.

If my clients have to stay at their parent's homes, I tell them that what is most important is that they not let this become a permanent return to a relationship in which their parents take over their care. If they regress a bit but catch themselves early, nothing is lost. After all, it does feel good to have compassionate, competent parents to turn to when things are hard and we feel we need some extra nurturing for awhile.

I also caution them not to write parents off without at least some exploration of possibilities for positive sharing. The premise of this book is that we all have the capacity to change and grow, and sometimes a crisis such as a separation will bring people closer together. I have provided one example of what can happen when parents maintain a spiritual perspective, and unless they are completely closed to suggestion and influence, it is possible that this can be used to shape our parents' responses by letting them know that we expect something similar of them. With our own faith in the healing and growth potential of experiences such as this one, we may want to try to sit them down and ask for what we need. What a wonderful opportunity for growth on all of our parts this can be.

The main idea is that we have to be ready to always accept people where they are, but we do not have to join them there. Our job is to be sure that we are growing from our experiences, and that we do not allow anyone to pull us backward. This requires keeping an open mind and an open heart, maintaining oneself in a self-loving and self-protective way, and closing off intimate communication when danger appears.

Siblings

Many of us heard as children that we should invariably side with a brother or sister because later, when no one else is there for us, family always will be. And indeed it is wonderful to face a separation and to find family members rallying in an affirming, approving, and supportive manner.

There is certainly no time when such nurturance is more likely to be appreciated or less likely to be forgotten. And having the myth of family constancy affirmed in the process adds feelings of being special and protected in a way that is hard to describe.

But experience teaches that the same cautions that apply to parents during a separation apply as well to siblings and other family members. Generally speaking, in spite of blood ties, siblings and other family have as hard a time being unconditionally loving as anyone outside of the family does.

In addition, there can be extenuating circumstances that make immediate support within the family less likely than with non-family associates; some "family-specific" reasons that they might prove unresponsive or negative, or at least not supportive in the way one might hope or need.

One of the worst experiences is to expectantly turn to a sibling for brotherly or sisterly support only to be questioned, blamed, attacked or rejected instead. When aid is anticipated but something less is given the sense of betrayal and the emotional letdown that results can complicate healing immensely.

This is a bad time to witness the explosion of the myth of family togetherness. Without that sentiment to hold onto, the prospect of marital loss can leave us wondering if we can rely on anything for permanence, and leave us feeling truly alone and vulnerable.

I have found that some of the problem reactions between siblings can be traced directly to unhealed wounds from earlier times. For example, in some families the sibling relationships never escape the influence of birth order, even after everyone is grown. In these families, older siblings who have not awakened to their dominant and superior ways may tend to reflexively react in a judgmental or admonishing manner toward younger siblings who are having difficulty. And younger siblings who have not abandoned their inferior roles may abet the situation.

This is more likely where parental attention and approval were in limited supply and had to be competed for, and where jealousy toward younger siblings and resentment toward older siblings created an undercurrent of insecurity and hostility that has gone unhealed.

I recall a client telling me of her younger brother being "glad" about her separation because he perceived her as acting superior to him since the time of his divorce several years before. When hearing this, my guess was that her brother's feelings had much older roots, and upon reflecting on their relationship as children, my client said she had to agree.

Problems also arise when siblings get attached to other siblings' mates, and integrate those relationships into the emotional framework of their lives. With the problem of jealousy and competition from the past in mind, it should seem entirely reasonable that a sibling would actually like an in-law better than the brother or sister who brought that individual into the family, and to have developed a stronger bond.

Sometimes they even become best friends, and speak of having found the "brother or sister" they never had and always wished for. After all, such relationships have none of the negative history that might be shared between siblings for having grown up under the same roof.

When a separation threatens that bond, old hostilities may arise and result in anger and resentment. Here a sibling might choose to support the new companion over a brother or sister if they think their sibling is somehow at fault, or if they are simply upset about possibly losing access to a person they care about. Their feelings may be understandable, but the rejection will seem bitter nonetheless.

A variation of this feeling of rejection that I frequently see occurs when brothers and sisters remain loyal to the previous mate after their sibling begins a new relationship. For example, a client of mine had been in a months' long relationship with a recently divorced woman who came from a large family that he described as "close knit," and as a group that would ordinarily get together in an instant for any family occasion.

When my client and his new companion decide to throw a family wine and cheese party at his house, almost none of her siblings showed. They both felt their message was clear, that the new man did not replace the old one, so that from that point on she found herself at odds with her family group.

What also happens in families is that one sibling's separation can send a chilling reverberation throughout the other sibling's marriages, causing them to draw distant. This effect is greater when the failing marriage seemed to be a good one, and its announced ending comes as a surprise. It is also worse where the couple had always joined with the other couples in an extended family way to celebrate holidays and share in each other's life. Because of the family ties, what results before any other emotion is fear; the thought being, "if it can happen to them, will it happen to us?"

From the perspective of the journey, having old wounds surface for any reason is actually good because it makes them available for healing. A marital separation is one occasion that often draws out feelings and attitudes among family members that may have lain dormant for years.

I counsel my clients to be aware of our tendency to return to past patterns under stress. Because separation is a family-relationship phenomenon, it often evokes latent family issues, and the behavior that ensues is a mirror image of what went on in the past. Our work is to become familiar with these issues and patterns without being pulled back into them, which is not easy because all of the participants are close relatives who perceive none of the personal boundaries that friends and acquaintances might sense. Things that are said here are usually of the no-holds-barred variety, and retaliation is swift, just as when we were young and living together.

Healing proceeds from remaining centered in our practice of being peaceful and compassionate. We especially have to be aware not to react immediately, but to let some time pass if necessary so that when we talk the intensity of the separation may have lessened, and everyone might be better able to be rational.

Perhaps the only benefit in the thin boundaries in family relationships is that they afford access that is not so automatically available elsewhere. This characteristic may allow our talking about old resentments in a helpful way, which for the sake of growth and harmony should probably be attempted before letting the relationships fade.

To me the important goal in this is not so much to restore family harmony as it is to end the mythology of family permanence so that everyone can gain in autonomy and shed unhealthy dependence. I know for certain that with effort and resolve we can move past the old roles, patterns, and expectations.

The best is when unconscious family bonds evolve to conscious bonds of friendship, as it is on this basis that fresh love and respect can develop. I recommend talking openly with parents and siblings about this desire.

But be forewarned: this can also be a time when for growth's sake unhealthy family bonds have to be broken, which can unfortunately mean having to end relationships that resist healing or thwart growth. It is often the case that being kin has no bearing on the similarity or dissimilarity of our places on the journey. Regardless of how close we may have felt at some time in the past, we may now find that our lives have really diverged.

Therefore, we may be forced by circumstances to re-think as objectively as possible our family relationships to determine if they are appropriate to the person we have become. They may no longer be, meaning that we may have to accept that, as with the marriage, what had been good with siblings has changed.

With the perspective of the spiritual journey to support us, we will see that there is no real tragedy in this, regardless of how sad and frustrating it might be. We know from our own separation that people are sometimes on quite different paths and that they may have to part to progress. And we also know that the separation can be handled with grace.

Usually relationships with siblings do not have to end altogether. We can at least remain friendly so that everyone feels open to sharing the various family occasions that are sure to arise in the future. We may have to accept less contact, and to expect that we may not be understood, as we would like.

When friends and other associates do not share the same perspective we have, we just stay away from topics that engender misunderstanding and conflict. We can do that with family members, too, as long as we accept them as they are, and do not require more than they are prepared to give just because they are family.

But do not give up hope entirely. As with parents, it may be possible to guide siblings toward more helpful attitudes and behavior. We can at least try. After all, it is not unreasonable to think that our positive energy might begin to resonate within them just for being around us.

Friends

The quality of support available from friends during separation often surpasses that of family members. This should not be surprising. Friendships tend to be autonomy-based: they do not carry the emotional baggage of having shared a household while growing up, including old competitions and jealousies, which makes it more likely that we will be listened to from an unbiased point of view and that our boundaries will be respected.

If they are recent additions to our lives, the chances are also good that friends will know us better as the people we actually are because there is no layering of expectation that parents or siblings may still have from our early days. And because we attract people who are like us, friends may better reflect the growth we have accomplished because they have come into our lives partly as a result of it.

When a separation occurs, there is usually no problem in maintaining friendships just as they are if prior to the split the friends have a clear allegiance to one or the other of the mates, as there is then less conflict regarding loyalty. However, serious conflicts can be anticipated if friends feel connected to both members of the couple, especially if the "shared" arrangement has been going on for a long time.

In these circumstances, friends often take sides. In my experience, they do this most often according to their perception of who is more blameworthy and who is more hurt. This is particularly true when they have not grown much, and when their customary values are similar to the person they champion and at odds with the actions of the one who they feel is at fault.

Once a position is taken, the feeling of awkwardness that follows usually makes being around former friends impossible. Sometimes things settle down after awhile and friendships are restored. But I have witnessed many instances where things never improved, and former friends permanently fell away.

Relationship changes like these are a normal occurrence on the journey. People who were right for us before might not be right for us now. What others and I have found is that a separation from the old connections allows new connections that could not be made without the disruption of life as it had been. New relationships invariably replace the old, and most often the new people who show up have been where we have been and think as we think, so that a whole new level of sharing happens.

What is most interesting is that the people who present themselves for relationship do not have to actually be new. Novel relationships can develop with parents, siblings, or former acquaintances if they are empathetic and compassionate and share a similar call to growth

This may all have to be initially taken on faith because the feelings of loss can be so intense. But in my experience, most people who have walked the path of divorce with a spiritual perspective feel that they have been rewarded for their faith by an unexpected admission to a group whose level of awareness is unavailable to those who have not gone through the process. The new connections often become some of the most important and trusted relationships they will ever have.

The Question of In-laws

I frequently have to remind clients that the reality of their relationship with a mate's mother and father during a separation may differ from their wishes and expectations. Regardless of how close we might feel to our in-laws and how we might have come to think of them as "real" parents, the fact is that parents-in-law always belong first to our mate, and I believe that our mate has a right to expect that sovereignty to be honored.

This position regarding sovereignty has important ramifications in regard to how we might access our in-laws, the basic one being that I think our mate really should assent to our addressing them for support, nurturance, or guidance before we approach them. This means that even if we have relied on in-laws this way in the past, and although we may now feel all the more compelled to go to them, we should wait. This is especially true if our mate is hurt or angry and has gone to them for aid, and has asked us not to.

Problems with this position usually first arise when a mate refuses to inform his or her parents that a separation is under way. Earlier in the chapter I noted that some people put off telling their parents about the changes almost indefinitely. This can make an ongoing relationship with in-laws feel extremely awkward and even dishonest.

However, as justified as we might feel I think it is best to resist temptation to tell the in-laws of the separation before a mate has done it. No one who cares for them will feel right about their being kept uninformed, but there is a great risk of violating important boundaries if we act in haste.

I recommend giving a mate ample time to make a statement, and if too long an interval passes with no indication that an announcement is forthcoming, to give fair warning that the truth of the marital situation will be revealed without approval. If in the meantime the in-laws grow suspicious and ask about a problem, the boundaries become less clear because we should never be put in a place where we have to lie. We may at this point refer our in-laws to their child for a discussion, taking care not to use this circumstance to give our side of the story before our mate has a chance to tell the story.

When afforded the opportunity to approach our in-laws, I believe a discussion with our partners about how it is to be done and what limits there might be on what is said needs to occur. This does not mean that we cannot spontaneously relate personal feelings of affection and sadness regarding our in-laws, but it does restrict what we can say to them about our mates that is negative. We have to remember that those people will continue to be associated where we will not, and therefore we have to avoid trying to poison their feelings in any way.

This also does not mean that we have to allow wrong information to pass uncorrected if it applies to us. We need to be careful how we define this, however, because when we are feeling hurt and angry and defensive, achieving a balanced explanation can be difficult.

If the emotional state in the separation is rancorous, a discussion with a mate about speaking with his or her parents may not be possible. In this case I suggest waiting to see if the air eventually clears enough to allow this discussion. Failing this, it may be best to let life take its course and hope for a time when the worst of the feelings pass and access is allowed.

If the in-laws have not made contact in the meantime, it may be that they need time to process their feelings, or it may also indicate that they have sided with their child, which is an additional reason to wait for an opening. It is natural, after all, that parents would sympathize with their child and want to defend and protect him or her, and it is unkind to force contact or to try to move between their child and them, or to expect support at their child's expense.

Likewise, I recommend resisting the impulse to ask in-laws to try to persuade a mate to reconsider if he or she initiated the separation. This includes situations where we believe that our in-laws want this, too, as this also puts them in the middle of a problem that is not theirs, and is disrespectful of the mate's autonomy.

Many times the bitterness or pain a mate experiences is so profound that we are denied access to our in-laws forever, and sometimes our in-laws accede to this because of their own similar feelings. In this situation we may just have to live with things feeling unfinished and accept the ending as it is presented.

After a time with no contact, we may consider a note letting our former in-laws know that we wish them well and are grateful for what was good. It is hard to say what this might do for them, but it might give us a sense of closure. I would caution, however, that no contact should be attempted if the desire arises as a result of loneliness, nostalgia, or a sentimental fantasy about a reunion of some kind.

We may also want to just leave the ambiguous ending alone. Sometimes it is best just to accept the change, to do our well-wishing in the privacy of our hearts, and to remain open to friendship if our paths should ever cross.

It is a harsh fact of married life that even when divorces are amicable, many times relationships with in-laws are lost. They came with our mate and they leave with our mate. It is our work to accept this and move on.

The emotional relationship may take time to die, but it usually will if given the chance. It may sound strange that this could happen, but if the intimacy of a marriage can fade, it makes sense that any other bond can fade, too.

The key points to keep in mind are that in-laws are not truly our family, and that our relationship with them, and our access to them, hinges on the state of the marriage. It is also important to keep the journey in mind when we consider our loss, as from the spiritual perspective we can assume that they came into our lives as part of an opportunity to grow. If they have to leave us now, it must mean that our further growth no longer requires their presence. This may not be a design that we ever had in mind, but our work is simply to have faith that the changes are necessary and right.

Consulting a Therapist

Sometimes a person's inclination to consult friends or relatives first proves to be a good one. But quite often the intensity of a separating person's needs outstrip the supply of patience and understanding friends or relatives have available, or their proffered views are biased, or they wish not to get involved for any number of reasons. And sometimes they are just as perplexed by the situation as anyone and are in no position to give helpful direction. It is at this point that many people consider contacting a professional therapist for help.

There is no guarantee that a trained therapist will prove a competent guide, of course, but for the reasons I list below I believe the chances are that he or she will do a better job than friends or relatives. And I also think that it is possible to find one whose personality is a good match to the seeker's so that the new relationship can rapidly feel as comfortable as that with familiar others, with the additional advantage of not having to worry about wearing them out.

Therapists are professional listeners; they are paid to supply that particular service and are usually prepared by training and intention to do it well. Being attended to without fear of interruption, criticism or judgment is a rare experience for most of us, and is especially welcome at a time such as this when we are in the throes of extreme emotion. For many people it is the most memorable aspect of the whole therapeutic encounter.

But more than just being willing listeners, competent therapists are also guides. They not only can support people through the adjustment process, but unlike well-meaning friends and relatives, can also help them grow in self-awareness and self-understanding for having had the separation experience.

I recommend searching for a therapist who seems peaceful and grounded. No characteristic is more helpful during the early months of a separation. When calmness and stability are in short supply just being around someone who is peaceful can make almost anyone feel immediately better.

This does not mean that a therapist has to have a perfectly ordered life to be helpful. In fact, it is a mistake to think that we have to find perfection in another in order to begin to heal. Like all other human beings, therapists still have their own work to do, and the wise ones know it. But it is an advantage to meet with one who is at least relatively more steady and composed than we are so that his or her personal energy can calm ours.

One caution at this time is to avoid authoritarian therapists whose main appeal is a charismatic self-confidence and self-righteousness. I bring this up because many people who are in a separation are vulnerable and it is not uncommon for those of us who feel insecure to find dominating individuals attractive for the order and control they might provide. Part of the work of therapy is to transcend emotional dependence and rise above unthinking compliance, so that what is actually needed is an atmosphere that nurtures independent thought and experimentation with old boundaries.

As a rule, no one knows what is best for anyone else. Our individual paths are mysteries even to us, and what someone might proclaim as right for us might well be right for him or her, but that is all. It is difficult to prosper spiritually under domination. An authoritarian persona can harm a vulnerable spirit; therefore, a brusque and opinionated style should warn us off.

A therapeutic atmosphere encourages candor and supplies the security and confidence needed for unreserved self-exploration. Being with a nonjudgmental listener provides the best backdrop for revealing ourselves; we should feel drawn to becoming more honestly self-aware. If we find that we are being lectured instead of listened to, or discover that we have not been completely forthcoming for fear of criticism or judgment, it is time to seek a more suitable setting.

A client also should never hear a condemnatory tone about a mate. When a therapist joins a client in angry judgment about a mate, it prolongs the healing process. Feelings of indignation and anger toward a mate should be diminished by session's end, not inflamed. If any sort of antagonism is promoted, or if blame is being laid in any direction, then it may be time to look closely at the kind of guidance that is being received.

Therapy should never promote ill will. Bad feelings should be its grist, not its byproduct. All of our feelings have a function, but if the negative ones continually dominate consciousness, they can be draining and damaging. So, while we need to acknowledge our negative feelings, we also have to move beyond them to get better.

The one emotion that no therapist should inhibit is sadness. Endings such as a marital separation are often sad, and usually the more significant the ending the greater the sadness is. We have to be allowed to be sad for as long as it takes that emotion to pass.

As an aside, it might be said that typically, the more developed a person's spiritual perspective, the less sadness there is in his or her life because the recognition of the benefit of every experience always balances the feeling of loss. But we usually have to work through a great deal of sadness on our way to that higher consciousness.

Two Perspectives on Healing

In my experience, most people who are new to separation enter therapy largely in hope of regaining their emotional bearings and positive self-regard. For example, when I meet with clients who initiated a separation against a partner's wishes, they usually require abundant reassurance that what they have done is all right because they feel so bad for it. And when I meet with clients who have been left by their mates, they usually require liberal amounts of reassurance that they are still worthwhile because they feel so rejected.

In any case, because the pain is so severe, nearly everyone enters therapy needing reassurance that the suffering from what they are going through will end and that it will prove to have been necessary, even though it may not seem to at the time. Providing this reassurance during the early trauma of separation is what most approaches to therapy have in common.

I tend to divide what comes next in therapy into two distinct approaches to the healing process after separation. I call one approach restorational, because it views healing primarily as a matter of restoring a client's life as close to its usual order as possible without encouraging fundamental modification. In a sense this orientation perceives the threat of fundamental change as the presenting problem in therapy: the client is unhappy for his or her loss and would just like restitution in the form of something similar. This approach mainly involves a therapist providing emotional support while an individual adjusts to loss and its aftermath, prior to reestablishing things pretty much as they were before.

I refer to the other approach as transformational, which implies that its goal is to help a client move forward on his or her spiritual path with no intention of returning to a former state. Thus, it looks at healing from a fundamental change and growth perspective, and uses the separation process as a starting point for the work of personal spiritual progression. It views separation as an opportunity for gain rather than as a problem to be coped with until we recoup our losses.

Either therapeutic approach requires hard work on a client's part and skill on the part of the practitioner since separation is a difficult circumstance with extraordinary emotion. Moreover, both of them are helpful, depending on the desires and orientations of those involved. Nevertheless, each of them unfolds quite differently from the other in crucial ways.

The restorative approach begins with someone's life having been fragmented by the separation experience and ends with restitution to normal living. It is similar to rebuilding a house to its original appearance after it has been knocked to the ground, using as much of the original materials as can be found. Things are not quite the same as before, but if the resurrected house has a reasonable resemblance to the original, the client and therapist feel satisfied.

This kind of resolution is the one that tends to naturally occur over time without assistance. However, a skilled therapist can accelerate the process by providing emotional support, by encouraging restorative activities such as becoming socially active again, and by recommending other resources that will aid adjustment, such as reading materials and support groups.

The heart of this therapy is the free expression of feelings in the presence of an unconditionally reliable and compassionate professional ally who is affirming and reassuring during hard times. The therapeutic experience is often a memorable one for which a struggling client is usually enormously grateful.

By contrast, the heart of the transformational approach is to avert a return to a "normal" life without first having gained a new way of looking at it. Only then will the separation experience seem worth having.

Transformational therapists start where all good therapists do and provide the basics. Then they move beyond them as soon as possible by introducing a perspective into all of the discussions that is designed to lead individuals to think differently about life for having gone through the separation experience.

It does this by promoting the idea that there is a purpose to what has happened that has to do with his or her spiritual growth. It uses the actual events in his or her life as the teaching tools they in fact are, and once seen from this spiritual perspective, everything in life begins to make new sense. The therapist helps the client generalize from the separation to other aspects of the journey, teaching him or her how to look for the "lessons" they have to teach regarding life.

This spiritual method naturally becomes the standard practice once the client's perspective has been opened to new possibility, which has enormous repercussions regarding growth. After this, there can be no return to "normalcy." Even if appearance seems to belie this, the client knows from within that the way he or she looks at things is forever changed.

A couple I worked with provides examples of both orientations to healing. She decided to end the relationship after over twenty years together. In the course of his restorational healing process, he soon joined a divorce support group, met a woman there who he found attractive and courted and married her about a year later. His son later described his perception of the process as his father simply filling his ex-wife's empty chair at the supper table, which from a fundamental-change perspective is metaphorically just what he did: he replaced a missing piece to reprise the life with which he was familiar.

His ex-wife, on the other hand, joined a self-help group that had as its function becoming less dependent on others, and was a regular member for several years. She read voraciously on personal growth, and completed a course of self-study that is designed to change an individual's fundamental orientation in life from fear-based to love-based. She had several relationships, and progressed through them on her way to learning how to be comfortably on her own.

A few years later, she met, lived with, and married someone who was on a similar transformational path, and together they continued to view Life as an unending spiritual growth workshop. Interestingly, her new mate's ex-wife had followed a restorative path similar to her own ex-husband's.

This is not to denigrate any relationships or paths to healing in any way, of course. Both of these individuals suffered greatly through their separation and divorce. Both worked very hard to bring their lives back to balance, but their paths could not have been more different. This example simply illustrates restorative and transformational orientations to healing and how each path was followed to either re-establish the status quo or change lives.

As with anything else having to do with healing and growth in the separation experience, the key points in finding the right therapist have the concept of the journey as their center. It is ideal if a therapist is as conscious of the spiritual journey just as we are, but it is not necessary that we be exactly at the same point. We can always use our perspective to bolster or complete the therapist's.

What is essential is that he or she is a good listener; that he or she not be authoritarian; and that he or she have a transformational orientation so that we will be certain to remain optimistic about what we are going through, and to maintain an essential growth perspective.

Clergy

Because marriages are frequently solemnized through a religious ceremony, it would seem fitting that the clergy would have a role to play in the separation process, too. This is especially true for divorcing people who fear that they are violating a code of faith, or who feel guilty for wanting a separation regardless of justification, or who think badly of themselves for just being part of a marriage that is ending.

Some people also want to inquire why God could allow such a thing to happen or wish to be comforted by scriptural wisdom from an expert. These are the usual occasions when people seek guidance from a member of the clergy rather than a lay therapist.

Since love relationships involve our hearts and souls, they are part of the spiritual side of our nature. The spiritual dimension is what gives love its mystical feel, which is why even non-believers will sense the Divinity when in love, and is probably at least partly the reason many feel that marriage is specially ordained by God. In this way, a love relationship cultivates our spirituality, which is also why when one ends in separation, as much for non-religious people as anyone else it can feel like a spiritual transgression.

Some religious doctrines prohibit divorce, and others strongly discourage it. The Catholic religion, for example, does not recognize divorce but will allow a de facto version through the process of annulment without which a divorcing person cannot marry in that religion again. The prospect of censure or exclusion can make an unavoidable separation all the more complex and hard to bear. In these instances, consulting with clergy may be an indispensable part of the healing process.

For these and other reasons religious professionals would seem the perfect spiritual guides at this critical time. In fact, many ministers and priests have taken training in counseling and psychotherapy, and some have advanced degrees in psychology or similar fields. Therefore, they may be able to combine sound spiritual guidance with effective therapeutic skills and prove very helpful. What actually happens when they are consulted can have a significant impact on whether separation activates new spiritual growth or hinders it.

If I have a caution about the clergy, it has nothing to do with questions of innate goodness or helpful intentions, and only to do with my belief in the value of flexibility as a precursor to fundamental change. In my experience, we have to be careful not to assume that because someone has religious training that he or she automatically understands what is necessary for another individual's spiritual progression.

I believe that a person's spiritual development can actually be inhibited by unthinking adherence to a particular religious doctrine. The truly spiritual is essentially beyond imagining and is therefore beyond our ability to interpret, define, and prescribe. The way I see it, spirituality is all-inclusive rather than exclusive, as religions tend to be. It subsumes all religions rather than being subsumed by any of them, and it is timeless and belongs therefore to the realm of non-tradition, as tradition implies being time-honored and time-bound.

When clerics are in fact spiritually advanced, I think it is because of something unique about them as individuals and not because of their religious training. For while it is true that an inclination to the spiritual dimension draws individuals to become clerics, the calling may be neutralized by the need to be viewed as an expert in a particular doctrine of a particular church.

This means that a person's ability to guide others may be limited to certain spiritual beliefs and practices. Like everyone else, clerics may be unenlightened in their spirituality if they have not done fundamental healing work of their own, which to me usually requires moving beyond rigid conventional religious thinking.

It is each person's responsibility once he or she becomes aware of the spiritual journey to be open to discovering new meaning to his or her progression in all of the experiences that confront them. This especially includes any person who is in a position to guide the spiritual healing and growth of others. If cleric-guides and their clients remain locked into a conventional perspective, they may not use separation as an opening to further awakening the way a transformational perspective would.

I have too often listened to clients who mistakenly turned their journeys over to someone who automatically disapproved of their situation, and who peremptorily explained it as against the will of God without exploring what the experience might mean to them personally. The worst instance occurred in a congregation whose minister and some of the elders had actually experienced the benefits of divorce and remarriage but told my client that she needed to forbear and go back to her abusive husband. When this happened, a pained spirit resulted where support had been anticipated, which delayed her healing and growth.

Therefore in keeping with the spirit of the transformational journey, it is important that the individual takes care with whom he or she confides at this time of special vulnerability and possibility, and that they choose to work only with guides who are open and flexible in spiritual matters. These clerics certainly exist. No one on a spiritual path can afford to risk becoming stuck in repetitive patterns, as these are defenses against fundamental change.

The standard of care that I have applied to other therapists applies just as well to religious professionals. They should readily and unconditionally provide support, affirmation, and compassion. Judgment and criticism, whether of a client or the mate, has no place. In addition, there also needs to be an emphasis on the growth potential of the separation process. This standard precludes leading anyone to feel sinful or immoral.

As the woman whose congregation rather hypocritically and coldly let her down learned, sometimes we have to separate from a particular religious organization for the same reason we have to leave a marriage: it no longer serves us spiritually.

The lesson on the journey is that, although it can feel good to return to the stability of a religious group the same way any homecoming feels reassuring when we feel lost, we may find that in the process of change, one can never really go home again. Home now lies in a new direction.

Attorneys

While it is possible to do much of the preparatory work for a divorce without a lawyer, for most people legal consultation is a usual component of the separation process. Attorneys are conduits to the courts and are the persons who are most familiar with the legal and financial aspects of separation.

A competent attorney can help us regarding child custody concerns, child and spousal support, the fair distribution of marital assets, and other complicated matters at a time when most of us are too distressed to think objectively about these things. In addition, the best of them make us feel that we have a trustworthy ally during this awful time.

In my experience, it is only the coolest of individuals who can decide to consult an attorney about separation without feeling guilty or frightened or sad. Even people who are angry and are certain that they want a divorce feel shaken. I know for certain that I am not the only one who put it off for weeks, most likely because of the place that lawyers hold in the separation process. Attorneys symbolize the true beginning of the end of the marriage, which makes them the de facto gatekeepers to all of the bad imaginings that go along with that possibility.

I think that it is advisable that both spouses have their own separate legal consultants somewhere during the process. This is partly for the sake of having more than one perspective regarding the appropriateness of the final settlement. But I recommend it also from a personal growth standpoint, even when the atmosphere between spouses remains one of relative goodwill and cooperation. This is a time when operating independently and taking responsibility for legal and financial matters can be practiced in anticipation of having to do such things without the partner in the near future.

As with anyone to whom we might turn for assistance during this critical time, there are certain essentials that should be looked for in an attorney so that an atmosphere appropriate to the spiritual journey can be promoted. Assuming first that a particular attorney has been chosen for consideration based on his or her reputation for effectiveness and/or the recommendation of someone we trust, I suggest looking for two particular qualities so that we can have peace of mind in his or her care.

One of these has to do with an attorney's willingness to be a listener. Not all of the legal aspects of separation and divorce are technical. The settlement process is a time when we can do significant personal healing and growth. But in order to use this part of the separation process in a growthful way, we have to avoid feeling like we are just along for the ride and that someone else is making the decisions for us. We have to be active participants.

This means among other things that we need to know that we will be consulted about our point of view about the settlement and that we will be heard in a way that contributes to the outcome. Taking personal responsibility helps mark this passage on the journey as our own.

Therefore, it is in our interest to have an attorney who will guide and advise without trying to take control away from us.

Finding a willing listener can be more of a challenge than might be imagined. In my experience, attorneys tend to be independent, assertive, and pragmatic by nature. Also, their primary work is taking care of our legal business, not nurturing us. Therefore, many attorneys will automatically try to take charge of the legal component of the separation without thinking about what his or her client might require in terms of personal healing and growth.

The second quality has to do with an attorney's predisposition to decency and fairness. While we are ultimately responsible for making certain these qualities guide the process of arriving at a separation agreement, it is our attorney who will often do some or all of the actual negotiating.

The desire for decency and fairness applies equally to the manner in which our attorney and we will deal with our mates and the manner in which we will allow ourselves to be dealt with in turn. Thus, while it implies always being compassionate and just toward a spouse, it also means being appropriately attuned to protecting and promoting self-interest as well in the event that a spouse behaves irresponsibly and does not reciprocate.

How this might support fundamental change may be seen, for example, in the case of a person feeling undeserving because of wanting a divorce, especially since feeling unworthy at this time usually reflects similar feelings throughout the marriage. Deep healing will stem from consciously requiring a fair settlement and decent treatment in spite of the uncomfortable feelings, particularly when challenged with unreasonable demands or intimidating gestures from an angry mate.

There is no spiritual gain in having given up a fair share of the joint assets. Feelings of unworthiness belie any thoughts that we are simply being generous or non-materialistic, which are spiritualized rationalizations for not feeling deserving or for not having courage enough to take what is proper. Here an attorney can support healing by advising us about what is appropriate, and can affirm us as worthy persons.

Of course, an attorney can have a negative influence, too. People who are separating are open to manipulation because of their feelings of fear, guilt, anger, and entitlement, and it would not take much for an attorney to inflame any of these. For example, I know of an instance where an attorney tried to empower a client's feelings of victimization and entitlement so that she would agree to go after a settlement from her wealthy husband that at best sounded greedy. My client got another attorney. Likewise, I know of an instance where an attorney tried to move a guilt-ridden client in what we determined was a too conciliatory direction in order, perhaps to get the settlement over with quickly, or perhaps because he really believed that it was right.

What must be kept in mind is that attorneys are normal people. Therefore, they think and behave as most other people do, which means that they are frequently being led by unconscious conventional values and expectations.

Thus, an attorney who believes people are wronged when a spouse decides to leave might reflexively encourage feelings of victimization, and entice an attack to punish a mate or to try to take more than is fair in compensation. An attorney who believes that men are supposed to take care of women may play on a client's sense of obligation and encourage a settlement on that basis.

Likewise, an aggressive attorney may naturally seek litigation and make the whole situation more adversarial than it needs to be. And an attorney who is too much the peacemaker may promote a settlement without enough hard negotiation.

Passively acquiescing to an attorney's perspective or style could lead to an unfair settlement while also reinforcing attitudes that waste valuable healing time and inhibit spiritual progression. It is our work to see that this does not happen. Fortunately, there are many excellent attorneys to choose from who can assist us in just the right way.

As with finding the right therapist, the essential features to seek in a lawyer are those that reflect the spiritual journey, although we should not expect a lawyer to think or speak in those terms. All that is really important is that we feel that our attorney recognizes this path as ours, that he or she allows us to contribute significantly to the outcome of the settlement process, and that he or she helps us accomplish closure in a responsible, fair and decent manner.

Reflections

Sit quietly, breathe slowly, and open your mind.

Silently read the following:

- Healing and growth are the most important considerations in my dealings with others.

- I will protect myself appropriately when around people who promote guilt, shame, anger or entitlement, and I will remain vigilant against negative thoughts and behaviors.

- I am aware that family and friends may not react well to my separation, and that they may not be able to provide unconditional support and love.

- I am prepared to accept people where they are, whether or not they can do the same for me. I choose to keep an open heart.

- I acknowledge my mate's sovereignty over her family. I realize that old bonds sometimes have to be broken for growth to occur. I trust that where there is present relationship loss I will experience future gain.

- I choose to work with professionals who encourage healing and growth.

- I choose to be fully engaged in the settlement process, and I realize that taking personal responsibility for the outcome marks this passage as my own.

As you repeat each phrase, again note the affirmation you feel.

Write the phrases, thereafter reading them aloud once more.

Dedicate yourself to using this part of the separation well, imagining that you will always be glad you did.

6
On Your Own

For many of us the most profound challenge in separation is that of having to be truly alone. This is something that is never easy, but it is even more difficult after years of being used to someone's daily company, regardless of the quality of the relationship. The longer we are in someone's company, the harder it is to be alone. Even a previous divorce does not protect us from this reality; each new attachment reestablishes the challenge of having to adjust to unfamiliar and usually unwanted solitude.

Some of the best opportunities ever for progressing on our paths occur once a separation is irreversibly underway and we have to really begin to function on our own. Now, this clearly is one truth that is more easily grasped in hindsight, once the terror and sadness of the separation have abated. Nevertheless, it is a fact of the spiritual journey that if we can face the challenges of being on our own with a positive attitude, we will free our creative energy and grow right from the beginning of the experience.

As with many other aspects of the separation process, learning to be alone is hard for both spouses. I have found that neither the one who leaves nor the one who stays behind has an advantage that is not countered by some disadvantage. For example, it is no easier to wake to aloneness in a familiar house with all of the reminders of the other person's having been there than it is in a strange apartment where nothing is familiar at all. The presence of children is but a minor comfort. The pain is in missing the presence of the other, in the vulnerability that we feel when being newly on our own, and in the fear that inevitably arises that we may be alone forever.

I have described in previous chapters how the fear of being alone keeps us bound to unhappy marriages, how it explains the need many of us have for a lover if we are to successfully leave our marriages, and how it may motivate us to immediately replace a partner once a marriage ends. It also explains why we tend to become so quickly (if only temporarily) bonded and dependent in new relationships in the aftermath of separating, and it is what inspires sympathetic couples to play the role of matchmaker for us when we are newly single. Because we cannot tolerate the thought of being alone for even a short time, we force the issue: we try to take control and make love happen instead of trusting that it will come when it is time.

Being alone when we are newly separated does not mean that we should attempt to remain completely socially isolated. That is more than most of us can bear, especially early in the healing process. Too much alone time can even be unhealthy, especially if our mood and energy are low because then isolation might lead to depression. We need contact with our friends and families to support us.

While I will address new relationships more specifically later in the chapter, let me say here that seeking a new love is natural and normal; not everyone is ready to be without an intimate. And a new love may prove beneficial if the new relationship allows us to practice opening our hearts again, and we progress in our capacity to love in general. In the case of love, practice does make perfect.

What I am simply recommending is that we try to reframe this period of "forced" aloneness as a spiritual training ground in which we undertake periods of voluntary solitude until our fear dissolves, rather than thinking of it as only a time of loss and avoiding it as we usually do. We might think of it this way: the compulsion to replace one person right away with another is not likely to result in the highest love relationships.

We can significantly speed up our growth as loving beings and enhance our spirituality if we act on faith rather than out of desperation and allow ourselves some time to get used to being on our own. As long as we have to have someone in our lives, we will remain dependent on that person for feelings of security, and if that person leaves, we will have to find another. I believe that it is better to allow the process to unfold, and to use the experience to work on overcoming our fear.

In keeping with the concept of fundamental change, it is time to understand that it is simply a common error of perception that causes us to interpret this healing interlude as a tragic disruption of our interpersonal lives. Separation is not a deprivation, for it is at that point when we feel abjectly alone in life that many of us begin to seriously look within for emotional sustenance. This is the challenge that we all ultimately have to face and master. And as everyone who has faithfully walked this path has learned, when we stay with our fear rather than seeking refuge in yet another human relationship, we find that we are not alone at all.

When we take the time to be by ourselves we have the chance to locate something that is not attainable through relationships with our fellow human beings, regardless of how good they are. This "something" is a direct, one-to-one connection with the Source of all love; and as our revered saints, mystics, and guides have always taught, it is found within. Our typical people- and activity-filled lives interfere with this discovery in ways that we do not recognize until that busyness ceases and we are on our own.

The security that comes from this intimate inner connection forms the basis for relationships where we come together with another out of choice, not need, and it allows our bonds to be increasingly based on love, not fear. This includes all relationships, including those with parents, children, friends, coworkers, and all significant others. Most importantly, all of our relationships remain secondary to the primary spiritual relationship we have developed with the Higher Source, which is as it should be.

Thus, we grow spiritually from acknowledging and living with our fear of being alone, which is brought home to many of us for the first time through our experience with separation from our marriages. The task for everyone, the newly separated and all others, is to have faith enough to leave things alone, to trust that we will be provided with what we really need, and to not allow relationships with others to take us away from us.

A young woman with whom I had met several times just prior to her separation really took this advice to heart. Her parents had been clients of mine, and had referred her to me because they were concerned that she might have acted impulsively in seeking a separation. They knew that she was unhappy in her relationship with her husband; however, they also perceived that she was hesitant and worried about leaving, which made them believe that she was ambivalent about her choice, and they hoped that therapy might restore the marriage.

What I discovered early in my work with her was that she found her marriage lifeless and unfulfilling, and that she really did want to leave it. She told me that she and her husband had done fairly well in the early years of their relationship, but that over time they had become more like roommates than lovers, and that lately they had even been sleeping apart. In her mind they were already emotionally separated; it was now just a matter of actually starting to live apart and making what had already been occurring official.

The hesitation her parents had perceived was real, but it mainly reflected her fear of being alone rather than any serious self-doubt or second-guessing about the value of the marriage or the necessity to leave. She said that having never been fully on her own, she found she was apprehensive at the prospect, and like most people she anticipated the worst.

As a hedge against her apprehension about her first weekend in her new apartment, she arranged to have a friend stay over. Then, in case she had a really bad time of it, she called and asked to see me a week ahead of her regularly scheduled meeting.

Not surprisingly, however, she reported in our Monday evening session that her preparatory work in therapy regarding the necessity of facing her fear resulted in her being able to ask her friend to leave after the first night so that she could do what she knew she had to. She said that she had found her first night of solitude more than a little unnerving. The reality of the shift from sleeping in the house with her husband nearby, to being totally alone in an apartment frightened and depressed her, and made her wonder if she had made a mistake in leaving him. She confided that in her deepest gloom she had even considered calling him to ask about returning home, but she had resisted the impulse and remained fully present with her fear instead.

The more we talked about her experience, the clearer it became to her that she had successfully completed a rite of passage: her dark night alone represented an initiation to the next phase of her spiritual journey. She realized that life had purposefully challenged her to relinquish her hold on a marriage whose continuation had come to be based more on the fear of leaving than on anything resembling love, and had provided her with a chance to choose a path of healing and growth instead. For her, any possibility of love now lay in the direction of healthy change.

She saw that when she deliberately elected to embrace that gloomy night of solitude rather than retreat from it, she had for the first time consciously acted on faith in her path in place of simply being led by fear-based unconscious programming. Having witnessed the healing of her fear and its replacement by new feelings of personal strength and integrity, she became increasingly certain that her life had direction and meaning, and that all of her experiences made sense. She thus achieved a sense of connection with the spiritual dimension that had been previously unavailable to her.

Another brief example is a man who, like many of us, sought new companionship as soon as his separation began. However, after several months of working to overcome his fear he was ready to spend some quality time on his own, which he readily pursued.

He had built a tree house in his backyard, and while sitting alone in it one evening watching the sunset, some deer passed below him. He had always been a religious person, but he told me that it was at that instant, when he was apart and alone in that awesome natural setting, that he perceived his connection with God and all of Creation for the first time.

This was clearly a moment of spiritual transformation. He said that he knew then without any doubt that the path of separation, as initially repellent as it had been, had afforded him this epiphany regarding the unity of all things. His sense of meaning and purpose in life was affirmed as never before, and his fear of aloneness was gone forever.

Emptying Out

From a spiritual perspective, separation is a time of being purposefully emptied of things that are no longer relevant to the journey. Depending on the unique requirements of our individual paths, the dispossession process can be a modest one in which only a few major changes occur, or it can be extreme in that it seems intent on removing practically everything. How this is decided is mysterious, but we often understand it in hindsight when we see how we have been provided with an opportunity to move to the next higher level of development.

Emptying out can unfold slowly, allowing for a kind of trial-and-error learning regarding what serves growth and what does not, for the chance to deliberately and perhaps ceremoniously let go of what is dispensable, and for adjusting to the changes. But it can also happen with ruthless speed, providing no time at all for preparation, adjustment, or any feeling of voluntary participation.

It is in this latter instance of change, when one terrible loss follows another, that the perspective of the journey has its most comforting effect because it reassures us that all of our experiences are purposeful and are meant to move us forward. Without it, there may seem no usefulness in what is happening to us, which can result in feelings of spiritual alienation and despair. I have often witnessed this perspective help clients deal with otherwise unsupportable losses that they had not anticipated and would never have consciously chosen.

I had one client in whose life a sequence of losses was so rapid, relentless, and all-inclusive that it stretched her tolerance almost beyond comprehension. She was a middle-aged person who had lost a daughter in an auto accident a few years before I met her. Now in therapy because of an unhappy marriage, she reasonably decided to end her relationship with her husband because of his lack of involvement with her and his apparent unwillingness or inability to meet her needs.

Once separated from her marriage, her already precarious health unexpectedly began to deteriorate to the point that she no longer could work. Without her regular income she was unable to keep what had been awarded to her in the separation, such as the simple country home and barn and property she loved, and the horses and other animals she had nurtured and enjoyed.

To her immense credit, she was unwilling to be a passive victim of her circumstances, and so in spite of the blows, she enrolled in college with the intention of retraining for work that she would be capable of doing, and that she hoped would be personally fulfilling. Although she found getting to and from classes physically challenging, she discovered that she liked being a student, and she studied hard and performed well.

But in a short time her health worsened, and she soon became unable to continue with her college courses. Her future became increasingly doubtful. Try as she might, her efforts at adapting to her changing circumstances were thwarted and she was able to maintain little of the life she had known. Before the downward spiral of her period of dispossession had ended, her life had literally changed beyond imagining.

One night during this period she had a dream in which she was leading a young thoroughbred horse by a tattered harness that could not possibly hold if the spirited animal decided in the least way to resist her direction. The image in the dream suggested that she was going to have to manage her life without the kind of resources that normally would provide anyone with a sense of security. It hinted strongly that she was not really in charge and that life could go unpredictably and seriously out of control at any time. It also suggested that she was going to have to look beyond herself for help in managing things. Perhaps the only reassuring part was that the horse was staying with her.

Coming at the time and in the form it did, I thought the dream was a true blessing. The changes in my client's life were so persistent and had become so disheartening that it was hard for her to find a reason to carry on. At least now we had a message from the spiritual side that validated her plight as purposeful, even though it in no way suggested that the losses were at an end.

However, in spite of having a good heart and a loving nature, my client had long been a rather skeptical person who relied completely on her own efforts to manage her life and who kept her feelings to herself. To my knowledge she had not consciously thought in spiritual terms prior to that time. I am sure that a difficult childhood and the heartbreaking loss of her daughter cemented her apparently characteristic distrust of things spiritual. Therefore, the deep spiritual significance of the dream was not immediately apparent or helpful to her.

What helped tremendously was the fact that the dream came when it did, and also that it contained images that were familiar and dear to her in that she had tended and loved two horses for several years. When we discussed that dream from a spiritual perspective, that is, from the point of view that its timing and form were intentional and designed to be uniquely helpful to her, she began to acknowledge the possibility.

Also, having finally lost everything that had seemed important, she was placed by her circumstances just where someone with her rather closed, somewhat defensive perspective toward life needed to be if she were going to grow. She was confronted with the stark choice of despairing (which she told me was tempting), or beginning to look at things differently, meaning from the spiritual point of view we have been discussing.

She was apparently ready for transformation because she freely, if somewhat hesitantly, chose the latter, and from that point on she began to make a remarkable transition. She changed from living a relatively unexamined life in which she was just getting by day-to-day, to becoming a self-directed student of the spiritual dimension, accessing an eclectic array of literature and audiotapes regarding the perceptions of Christian and Buddhist teachers, and growing substantially in the process.

With her mind and her heart newly-opened, she began to understand how her difficult losses had contributed to her spiritual development, and with this inner growth she was able to find what was needed to ease the pain that her losses had left. She was truly grateful for having discovered her spirituality, without which she believes she would have been lost.

I once asked her if she had second thoughts about her decision to separate, since remaining with her husband would have meant keeping her lifestyle. (In fact, she always had the opportunity to rejoin him.) Her answer was a thoughtful and confident "no." Despite all of its difficulties, she was certain that the path of change was right for her, and she loved the contributions her spirituality made to her life. More than merely making the best of a tragedy, she felt that she had finally joined the "flow" of life, meaning that she no longer felt alone and isolated in the world, but an integral part of all of it.

For most of us, dispossession is less extreme; but the emptiness that follows the loss of access to our mates as companions, to accustomed activities, to comfortable belongings and surroundings, and to our friends is always hard to bear. Nevertheless, it seems that for many of us, some degree of dispossession is necessary if spiritual transformation is to occur: we have to be ready to give up the ordinary in life in order to find the extraordinary.

When I was experiencing my own losses, I learned to think of separation as a process of purification preparatory to heightened spiritual awareness. I often imagined a meteor streaking through the atmosphere, its lesser metals being burned away by the heat of its fiery descent until nothing remains but its essence. I frequently likened my experience to that of the Trappist monks, who are required to leave everything, including their names, at the monastery gate as they embark on their intense spiritual paths.

Above all, I regularly reminded myself what a friend had told me, that God never takes anything away that is not replaced with something better, which in terms of the preeminent spiritual gifts I was given, I soon discovered to be true. And I have had the opportunity to watch many others discover the same.

Empty Time

An important variation of emptying-out involves time. Most newly separated people, even very busy single parents, have to cope with now-empty time that had been filled with company and activities that routinely come with being married.

For example, most of us have to adjust to lonely hours in the late evening or early morning when our mate is no longer around. These can be eerily quiet times, especially when the children are staying with the other parent. And they can seem to be emotionally and spiritually barren times when we feel particularly alone.

Having this time completely to our selves can be invaluable. It allows for the healing we all need to do when a marriage ends, and it provides an opportunity for self-discovery that is unavailable when we are always busy. But we need the right perspective to use this time well, and thinking of it as a meaningful function of the spiritual journey is the best.

I remember one young woman saying that she "hated" being alone at these times because "I keep bumping into myself." This is, of course, just what we want to do as part of healing and growth. And since we tend to be more open to the inner dimension resources right before and right after sleep, one of the best places to "bump into" ourselves is in bed. I say this in spite of the dread we all have regarding the "empty-bed syndrome," by which we associate some of the worst feelings of loss, sadness, loneliness and fear with sleeping alone.

From the right perspective a bed can become not only a refuge where we may hide from reality during this difficult passage of the journey, but a vehicle for spiritual transformation that is perfectly adapted to the opportunities for self-discovery and personal growth that this passage has to offer. In fact, with this attitude, many people have found themselves looking forward to their private time in bed rather than avoiding it, and setting firm boundaries around what for them has become a sacred place, one that they wish to keep for their exclusive use - at least for a while.

Changes in setting that will help with this attitude shift might begin with votive lights and tapers strategically located around the room. I found that lighted candles always seemed to invite the proper spirits into a bedroom and to drive the gloom out. Candlelight invariably adds a sense of the sacred. A small table or dresser top can serve as an altar for candles of differing colors and scents, as well as for incense, and will assuredly convert a forbidding room into a sanctuary.

A journal for expressing thoughts and feelings, and spiritual and personal growth-oriented reading materials, are next-to-the-bed essentials. Writing about feelings has proved to be as helpful as talking about them, which is important to help with the grief that visits early in the separation process during these hours. Most people I talk to have their own favorite books they refer to for comfort, understanding, or guidance; and with self-expansion in mind, this is also a good time to try new spiritual reading materials on for size, as looking at things differently will never be more appropriate than now.

Such reading and writing materials lend an air of serious study and contemplation to the bedroom atmosphere, reminding us each night and in the early hours that what we are going through in our aloneness has great importance in the grand scheme of our lives. Together with all of the candles, they helped me think of my room as a monk's cell, a place of special calling away from the ordinary world, dedicated to deep healing and spiritual expansion.

A variety of extra pillows on the bed add psychological ballast to the bed, something to lean against and hold onto, and they make sitting up to read and think and meditate easier. A new set of personally chosen linens and a comforter or bedspread can individualize the bed and provide a sense of pride in ownership.

Having the kind of quiet time at the end of the day or early in the morning that can be experienced only when alone in a bed can be wonderful. There is peace to be found here, often beyond anything previously known. It is in just such an atmosphere that we can do some of the very best work we have arrived at this place to do. As intrepid travelers on the spiritual journey, we should not be surprised to find that after awhile we no longer need rescue from our solitude, for our solitude will have rescued us.

Other Resources

Taking time out in other ways in other settings will add continuity to the path of self-exploration that begins in our bed. The general idea is to pursue time alone for reading, writing and contemplation when possible in any place that promotes self-study. Parks are good places for this in good weather. The coffee shop chains that have sprung up everywhere have done so to cater to individuals, such as the newly separated, who seek a place to relax and read. Some of the larger bookstores have reading areas and coffee bars, too, making them ideal places to spend an afternoon or evening of perusing personal growth and other books at leisure.

Sometimes a church sanctuary is available during non-service hours, which can be a good choice because of the healing effects of all the prayer energy that has been shown to linger there. And although more difficult for many people to arrange, a retreat in a monastery can have special value because of the monastic dedication to spiritual healing and growth.

Even cemeteries have promise because they are often physically beautiful, they are usually quiet and peaceful, and they certainly are reminders of the spiritual dimension. But anyplace works if it supports the theme of deliberately seeking time apart for leisurely self-nurturance and personal development.

When we do choose to balance alone time with socializing, it is a revelation and a treat that we will happen upon people who are on paths similar to ours. Nothing seems more timely and welcome than encountering someone who is processing his or her life in the same manner that we are, and perhaps even reading some of the same books.

But even when opportunities to engage such persons do not readily occur, or at those times when we want to be around people-energy without actually interacting with the people, bookstores, coffeehouses, and other such places offer a chance to sit alone and still have other people around us.

Empty Space

Another form of emptying out occurs when we lose material possessions in the separation. This usually happens as we leave some things behind when we move out, or our mates take things with them when they go, or our things have to be sold as part of the division of joint assets. Sometimes the new residence has insufficient space for our things and we have to discard them before moving in.

The initial challenge in this part of the change process has to do with overcoming the emotional shock that hits when our formerly shared space sprouts gaps on the clothing bars in the closets, newly vacant spaces on living room and bedroom carpets, and empty picture hooks on the walls. (And unless it comes completely furnished, the new residence will have these unmistakable signs of change, too.)

These physical discontinuities can have a powerful psychological effect that sends us reeling. They can remind us of what used to be and make us sad; they can make us long for the sense of completion we felt when married; and they can ultimately influence us to try to restore a relationship that is no longer appropriate to our growth.

But there is an additional challenge that results from the downward change in the quantity of what we have owned, one that is essentially spiritual in nature, which is the problem we now have of contending with empty space all by itself. The spiritual aspect of this challenge is revealed when we find that we feel anxious and incomplete without our material possessions, as this indicates that something may be missing inside.

It seems to me that voluntarily reducing our material possessions is not something most of us would normally do. Just as we like to fill our empty time with activity, most of us are accustomed to filling the physical space around us with things that we like (and our basements, attics and garages hold what is not in current use). Not only do we tend to hold onto things rather than eliminate them, being a wealthy culture, we also tend to quickly replace what we do lose or eliminate, and so any sense of emptiness we might experience is only temporary.

Having lots of familiar things makes us feel comfortable, safe, in control, and prosperous: we feel embraced and enhanced by our things rather than crowded or overshadowed by them. This is why we can feel so exposed, diminished and vulnerable when our things are unexpectedly or forcefully taken away. It may also be why we tend to battle over who gets what, and it is what motivated one client to buy exact replicas of the things he left behind, and another to hire an interior decorator to completely furnish his new condo even before he actually left home.

To make the most of this opportunity for spiritual discovery and growth, I suggest resisting the impulse to cover over the feeling of emptiness that change has exposed. This means allowing the physical emptiness to stand in the immediate aftermath of separation and after the initial crisis has abated and life has stabilized to some extent and we feel tempted to start purchasing and possessing anew.

Now, I am not referring to things such as beds for the children's room in a new apartment, or a sofa or refrigerator, but the extras that we have come to think of as necessities because we are used to them. This includes items that bring excitement when we think about having them, and that we look forward to shopping for and are willing to go into debt to have now. They are things we may feel deserving of and entitled to, or that we demand for ourselves because they provide a look or lifestyle that we desire.

The list differs for different people. It can include decorative wall hangings, knick-knacks for placement on shelves or dresser tops, unneeded furniture that we tend to look at but not sit on, and clothes, tools, books, dishes and silver that we tell ourselves will be needed, but actually just create an opportunity for shopping and owning.   These things replace those that we had that were not used, either. If they were lost, they would be replaced again, too.

A spiritual perspective on this process begins with the idea that life has removed our possessions for a reason. Our work is to trust in the process and to quietly observe our need to accumulate things and fill space, and to reconsider what we actually need to get by. We can begin to practice a kind of voluntary material minimalism that may remove clutter from our spiritual paths and present us with a whole new feeling of control that comes with not needing things to make us feel fulfilled and happy.

Therefore, instead of shopping we can just notice our interaction with the spareness. We can start by deliberately sitting in large spaces, and then expand our focus area-by-area to take in all the empty space nearby. If we find one space that is more disturbing than another, we should focus on that spot and see what happens. What we often find is that even small empty space bothers us. Any exposed area may cause inexplicable anxiety. We want something there to break up the emptiness.

Continuing to live deliberately with spareness will deepen awareness. It is at this point that the perceptual shift starts: we begin to understand that it is not our environment but we who need filling.

Acquiring things is a superficial remedy that at best works only temporarily, so that we have to shop again and again, which is why we end up with so much stuff. This fear requires a spiritual resolution, which means we have to go inside to find it. Shopping and ownership can distract us from doing this inner work. But we avoid going to our inner dimension because we fear the emptiness that is there. We can easily manipulate empty physical space, but we have no such power or control over spiritual space. We may be more comfortable outside where we feel more in charge of what is around us.

We will learn to move to the spiritual dimension to find meaning and significance because ultimately our frustration and unhappiness with the material world will motivate us to try. But why are we so resistant?

My perspective is that mostly we are just afraid of the emptiness there because we are unfamiliar with it and we distrust it. Perhaps we even sense that we might find that there is nothing meaningful there at all, and since the spiritual underlies the material, if it is just an empty void, what must that imply about our lives and us?

With such a grand unconscious fear overriding all, it makes sense that we would busy ourselves filling small exterior spaces and keeping an outward rather than inward orientation. So, whether we recognize it or not, we distract ourselves from fear of the Unknown. Our clutter and the act of gathering it protect us from it.

Thus, our job at this point is to not do anything to try to establish meaning and purpose by getting things, but to sit with the open space that has come to us by way of the process of change. We have only to practice patiently waiting for life to unfold as it will, and see what it has in store. Streamlining our material lives after our separations will help us with this.

Of course, we can just as easily use existing possessions to distract us, and in a way the older things can present more of a challenge than the new ones. This is because their sentimental value can create a great resistance to letting them go. It is hard for us even to imagine leaving behind photos, clothing, books and other memorabilia that provide a sense of continuity with the past.

For me, having to move into a very small apartment that had no room for my stuff encouraged this process of streamlining. Sorting through my books, for example, I sat with each one deciding whether it had relevance to my life now. I sorted them into piles, and then sorted them again, letting go of another one or two each time. At every passing, my fear lessened and my courage at letting go increased. Soon almost every one of them was deemed expendable.

The joy I felt at having been able to let go was unforgettable. In the process, I consciously set a course of living lighter. Other memorabilia followed. I was amazed at the anxiety I felt at the thought of discarding things of the past, and was relieved when I found I was able to move on without them.

I discovered something interesting on the way, which was that, probably because it hints of another dimension, nostalgia feels spiritual. But going to the past to find spiritual sustenance is the same as trying to gain nutrition from the memory of a meal, or happiness from the fantasy of things we can buy in the future: it just is not there.

We are no longer the persons in old photos, and when we relish the feelings we get from any return to nostalgic times, we do not attend to life here and now. The stuff of the past forms an umbilical cord that connects us to a source of nurturance whose time is gone because we are gone. An umbilicus represents dependency and spiritual insufficiency. When we face letting go of what has protected us from independence, we will encounter the fear of emptiness. When we sit courageously, patiently, and faithfully with this feeling, we can heal it. But first we have to let go.

All of this being said, we do not have to become mendicants, or think that the desire we feel to acquire and possess things is bad. Possessions have a place. No one said being spiritual means being uncomfortable. Even Buddha preached a middle road.

We probably need our possessions to prop us up until we are able to stand spiritually on our own. Identifying with things of value and beauty can help us feel personal worth and attractiveness where these might be lacking inside. Old photos, postcards, notes and letters can help us feel connected through bygone relationships while we are forming a higher connection. All of these things are expressions of our humanness, after all, and they bring comfort, which in a compassionate universe is a valid reason for being. Our need is to be conscious of our material things, and not to allow them to inhibit our spiritual progress by hiding our fear.

I have found that envisioning life as a perpetual journey helps with the decision to streamline. If we are always on the move, we do not want to be weighted-down with too much stuff; we want a light load. The accumulation of unneeded things indicates that we have arrived somewhere permanently. Obviously, since life is temporary, this cannot be true. When we fail to perceive the journey we will begin to accumulate material things. Wanting them may be a cue that we need to become more conscious of why we are here.

The rule is that the more things we possess, the less graceful and efficient our spiritual development. Once we know better, we realize the wisdom in keeping what we have to a minimum, and in always being prepared to let go of what we have in order to move on.

In the process of experimenting with minimalism, I discovered that the spareness has natural beauty and that emptiness is lovely without further decoration. The more I practiced leaving things alone, the more accepting and appreciative I became of everything in its naturalness, including myself. This changed my concept of imperfection in Nature, as nothing can be imperfect to the spiritually attuned eye.

If we practice consciously leaving the empty space around us alone, we will learn to leave the rest of Creation alone, too. In the process, we will align ourselves with the flow and rhythm of Nature. The practice of a natural relationship with the environment will then provide the deep connection with life we all deeply desire. Our awareness of this relationship opens a whole new level of spiritual development, the result of which will be a diminishing dependency on the acquisition of material things.

Roles

For many people, a new life alone also means that many of the roles that normally got divided between two people now fall entirely to one. This is not as bad if there are no children or if we had been on our own for significant time in the past and had been accustomed to handling life's requirements. But having shared roles and duties with another can still make changing from joint to single life challenging under the best of circumstances as we get used to relying on our mate.

This change can be extreme for some people who depended completely on their spouses for certain things. I have known very traditional women who knew nothing at all of finances, not even how much their husbands earned, who were lost as to managing money and bills when the marriage ended. I have also known traditional men who could not prepare food for themselves because while married they never had to fix a meal. These examples may seem unbelievable in our modern world, but they are real. What is more, I think that the most conventional of marriages still encourage this kind of dependency.

Generally speaking, most of us find performing under the changed circumstances much different than occasionally substituting in a role if a mate was not available, because at those times we did not have to enter into the roles wholly physically and psychologically. Now comes a permanent change in role functioning that substituting does not prepare us for. It means if we do not do it, it does not get done. The toughest of these have to do with raising children.

So, for example, a man who literally has not changed a diaper may face the full array of child-raising duties with no back up, including such things as arranging for day care, shopping for clothes, and leaving work to pick up a sick child at school. A woman may have to learn how to throw a baseball on weekends, and to negotiate with a teenage son who is not sure he likes a female telling him what to do. Because most single parents have to work for a living and are tired by day's end, the at-home chores become additionally draining.

We also become solely responsible for social functions if we are to continue our involvement with friends and extended family. Thus, it falls to us to invite people for dinner and do all the cooking, to remember birthdays and anniversaries, and to make, carry out, and pay for the arrangements for all sorts of other social occasions without help. And we may have to attend graduations, weddings, reunions and other celebrations without escort.

Any adaptations we are able to make without becoming mired in anger or bitterness is progress. It may be inconvenient and tiring to play new roles, but in these we have an unusual opportunity to experience life differently, as only happens when circumstances require that we take over for someone who had filled those roles for us.

But there is more at stake in successfully making these role changes than we commonly know. Conventional marital roles can have a limiting effect on personal development. We share the load, which is good, but we usually share it according to prescribed gender-based roles that reflect the cultural biases we grew up with about who can do what. This is an unconscious practice by which we tend to promote a particular right way for men and women to behave in a relationship, especially when children are involved.

We can benefit from the experience of the new roles by expanding our perception of what is possible for us, which broadens our view of the limits of reality and eliminates the artificial limits of our development as whole persons. This is an exciting time in regard to becoming conscious and healing and growing in a truly fundamental way.

By nature, we are all both male and female. We may be aware of this in the abstract, but in many practical ways it has been hidden from us by cultural biases that do not favor androgynous behavior. While we are certainly biologically instinctively male and female in important ways, we are also conditioned socially about the limitations of the genders, and this becomes part of our belief system and expectations. The more traditional our thinking, the better we feel when we perform a role as a man or woman "should," and the more disturbed we are when people behave outside of role expectations.

Therefore, if a man is good with children, we see it as unusual and applaud it. But we do not really expect it of all men. When a woman is not good with children, we think it odd. In a divorce, when a man wants custody of his children, or worse, when a woman does not, we may be shocked. Such role reversals are just too far out of the ordinary, which means too different from what we customarily expect.

With forced changes in what is required of us, we can expand the maleness and femaleness that is natural to all of us in positive, healthy ways and in doing so begin to round ourselves out as human beings. To me, this makes what seem the worst of times actually some of the best. People really stand to benefit immensely.

For example, if we accept the model that a physical chore like changing a furnace filter is always done by a man, then in a marriage it would automatically fall to the husband to do that task. It might never occur to us that a woman should or could do that job. By doing it a man would be affirmed in his masculinity, and by having it done for her by a man, a woman would be affirmed in her traditional feminine image. The appropriate sex-role expectations would be reinforced for everyone, including the children who witness it.

For a woman on her own who needs a furnace filter changed, the first inclination might then be to look for the nearest man, and failing to find one, to let the project go. She may only fleetingly consider doing it herself. Therefore, facing the task of replacing a filter means challenging not only a physical barrier, but also an even more important psychological one. When she achieves success, her personal accomplishment would shatter a restraint in her belief system about what is possible for a woman, and increase the chances that other such beliefs might be shattered also.

This is true for a man, too. If, for example, planning a sleep over or a birthday party for a child was always a wife's job, then a man's successfully completing either of them can expand his sense of possibility. If we pay attention, we notice that the feeling of satisfaction is deep when we break through a barrier, and the breakthrough encourages further change.

I remember a very traditionally feminine woman excitedly telling me how she had cut a limb from a tree that was blocking her driveway. She had a sense of awe about herself at her accomplishment that caused her to glow. She had begun to cross the barrier between culturally determined feminine and masculine behavior and it made her feel masterful.

From a spiritual point of view, when men have to practice doing traditional female things, and women have to do traditional male things, we access and expand the non-dominant gender energy within each of us. This begins to push out against the resistance we have to becoming conscious of the mix of masculine and feminine in each of us.

The image I have of this is that we begin to inflate the flat side of us so that, like a coin that had been cut in half, we can now become full. Until we are rounded out, we unconsciously seek an opposite sex other to fill the flat side in for us. In effect, we are looking for our other half. This is why very traditional males end up with very traditional females, so that we would expect the captain of the football team to marry the head cheerleader.

The work we are here to do is to be both halves unto ourselves, which many of us may never accomplish without having to make a go of life as a single after being married, especially if we married young and essentially went from one family to another.

And it is not only important to our progression that we accomplish the role shifts, but that we become conscious of the dynamic interplay of the male and female energy that animates us. The more consciously we proceed with the new roles, even if we have no choice but to do them, the faster we will heal the old beliefs about our limitations as human beings, and grow. In my opinion, if we do not succeed in consciously doing this work of completion, we will have failed at one of the most important purposes of our lives.

There is another benefit to this personal completion that has to do with future love relationships. The more complete we are individually, the less likely we will be to attract incomplete people to us as intimates. We will not need to compensate for what is unfinished in us through a relationship, and we will not settle for anyone who has not done healing work similar to ours. Two incomplete people can never equal a complete one. Each of us has to achieve that on our own, and I believe we are meant to do just that.

We can be in relationship with someone simply for his or her good qualities without having to fit him or her into our system of needs. Likewise, someone will seek us just for who we are, not for what we can provide. We can have an emotional grown-up who is an equal and a companion. In sum, we may still prefer the company of another, but we will no longer be emotionally dependent on him or her. This is the ideal for healthy intimacy.

Breaching social barriers as complete individuals includes participating in activities alone that we had perhaps only attended in the company of a mate. As newly separated people we may tend to avoid dinners, or movies, or concerts, or vacations alone because we believe that these are meant to be done with others, and we assume that we will look or feel strange doing them alone. But there is nothing to prevent us from learning to enjoy any of these activities without company.

The food at a favorite restaurant is just as good when we eat alone. Movies are every bit as enjoyable. An orchestra transports the individual soul just as fully. And a sunset at the beach is every bit as beautiful. So much of how we enjoy such activities has to do with habit and expectation, and these can change. After all, our senses are always individual, not shared.

I remember reading somewhere that joy is for the person who is not afraid to be alone, and I found that this was true. One of the unexpected treasures was discovering that I could enjoy many of these things even more for not having to share them. This seemed to have mainly to do with the undiluted nature of the interaction between the event and me. I found that I did not need anyone's input about the event to add to my own pleasure. And very selfishly, I did not have to think about whether the other person was enjoying it, too. My experience was more purely my own, free of the moods, or tastes, or other idiosyncracies of anyone else, and therefore free of distraction.

Even though we may be happy in someone's company, we are better when we have learned to be joyful on our own. Our happiness is thereafter not dependent on anyone else. Once we have achieved such autonomy, we will want to be with others who have achieved it, also.

Holidays

The major holidays are times of great social and emotional significance. As repositories of cultural custom and tradition, they are laden with sentiment and nostalgia, and they kindle a feeling of kinship and goodwill among people that is not there much of the year.

On an individual level, they also serve as benchmarks of our personal success at feeling included in society and in life, which we unconsciously judge according to how close to the conventional manner of celebrating them we come each year. Failure can impact our happiness for months, and is the reason many of us feel a sense of dread when holidays approach and our proper participation in them is not assured.

Since for most of us holiday success involves being with significant others, separation at this time can be scary and depressing, especially if we anticipate being alone. Things are worse if we have children. The saddest aspect of all, however, is that none of the pain is necessary.

Take Christmas for example. Over generations, we have come to perceive Christmas as magical and extraordinary. The fact that most people in our culture have similar expectations about it indicates that the fantasy has become institutionalized: the perceived magic of Christmas is part of our belief system. We even have unconscious defenses against altering its special feeling, such as labeling non-participants as either unfortunate if they are incidentally left out, or Scrooge-like if they intentionally decline to participate.

We are emotionally dependent on Christmas and want it to remain unsullied as the pinnacle of happy times. Many of us work hard to make

Christmas perfect each year, which means assuring that it turns out just the way we have always imagined it should. We are nostalgic about it and enormously sentimental. It is nearly impossible for us to imagine a different perspective than the one that we now cherish.

There is unquestionable value in having a holiday attitude when it encourages love and compassion. I know of people who gather lonely strangers and take them home to share in celebration. Many people work at church-operated soup kitchens to serve holiday meals to the poor. Food and gift baskets are prepared and passed out in poverty-ridden areas by good-hearted souls. Who would want to change such acts of kindness?

But there is a downside to this belief. Therapists certainly see the casualties that occur when Christmas does not play out according to fantasy. This is precisely what happens to people with separation. The liability in the illusion is revealed in the despair that is generated for those for whom the day means being without significant others with whom to share. In order to enjoy Christmas magic we have paid a price. Rarely can anyone anticipate this day in solitude without feeling that he or she has missed something of great value.

A healing and growth perspective does not diminish the Christmas spirit but releases it from confinement in one certain day each year and thus expands it. At the same time, it offers a means of rescuing ourselves from our emotional dependence on it.

It is important to keep the image of the journey in mind when facing the holidays as a separated person. From that image we can reassure ourselves that the changes in our lives are necessary for our progression. This is particularly important at this time because of the powerful reaction we have to feeling excluded from normal festivities.

I saw the path of my separation as offering a meaningful chance to do something different. Following that intuitive theme, as the first holiday season approached, I fought the panicky sensations that visited me and chose to decline friends' invitations to share traditional celebrations with them. Telling myself that this might be my only opportunity to experience holidays on my own and to face the monstrous fear I had, and that I knew many others had, regarding that possibility, I decided to give solitude a try.

Even though I knew the experiment might turn out disastrous, I contacted a friend who had a small, isolated, primitive cabin on a nearby lake about using it for Thanksgiving. She agreed, and on Thanksgiving Eve I gathered modest provisions, candles, wood for heat, and my sleeping bag and set out on the adventure.

As would befit such an experiment, the holiday itself was gray, cold and rainy, and the cabin was dark inside, with only the fire in the Franklin stove to keep the chill away. In place of a holiday banquet, I ate the kind of simple food one does on a camping trip, except for some fish I caught, which became the unanticipated main course of my "feast."

Capitalizing on the opportunity to use that day differently, in place of socializing over dinner, napping on a full stomach, or watching a football game, I read, walked, meditated, and relaxed. The experience turned out to be wonderful. Far from what I had always feared, it was a time I will always remember for the peace and joy I experienced for having removed what I have come to think of as the emotional shackles of habit and tradition.

As Christmas approached, I again turned down heartfelt holiday invitations and made arrangements to go to the cabin. I felt some anticipatory fear because I had never done anything like this on Christmas, and was well aware of the warnings to find shelter from isolation. Taking the same view that I was being presented with a perhaps once-in-a-lifetime opportunity, I followed my inner guidance. After spending some time on Christmas Eve with my kids, I went out to discover how I would be without the normal ritual celebrations that I had always liked so well. Thanksgiving appeared to be a warm-up for what I sensed was really going to be the real test.

Again it was wonderful. Not only were there no terrifying visitations by ghosts of Christmas past, but no sadness, regret, longing or feelings of loss. I experienced nothing short of the joy and peace we associate only with the magical season celebrated as usual, but this time it was not dependent on holiday routines in any form. I found peace and joy without all of the material and emotional trappings. In fact, the feelings were heightened because they resulted from my having been liberated from the fantasy and its shadow side of holiday angst if things did not unfold as prescribed.

It was clear that I had made an advance, and that what I found was superior to what I had had in the past. I knew immediately that I would never return to the old way. As unimaginable as spending the holidays so differently would have been just one year earlier, I could now no longer imagine wanting a holiday feast at Thanksgiving or a conventional Christmas morning celebration. The path of marital separation led to a freedom I had no idea existed; I just needed to take a leap of faith to find it. I cannot remember a better decision.

The next year I did the same, but this time I looked forward to those days of simple solitude. Once more the experience was wonderful. Since then I have eschewed holiday celebrations and have learned to see each day as special.

I now see that my time alone was a great leveler. No longer was there an energy peak at one or two points in the calendar. Having exploded my personal version of the cultural myth of the magic of holidays, the energy was released throughout the rest of the year. From a spiritual perspective, every day is a celebration of the spirit of Thanksgiving and Christmas.

Some may think that, not being a custodial parent I was privileged to have the opportunity to take such time alone. To that I would say that I indeed felt privileged. But I would also say that given the same opportunity, relatively few people would voluntarily choose holidays in isolation over holidays with family and friends. I know this from having worked with many newly separated people during the holiday season.

Also, I believe I was provided with this opportunity so that I could face this common fear and learn what I have from the experience. It is no coincidence that I am in a position to share my discovery with people who because of their marital losses are confronted with holidays alone. Who better to encourage them to try on a different perspective than someone who has done it and knows the benefits?

I have met a few others who were fortunate enough to have made the same discovery. They learned that not only are those days survivable, but that they can be as enjoyable as any other days. No Scrooges here, they just gracefully transcended the holiday snare.

It is vital to our progression that we comprehend that none of the holiday sentiment that we have held so dear arises within us naturally. It is conditioned, and because it feels good, we have innocently made our hearts vulnerable to it. The fact is that there is nothing inherently different about a certain Thursday in November or December 25th that should warrant the feelings we have. The spirit of Thanksgiving and Christmas do not belong to those days. That spiritual energy emanates from within each of us and is potentially around all of the time.

I recommend to clients that they try being alone on the holidays, if only to honor the path of separation. If this is too frightening, I suggest that they at least plan to spend part of the day in solitude, while toning-down their participation in the normal rituals such as shopping, decorating and gift giving. Very often they find that something as uncomplicated as a long morning walk in solitude, or a simple meal in place of an elaborate one, can be easily introduced into the normal routine.

The idea is to deliberately do something different to change the pattern and see what results. People almost always experience something good. From there we then can work on further change toward independence. I find that the process is always a revelation.

Courageously facing the fear of being alone on the holidays represents another form of initiation to that aforementioned level of awareness that is not accessible if we continue to react to the holidays in habitual ways. This is no overstatement. Our holiday tradition amounts to a cultural compulsion, replete with anxiety because so much emotion is invested in their perfect unfoldment and a predictable spiritual letdown once they are over. This is unhealthy. Part of our work of awakening is becoming aware of the unconscious influence that holiday expectation has on us.

This awareness is a prelude to freeing and advancing our spirituality, which is ironic, since we believe that healthy spirituality resides in those very celebrations. When we do become aware, we will begin to loosen the unconscious grip of other cultural bonds, too. This is a function of the journey, to transcend the limits of instinct and socialization, and there is no better time to try than the holidays.

With children, it may be harder to experiment with time apart and other rudimentary changes. We do have to take their needs into account. It would be unkind to deprive children all at once of what we have raised them to expect. This is all the more true with the first holiday cycle because of the emotional difficulties they already face with other changes in the home. If we choose to keep holiday rituals essentially intact, we can honor their spirit without giving in to emotional and material excess. A moderate alteration is a sensible beginning. We can request children not to buy us gifts, or to be very spare about it, and we can reintroduce the primacy of spirituality. We can begin to inform them about our changing perspective if they are mature, but leave it up to them to decide what to do in terms of their own practices as they become independent of us.

Through such an approach we can allow them to celebrate holidays in a familiar way while introducing a growthful alternative. Our own comfort with the changes, particularly with being alone, will present them with a model for living that is different than they are likely to see anywhere else. I consider that a marvelous substitute for gifts of the usual kind.

Each small change has a cumulative effect. With each one we increase our freedom and independence from the limits of conventional life. Separation is a road to this end.

New Relationships

Most therapists will advise their newly separated clients to take their time getting into new relationships. Many clients will voluntarily proclaim abstinence anyway, believing the last thing they need is another involvement. But neither the advice nor the proclamation stand up well against the reality of the unfamiliar loneliness and fear we experience having left the familiar presence of a mate. If we had someone in our life, we usually want a new person to take his or her place. We are just not used to being alone.

I have learned from personal experience and from working with separated clients not to direct relationship behavior at this time, but just to patiently and faithfully work with what develops. As we have seen with love affairs, people's relationship paths have their own wisdom and timing. Our job is to find the value in those experiences that develop naturally, not try to create valuable experiences ourselves. The guiding principle is that what we need eventually comes.

Working with what develops sometimes means initially helping people to adapt to life alone, at least for a while, and sometimes it means assisting them in their interactions with new love interests. The former is usually less complicated than the latter. We have to face being alone sometime, for that is the nature of separation, and I believe we benefit from a fallow period once leaving a relationship.

Besides, there is wisdom in waiting because we are so emotionally vulnerable and unstable at this time, and unsure of what we need and who we eventually will become once we heal and grow. This wisdom notwithstanding, whether forced or not, relationships happen, and we have to manage them.

If we do venture into relationships right away, whom we attract as an intimate has to be somewhat suspect if only because we are in such generally poor emotional shape at this time. Most of us actually have little to share other than our grief and struggle, seasoned perhaps with our dependency, and topped with our gratitude to the new person for saving us from having to be alone.

And we might wonder who would want a relationship with someone in our condition. Perhaps it would be another person in a position similar to ours who is also desperate for succor. Perhaps it is someone who finds the intensity of our emotional need attractive, or who might enjoy the feeling of dominance and control he or she automatically has because we are so needy. Or perhaps it is just someone who has a good heart but is naive and inexperienced.

This does not mean that these relationships never last: they sometimes do, and they may prove more satisfying than the previous marriage if everyone works at continuing to grow. However, one of the chief problems with an early involvement is that it tends not to last, and we are emotionally vulnerable. Because we have not yet healed from the primary loss, we risk real hurt with another one. In fact, in our weakened state the new loss can seem worse than the original one. This is all the more true if we felt rejected by our mate and need reaffirmation.

When a first relationship endures, we might discover that over time the new partner begins to appear significantly similar to the person to whom we had been married. This is good to the extent that those qualities are the positive ones; but we are likely to find personality issues of the kind that made the marriage untenable.

This is to be expected for two reasons. One is that we tend to draw people to us who reflect our level of healing and growth. We fit best with people who are like us, and because we have not had the time to do the work of personal change, we are most likely to develop a relationship that mirrors the original one.

The second is that, because we are here to heal and grow, life will provide us with the motivation to do just that, and with reminders of the work that still needs to be done. Therefore, if we have not moved forward as needed, the new relationship may frustrate us in the very ways the old one did so that the need for change is not ignored.

In my experience, however, the relationship with a new person usually does represent a progression, if only in terms of being a "bridge" between the person to whom we were married and the higher level of relational ability we are destined for as we continue to heal and grow.

The most common examples of a "bridge" relationship that involves remarriage I can think of have to do with abused men and women with whom I have worked who married their new mates because they seemed "safe." As we know, feelings of safety need to come from within, which is precisely what occurs when we do our work. When my clients eventually found safety within, they also found that their new marriages were no longer appropriate for them. Now they faced parting with people who loved them for the nearly inexplicable reason that they simply no longer "fit."

In every instance, my clients felt as if leaving on this basis made them as abusive to the new mate as their old mate had been. In a sense, they had used the new person as a stepping stone to healing old fears, and having done so they had to deal with selfishly breaking a nice person's heart. In some instances this was further complicated when children were involved because of the bonds that had been formed between them and the stepparent.

But the changes could not be avoided if these people were to grow. On the spiritual journey, once the conditions that promote a relationship change, the need for the relationship changes, too.

What seems most important is that we consciously try not to force a premature conclusion to our transitional healing process by making "permanent" relationships happen.   Forcing intimacy hinders our developmental work, part of which, ironically, is to prepare for healthy intimate relationships.

Many of us do not intuitively grasp the fact that we have personal work to do. We believe that all we really need is to find the right person to end our troubles. But progressing to the point that we attract a right person requires first becoming the right person.   If this could have happened in a relationship, we probably would not have seen our marriages end. We have to suspect that we are out on our own because we have inner things to take care of that can only be accomplished on a "solitary" basis.

When it comes to love, we can only get as much as we can give. Right interaction with others demands that we be emotionally self-supportive and self-sustaining. This means having a healthy relationship with our inner self.   Paradoxically, then, the appropriate context for healthy mutuality is healthy individuality.

As was emphasized previously, there is an "us" that we can only know from the personal experience of being completely alone. I might summarize this point by saying that it is our willingness to be alone that prepares us for interaction with others.   In effect, by consciously isolating ourselves, we make ourselves available for intimacy. Nights alone, holidays alone, handling sickness alone, walks alone, all of these things have an eventual transforming effect.

What this solitary work also does is to provide us with a sense of appropriate boundaries with anyone with whom we become deeply involved. With an appropriately developed sense of distance from others, we are less likely to try to control them, attempt to make them meet our needs, or get them to conform to our styles. We have the capacity to see that we are individual souls walking individual paths and we honor the path of another by leaving his or hers alone and taking responsibility only for our own.

As we first become aware of it, we may find this sense of distance disconcerting.   This is because true autonomy is so rare.   We have always been encouraged to mesh instead, which is a perspective on love and relationships that has to change if we are to grow.

From this detached perspective, we are able to observe our behavior and that of the other person in a unique way, and thus be able to own what is ours and allow them to own what is theirs. We do not confuse their problems with ours, and they do not confuse ours with theirs. By not believing that we should take on the other's emotional work and not asking them to take on ours, we will also avoid feelings of guilt and anger. This is an advantageous arrangement for continued healing and growth.

If we have done this preparatory work, we will ultimately attract intimates who have been through a similar process. Being with someone who has been where we have been will make us feel appreciated for the healing and growth we have done, and because we will be on similar paths we will always have important things to talk about as we continue our work. I cannot think of a better means of assuring a sense of significance to our joint lives.

After separation, it is hard to know for sure when the right person will enter our lives. Sometimes we go for long periods without a significant other, which can make for some lonely hours. But the more work we have done on individuation, the more patient we can be, and the more we can trust that we will know when a relationship is right. In the meantime, we have but to look to our paths to always uncover the next piece of work that is needed. It rarely actually requires the presence of someone else. When it does, we will know. That person will show.

Reflections

Sit quietly, breathe slowly, and relax your mind.

Silently read the following:

- I choose to face my new aloneness with courage and curiosity. It will be interesting to see what happens.

- I seek self-completion. I will use this time to develop as a whole person.

- Material changes that lighten my load are appropriate to my journey. Living voluntarily with material spareness will promote my spiritual growth.

- This is my best chance to end my emotional dependence on relationships and material possessions.

- New roles will expand my perception of who I am and what is possible for me.

- The major holidays provide an unusual opportunity to change and grow. I will not fear them, but will endeavor to look at them for their possibilities in making a new life.

- It is more important to be the right person than to find the right person. My search begins with me.

- I will no longer try to force change.

Repeat each phrase with conviction. Note the affinity you have with them.

Write the phrases taking care to attend to their content.

Say each phrase aloud to bolster your identification with the new perspective. And remember that life does not take away what is important without compensation.

7
Coming Full Circle

In this final chapter I wish to share some important concepts that have come to me from reading and contemplation during my own healing process, ideas that form the basis of my life now and that I believe will be of value to anyone who seeks continuos spiritual growth. It is meant as a guide for taking the new higher consciousness that we have been working toward beyond the divorce experience and into daily life. The path of fundamental change is not an easy one to find and follow. We have discovered that it requires not only that we traverse separation and divorce without becoming lost in the wasteland of anger and guilt; it also requires a willingness to expand our awareness in all directions. We are on a road less traveled whose guideposts are honesty, courage, love, and compassion, which lead the way to higher perception. Those who take this route follow the alchemists who learned how to turn lead into gold, our wealth being the knowledge that we are more than we thought, and that everything in life has meaning and purpose. Once on this path, we are positioned to heal and grow for the rest of our lives, but doing so requires constant work.

What helps to assure ongoing healing and growth is a daily practice of conscious awareness that promotes faith and confidence. One that I recommend contains several essential considerations that should remain refreshing, challenging and enlivening for a lifetime. They include some ideas that have already been discussed but that will benefit from reiteration, and some new ones.

These are:
- seeing life as a journey;
- believing that things happen for a reason;
- having faith in abundance;
- being vigilant against victim consciousness;
- taking responsibility for our feelings and behavior;

- becoming familiar with the dark side;
- honoring the mystery of the spiritual;
- sensing the unity in all of creation;
- practicing a peaceful response at all times.

I have found that each of these alone is sustaining, and that they also interweave with one another to create a conceptual and practical matrix of relevance to any situation I have encountered. When practiced continually they can help maintain faith and optimism.

Life as Journey

The first of these essentials, viewing life as a journey, can add a sense of movement and rhythm to an otherwise routine and predictable passage. It is also a means of sustaining ourselves spiritually when circumstances are especially tough. Life is wondrous, but as we know from separation, it is not always wonderful. If we perceive life as a journey, and see each day as a paving stone of a worthwhile path, we will find meaning in every endeavor.

This is especially helpful during times of transition, when fear and insecurity reign and time seems to stand still. If we picture the journey, we can perceive the perpetual movement that is there and remember that things were not always so bad and trust that they will change again. In this way, instead of feeling that we have entered a spiritual blind alley, we see a tunnel with light at the end, and a passage where there appeared to be no way out.

When we are on a journey, we know that we have come from somewhere and that we are going somewhere, and that every experience is part of a purposeful flow. However this awareness arrives, as a sudden intuitive insight, or after a long period of reflection reveals the necessity of an experience, it will usually confirm the rightness of our path and the value of our suffering and hard work.

The perception of a purposeful flow is not meant only for relief after we have struggled. We can also have a continuous interaction with it that adds joy to every moment. With it as a guide, we can play with coincidences and random-seeming happenings that, because of their timing, and content and pattern, form the links that tie people and places together in a remarkable chain of significance. What a treat it is to be able to see things this way.

As we become more sophisticated about linkages, we will see the obvious meaning of events that had previously slipped our notice. These are relationships that we intuitively know are beyond accident or chance. With foresight, we can stockpile these discoveries in memory to use later when others do not become readily clear for whatever reason. This way we can use the concept of the journey to validate every phase of living, no matter how befuddling it may be at the time.

At some point we have to begin to constantly reference our spiritual nature in order to understand that the journey essentially applies to the spirit. While we perceive our experiences in largely physical ways, it is not the person we see in the mirror who has walked the path of our life. The body actually has no control over the process. In a sense, physical life is something that happens to a body, and eventually depletes it and renders it expendable. For all practical purposes, the body is a temporary container for the spiritual being that dwells within, and when the physical container wears out, the spiritual being continues the journey on a non-physical plane. Time tells the story: the infinite is in the finite.

Having become conscious of the fact that we are spiritual beings on a journey through the human dimension, we can view life as a meaningful adventure from beginning to end. Without the concept of a journey, however, there is not much relevance to having a physical existence. We would merely be around for awhile and then we would be gone. There would be no more meaning in making one choice than there would be in making another, except perhaps comfort or convenience. None would have any lasting value, and conscious awareness in life would be pointless. But the linkage we perceive between the events tells us differently.

An interesting feature of a conscious journey is that we begin to recognize that others are on journeys, too, and that what they experience forms a purposeful chain for them just as what we experience forms one for us. This recognition is a joy in itself, especially when others are as aware of the fact as we are, and can communicate it. This adds meaning to our interactions, and it further serves to affirm and reinforce our faith in the reality of our own journeys.

The concept of multiple and varied personal journeys also provides us with a frame of reference for observing the lives of fellow travelers that will help keep us from being critical or judgmental, and will foster compassion. Knowing that all persons we meet are on paths of their own, and that what they experience is necessary to their progression, we will be more inclined to be kind, understanding, and respectful rather than to compare ourselves with them or feel competitive.

Paradoxically, the knowledge that we are walking separate paths leads to our feeling more connected than separated. With time we will notice a sense of kinship and affiliation with our fellow beings that we did not have before we knew them as fellow travelers. We seem different mainly because we are all at different mileposts on the path of healing and growth, but beyond that we are more fundamentally alike than not.

Our sense of connection with others who are presently also on journeys, together with those who have passed before us and will come after us, provides a feeling of continuity over generations and lifetimes that is very reassuring and can deepen our commitment to our work. It is nice to think that we are not now and have never been truly alone in our travels. What we are doing has been done and will continue to be done by others who are essentially trying to do what we are. Someday maybe we will all get together to share.

The journey perspective also affords a rearward view on our life that permits us to see how far we have come. The sense of progression is satisfying, and serves as motivation for further growth. We also like the feeling of mastery that comes with experience. And as is true with all travelers, the more we experience, the more we know what to look for and to avoid, and the better prepared we are to get everything out of the journey that is there to get.

Things Happen for a Reason

The concept of things happening for a reason is so common as to seem cliché. Nevertheless, for a person on a conscious journey, it is true: what happens to us is purposeful. We reasonably assume that on a path of healing and growth, things occur to aid our development, and we therefore tend not to dismiss any events that occur in our own or other people's lives as unimportant. We look for the meaning, or lesson, or value in all of them because doing so is important to accomplishing our purpose in being here.

Although my sense is that there is a connection in everything, some events can still give me pause. Difficulty arises with random-appearing acts of nature, including human nature, such as drought and starvation, war, and unexpected death, things that seem to cause meaningless fear and suffering, and tempt us to ask whether there is a God in the Universe.

As a person attracted to the realm of metaphysics, I like the idea of a connection between events and our paths. But as a psychologist, I also possess an inclination to scientific skepticism. Many of my colleagues would say that because humans want to create order out of chaos, we use our imaginations to see patterns and relationships where there really are none, and to rationalize what happens. Even then, because this is a superficial solution, we still tend to wonder why bad things happen to good people, and good things happen to bad people.

For me, it is not enough to say that we suffer simply because it is God's will, or that the reason for our suffering must remain a mystery. What has really helped is being able to actually see connections in the lives of people with whom I work, as well as in my own. Examples of events supporting our healing and growth are as numerous as they are reassuring.

One example of things happening purposefully is a client I had been helping through her early separation. She got to the point of having an attorney draft a letter to her husband about her intentions to leave, but fearing his reaction, instead of giving it to him right way she carried it with her for several weeks. In the meantime she kept herself busy with separation activities, including going a health club six evenings a week.

One night while leaving the club, she told herself that rather than being out all of the time she should be at home "taking care of business". A few moments later a car spun on the slippery road in front of her, and she hit it and then a concrete bridge abutment, injuring herself slightly and destroying her car.

The car she was driving was an older second car that allowed her to get out so frequently because her other car was a leased vehicle with a mileage limit. As she put it, the accident "clipped her wings," which meant that she would have to be at home nightly to face her husband and her unhappiness. The attorney's letter then became her remaining means of escape, which from a developmental perspective was appropriate.

Two other details about this event became compelling regarding the extent of the emotional separation. One was that when her husband visited her in the emergency room, instead of being overtaken by the emotion of the moment, as we generally are, she asked him to wait in the hall while she dressed. Also, she decided against replacing the car because her husband used it, too, and she did not want to resume that simple association. She would thereafter have only her car, and he would have only his own.

Was her accident purposeful? She certainly believed it was. Circumstances required her to complete an important step in the separation process that she had been avoiding, and it gave her additional information to support her decision.

Another example is a client who struggled with multiple obsessions, including child abduction, murder, and homosexuality. Her impulses had become so insistent and terrifying that she considered suicide rather than face giving in to them, which she feared was imminent. Reassurance from friends and others that these were just fantasies was of no help. A combination of psychotherapy, neurofeedback and medication brought relief, although the obsessions never ceased completely.

What came of this struggle was that she learned deep compassion. In having encountered her own powerlessness for inner control, she began to understand that uncontrollable urges could drive her fellow beings to the abhorrent acts for which they are condemned. She began to comprehend our nature differently, and could henceforth see that God was in everyone. As a result, she arrived at peace regarding issues that continue to plague most of us. She often commented that it took all the horror she had experienced to open her heart to the level of acceptance, understanding and compassion she had attained, and that she was grateful for her difficulty because it had ultimately brought serenity.

A most encouraging example of the possibility that we will at some point be able to see how even the worst of things are purposeful is that of a young woman who was dying of cancer. At one dramatic point on her deathbed she made the statement (to no one in particular) that she understood how her suffering made sense in her life. There was no artifice in this, just the mysterious clarity of vision some achieve as they are dying. I did not know her well enough to judge whether or not this insight was consistent with her usual view. I feel confident that even if she had not been mindful of the journey, her late grasp of the relationship between her disease and her path was meaningful to her spiritual progression.

Becoming conscious of the purpose of life is a process that unfolds through various levels of awareness, and we do not need to know what is happening to benefit from it. Therefore, while still in a rudimentary phase of consciousness, we are healing and growing. It is just that it is easier on us emotionally if we have at least a simple belief that what is happening to us has value, and we do assimilate life lessons more efficiently when we are conscious of the process, which eventually occurs.

Thus, when we are not awake, and it is time to become mindful of how we are using our time, a setback or disappointment may force appropriate change. It is also true that we require multiple lessons in the areas where we have been the most resistant and blind. And they come late in life, too, as with deathbed regrets where people review their life and with deep remorse discover that they have misused it. Apparently, sometimes our lessons have to encompass an entire life in order to get through.

Once we understand that we experience what we do in order to progress, we can have compassion toward others who are suffering without feeling guilty if we seem to have it better than they do, and without thinking we should intervene in their lives. We learn the wisdom of restraint if it appears that natural and needed lessons are occurring that may change a person's thinking or behavior. This does not mean that we will immediately, or even eventually, comprehend the meaning of any particular event for someone else. Sometimes we have to take it on faith that a purpose has been served.

Faith in Abundance

Abundance consciousness means having faith that we will be provided with what we need to sustain healing and growth. For persons on conscious journeys, this spiritual concept embodies every aspect of life, and is a centering thought against frustration and fear when we do not get what we think we should have or when we are afraid that what we have will not last.

The opposite of abundance consciousness is scarcity consciousness, which is the fear that what we need is in limited supply. In my opinion, a belief in scarcity is the foundation of our feelings of insecurity, the root of competition and aggression, and a source of great personal unhappiness. It is also the predominant consciousness on earth. Until we expand our consciousness to acknowledge the spiritual nature of our journey, we will hoard basic material and emotional resources rather than share them, which only adds to the insecurity of the world.

Because life can be hard, achieving abundance consciousness is a challenge. We all have witnessed suffering and death, and without it being specifically discussed, we have been encouraged to consider faith in abundance naïve and dangerous. The problem with this reaction is that true security is a state that emanates from within. This means that to be at peace we have to go to our inner world and transform fear into faith, trusting that our paths will provide what we need, and not over-invest in trying to control the outer world to insure a constant supply of what we want.

To accomplish this, I believe we have to do two things. The first is to accept suffering and physical death as facts that cannot be overcome. We may endeavor to reduce suffering and premature death, of course, but all hope of substantial change in this regard starts with personal change, including the faith that by altering our personal perspective, the world might eventually change, too. If we refuse to accept our physical destiny, or we wait for the world to change before we do, we will never feel secure.

The second is to learn that there is a difference between what we actually need and what we think we need. This is not easy to do. Ego, habit, desire, dependency, and willfulness can make us feel certain that what we crave, grasp at, or are attempting to hold onto is correct for us when it could be the opposite, as I have seen often in myself and many of my clients. The journey makes the differentiation possible. When I look to the past I can see how life has provided the support I needed to be where I am. But what I thought was best and what life offered was not always the same. I know now that much of my suffering resulted from insisting on having my way when my path was urging me in another direction. In the end, when I compare what I wanted with what I got I am humbled, and I often feel apologetic for being ignorant, demanding and impatient.

The stories I most enjoy retelling about abundance involve an apartment I was forced to take, a relationship I wanted to keep that was inappropriate for me, that same apartment that I was later asked to leave, and the eerily accurate predictions of two gifted seers. In the first of them, having left my marital residence, I went to live temporarily in a friend's unsold condo. After about five months it was sold and I had to leave. I encountered slim pickings for another residence that was convenient to my offices, immediately available and inexpensive.

Another friend came through in the eleventh hour with a small, spare, dark apartment in the basement of the house of one of his law clients. I was fortunate to find adequate shelter, but after my house and the comfortable (albeit unfurnished) condo, I felt depressed at how low my fortunes had sunk. Nevertheless, circumstance dictated the move; and while I expressed gratitude to my friend, I was not sure I felt any.

That place became a cocoon for my metamorphosis. It was a true monk's habitat, a spiritual retreat from which a person emerged that I could not imagine myself as having become in any other physical setting. Having little of the material comfort or distraction of my former property and possessions, I was required to go within.

I healed and grew in that apartment's embrace. I read and contemplated, discovered meditation, practiced being alone, and developed an appreciation of simplicity. I began to understand the concept of spiritual abundance, and by losing material things I was in position to gain something of greater value, which was learning the difference between need and want, and wanting fewer things than ever before. I chose to remain in that miraculous little place for as long as I could.

The second story involves what turned out to be a transitional relationship, only I did not want to believe that at the time. During its stormy course, the seers I had happened to consult about my path told me that I needed to let it go, as it had completed its purpose, but that another relationship was coming that would serve my progression well. These were wise and caring people who knew leaving would entail grief, but they could see the abundance in store for me and therefore were frank despite my pain.

One of them confidently described the new person and the relationship in detail, and the other predicted within a week when she would arrive. Thinking these men mistaken and perhaps foolish, I perceived no value in their readings, and I chose initially to believe neither of them. Before long my continued unhappiness convinced me to end the relationship, which I did with much grief.

When the woman who has since become my mate showed up as predicted fifteen months later, looking and acting just as described, I took the meeting seriously. I was not sure initially that she was right for me, but the predictions were on tape and their accuracy could not be denied, and I found it hard not to trust in an event that had obviously been in the offing the whole time. And so I gave the relationship a chance where without spiritual guidance I might have hesitated.

As it turned out, our relationship has been perfect in terms of my path (and hers). I could not be happier or more grateful. I have learned that I could have more than I could even imagine, and I received more than I would have believed was in store; but how well I remember the struggle to let go of what I wanted and trust that I would be provided with what I needed.

What helped my faith in that relationship is something that is part of the third story, which also began with one of those readings. Besides the relationship changes, I was told that I would have to leave the apartment in which I had by then lived for nearly two years, but that I would be attracted to a place that I thought was beautiful, and it would be available. I had no desire to leave my cell, nor at that time was there any indication that I would have to, and therefore I put little stock in that aspect of the reading.

Three months later, my landlady's son asked me to leave the apartment within two weeks because the house was being prepared for immediate sale. I had not anticipated having to move, especially not so abruptly. Remembering the frustration of the previous search for a residence, I was not looking forward to another.

On that very day, as I drove to my office I passed a farm whose beauty I had long admired, and recalling the seer's words, I uncharacteristically turned around in the first driveway, and went back to the farmhouse. I knocked, and when a woman came to the door, I asked if she ever rented space in what appeared to be a carriage house. She said they did, and with a look of puzzled amazement related that their tenant of twelve years had just informed them that he was leaving. She and her husband had not even had time to think of what to do about the news.

I was in the carriage house within two weeks. My only hesitation was the higher rent, but because of the spiritual guidance I had received, I believed I was supposed to be there, and out of my growing sense that I would continue to be provided with what I needed, I agreed to it.

The new apartment was as bright as the former one had been dark. The cocoon had opened, which was just right for my development. I walked the many acres of land daily, stood for hours in the fields getting to know their healing energy, and felt my spirit soar. It was abundance beyond comprehension. My future wife and I first met there five months later. By that time the outcome of the predictions and my experience on the farm, as well as other encounters with abundance, had expanded my abundance consciousness, and having learned not to meddle, I trusted in the meaning of her arrival.

Not everyone wishes to consult seers for guidance. I consider them part of God's abundance, their progenitors being the prophets mentioned frequently in the Bible. The two I consulted helped me understand that what was right for me was waiting for me. They could literally see it and I just needed to have patience and faith. Perhaps I needed tangible proof that good things do not just happen accidentally or randomly, or that I had to be in control and make them happen. The readings and their outcome provided the proof.

It seems to me that there are constant manifestations of abundance in all of life if we can just see it. One of the important mileposts on the journey is when we consciously shift emphasis from material wants to spiritual needs. Qualities like patience, courage, faith, peace and simplicity are what we ultimately want over anything else, and anything that helps us to find them, including personal losses, is a manifestation of spiritual abundance.

When I first heard that God does not take something away without replacing it with something better, I did not think in terms of losing the desire for some object as an improvement over the object of that desire. Of course, it is an improvement. From this perspective, most of us can think of examples of things not going the way we wished or planned only to have found that life provided well for us after all. From a spiritual point of view, perhaps the only way to be certain of what we need is to wait and see what we get, and then work with it rather than doubt or reject it.

Victim Consciousness

Anytime we believe we have been put upon, inconvenienced, or pessimistic we may be under the influence of victim consciousness. It is a way of looking at life negatively if it does not work obviously or immediately to our advantage according to our expectations. It is a predisposition to look first to what is wrong and to continue to feel that way even if things later turn out to be beneficial. The most prominent emotions associated with it are self-righteousness, self-pity, and depression.

Victim consciousness is an outgrowth both of the survival instinct and social conditioning. It is more than a habit; it is a perceptual filter that reviews information about the world in terms of scarcity, threat, competitiveness, and potential loss, and sharpens the bad and dulls the good before letting it through to our conscious minds. It subtly influences us to look for peril at the gate, the wolf at the door, and danger around the corner. It involves feeling trapped and alienated by our experiences; it says that life is not to be completely trusted; it hints that we do not really belong here; and it warns that we will be exploited if we are not careful. It begs the question: If we are at the mercy of caprice and fate, why risk opening our hearts? In its highest form, even God is suspect, which makes healing it a spiritual priority.

Negative comments and complaints are the most readily identifiable expressions of victim consciousness. One example of this is in an old joke I enjoy about two people in a restaurant. As they are eating away one says, "This food is lousy," to which the other replies, "Yes, and the portions are so small." Another example is a prosperous but curmudgeonly friend of mine, who after living his whole life on a beautiful tract of land in a wonderful geographical area, replied to my observations about the bounty, "Life is a constant battle against Mother Nature." A third example is a 96 year-old woman I heard about who, when told the illness she had developed would eventually take her life, said with anger and dismay, "Why me?"

In these stories, real or mythical people have enjoyed Life's bounty but could in all sincerity not see it that way because victim consciousness tainted their view of reality. They saw what they were prepared to see. I know for a fact that my friend was not entirely unaware of his good fortune, but he could not express what was literally right in front of him because it would mean softening himself and trusting that he would not receive some terrible surprise for having done so. Instead of being openly grateful, he continuously looked for disadvantage, and he really expected to find it.

We may wonder or laugh at his and the others' small-mindedness, but maybe we can also see something of their attitude reflected in our own. Every time we complain or make a negative comment or support this in someone else, we should look closely to see what our expressions represent. We may be innocently and unwittingly supporting the view of victim consciousness.

It is important to realize that victim consciousness is more prevalent than we know: it pervades what we read, see, hear, talk and think about. It is in a child's claim that his sibling's cookie is bigger than his own, a neighbor's accusation that the government does not give a damn about the common citizen, and in many other charges we make of advantage-taking, betrayal, or abandonment. Since claims of victimization are at the center of much of our most dramatic human interaction, from lawsuits to war, victim consciousness dominates mass media productions, such as the news, which by highlighting the victim perspective serves to reinforce it.

Most of our expressions of victim consciousness, such as complaints about the weather or a long line at the checkout, are relatively innocuous. The problem is that because they habitually make up part of our everyday thought and conversation, without our knowing it they help maintain a negative frame of reference toward life. Then, when things are not in our favor, what seemed harmless can explode with blinding speed.   We all know of instances where something of relative unimportance has overtaken good sense and self-control, such as when frustrated sports fans become destructive mobs, and road rage imperils drivers in traffic.

When we are in a victim mode, we constantly look for confirmation that our fear and hostility are warranted, and with persistence we will find it. In this way a victim-perspective can become a self-fulfilling, self-reinforcing cycle, and can serve as a foundation for withdrawing disgustedly or suspiciously from others or for striking back at them.

In a society in which victim consciousness prevails, all relationships, whether with people or the environment, have a me-against-you, us-versus-them basis, with the sides changing according to circumstance. Naturally, our side is always good, which means that the other side, whoever they might be, is automatically bad. Because of our incessant fear that we will be left out of our rightful share of whatever is being contested, we feel justified in being antagonistic, competitive and aggressive.

The essential rivalry is not for some lofty prize, but for the right to feel damaged or threatened by the other. The highest achievement of all is to be able to claim the title of underdog, as this entitles us to retribution and compensation, and justifies remaining skeptical and defensive about goodness. Furthermore, from this position we can feel morally superior even if we never accomplish anything else. Thus, we may actually prefer to believe that life is against us, our motto being bad things are bound to happen.

Ongoing conflict is needed to maintain a victim perspective; the sense of struggle has to be perpetual. Therefore, real peace will create disharmony, and healing and growth will threaten stability. This is truly a no-win situation; in fact, we have to lose because if we win at all, we will have to quickly reframe ourselves again as victims or risk feeling disoriented. We may say we want security and serenity, but very few of us stay with it when it arrives. In order to remain sufficiently guarded when no real threats exist, we manufacture them. These can be imagined scenes of victimization that generate internal dialogue and visceral reactions just like the real thing. They can also be stimulated through identifying with someone or something that we read or hear about, which is why talk shows that take moral and political positions are so popular. When times are good, the shows create or exaggerate conflict and give us an opportunity to feel threatened by people who are not like us, so that we can continuously align, hone and fine tune our negative filters. When times are bad, they let us know who is to blame.

Love is always conditional in victim consciousness; it has to be because we constantly fear that we may be taken advantage of. It is hard to let people be who they naturally are and not want them to change according to our standards or to be just like us. We are, therefore, in danger of trying to manage relationships rather than just comfortably relax into them. Affection, affirmation, and good will might be given and withdrawn according to whether or not we feel sided with, and rejection can result from nothing more serious than someone's not supporting our opinions.

With victim consciousness, we are likely to find more reasons to exclude people from intimacy than to include them. Contentment, compatibility and companionship are always at risk in this state. This makes it vital to avoid conflict even if disagreement is warranted, to admit failings and guilt whether appropriate or not, to attempt to make up right away without processing things, and to unconditionally promise to never again do whatever was offensive.

Because it is such an integral part of normal everyday life, healing victim consciousness requires mindfulness and disciplined effort. Even though I work with it daily in clients' lives, when at odd times it pops up in my life, I am always surprised by its seductive power.   It seems instinctively and unerringly to target my desire to pull away.   And although I have become skilled at seeing it for what it is, I have to work hard not to give in to its inducement.

Having models to emulate helps not only identify it, but to show an alternative.   I have mentioned the former Amish client, who would not cave in to victim thinking regardless of her circumstances.   I also know a remarkable woman who chose not to feel victimized and condemn her best friend for having an affair with her husband, and they have remained friends. I speak daily with people whose lives are hard, whose feelings have been hurt, and for whom the temptation to feel victimized is strong, but who take a more spiritual course.

It is important to understand that we are not talking about passivity or fatalism, but about a way of actively perceiving opportunity, freedom of choice, gratitude, peace and joy.   All of these people are good to themselves and loving toward others.   They deal openly, honestly and responsibly with their circumstances.   They are courageous and straightforward, experienced and sophisticated, and nobody's fool.

Christians and non-Christians can look to Jesus as an example of non-victim thinking.   He was a teacher and healer who was loathed and feared by some followers and religious leaders who could not tolerate his message about love.   He would not validate most people's perception of themselves as victims of Rome, and instead of leading a civil rebellion as was demanded of him, he took a non-interventionist, spiritual posture and told his followers to love their captors and to pay their taxes.   He sought a fundamental change in consciousness and he was subsequently prosecuted as a criminal.

Here we have no better example of victimization if we want to see it that way.   But I think Jesus would have been the last person to label himself a victim. He did not complain or defend himself as most of us might, but remained silent. While dying, he asked that his persecutors be forgiven because he knew that it was their victim consciousness that made them afraid of him and blind to his healing message, and that if they had known better, they never would have behaved as they did. He is revered to this day for having done so.

I suggest an approach to healing that encourages change by increment. First, we need to shift from pessimism to optimism. This has to be a deliberate, rational, conscious decision because we might not discover how pessimistic we are unless we act on the possibility, and there is not much normal reinforcement in the beginning to do so. We can set the stage for this work each morning in bed by saying several times how much we look forward to the day. Whether we actually do is immaterial; it is the positive effect on our outlook that we are after. Having done this, we can change ambivalence about getting out of bed into enthusiasm for the whole day, and eventually for life. We can repeat this ritual at anytime, and should.

It is a good idea to stop watching television news and listening to radio news broadcasts, and to avoid other media such as newspapers and newsmagazines because of their negative content. This is especially important in the morning because it influences our mood and outlook. At night, the news provides the emotional material we take into our slumber and an important part of what we process in our unconscious mind until morning. So, we start and end the day with bad news and heightened victim awareness.

Intuition dictates, and psychological studies have confirmed, that the news causes readers and viewers to believe that the world is more dangerous that it actually is. We are bound as a result to suspect that we will be victimized. We experience fear even without confronting any danger. Our imaginations can make us vicarious victims of acts or accidents that have little or no chance of ever occurring in the average life.

Next, I suggest simply just paying attention to any victim inclinations that arise, such as are usually revealed by our complaints or other reactions to real or imagined wrongs. This will familiarize us with them without reinforcing them or sending them back into hiding in unconsciousness. If we just sit with them, we will decrease their power and we will be less likely to react automatically to them in the future. When they are strong, it helps to repeat over-and-over that we are not victims, especially when everything in us wishes to debate the point. These repetitions create a non-victim association with our usual victim impulses.

Giving in to victim thinking validates it. If we do act-out, we should apologize immediately to whomever we may have hurt (including us) and resolve to do better. No self-punishment is warranted; feelings have to surface to be healed, and in the process they sometimes just get the upper hand. It is thrilling to note when we no longer react as we used to under identical circumstances.

When we are composed we can look for what we might learn from an experience. If it is not immediately seen, we can work from the assumption that information eventually will come, and then wait for its arrival. One tip is that usually there is a pattern to the expressions of victimization and the lessons, as we tend to feel victimized more in one area of life, relationships for example, than another.

What can make this difficult is cycling in and out of control when we are dealing with our victim feelings. We may float between being clear of the value of an experience at one moment and feelings of anger or resentment about it in the next moment. The seesawing can go on for hours and days. The conflict results from our spiritual-human dynamics, where spiritual consciousness is threatening to take an ascendant role over our more human tendencies. We may have clarity from the spiritual perspective and then lose it when the human perspective cycles through. But because we are on a path of progression, all we have to do is remain steadfast and our negative thinking will eventually yield.

Further, I suggest instituting a practice of always being grateful for what we have. Saying thanks has a cumulative effect on our optimism: it helps us feel good and reverses victim thinking. We have good reason to forgive ourselves for our errors in the time prior to knowing what we now know, and to feel compassion for others who are not aware of this alternative. No one actually chooses to be there, and no one would wish to remain once experiencing the peace that healing can bring.

Taking Responsibility

Transformation requires that we take responsibility for our feelings and actions. This is not simply a matter of being conventionally moral or virtuous, and it has nothing to do with the concepts of taking blame, being honest with others about what we have done, or being willing to accept our punishment. It is a high level learning that liberates us from much of the limitation of unconscious living by recognizing a fundamental truth, which is that our feelings and actions are centered within, and that we are the only ones who really have control over them. What is so important about this is that it is only when we locate the center of our reactions within us that we have any hope of healing them and moving beyond them. Once we realize that no one else can really make us do or to feel anything, we can begin to take charge of ourselves in a new way, and to manage our energy consciously rather than have it at the mercy of untold influences. This takes commitment and mindfulness, because our inclination is to place the responsibility for what we do not like in ourselves outside of us. But this is our energy that we are trying to get rid of, and we want to have as much of that available to us as possible. Therefore, we need to transform it, not dismiss it.

Looking inside as the source of our feelings and actions is also a path to peace and happiness. This is for two reasons. One is that we have such little practical control over what goes on around us. It is hard to predict what others might do, or what the environmental conditions are going to be, so by not relying on them for our happiness, we are less likely to be disappointed and frustrated when they prove naturally changeable.

Even good people will do things that we do not like, and they can thereby easily let us down if they do not meet our expectations. The economy and the weather are essentially unpredictable, so that if our happiness depends on how our investments are doing, or if the ball game gets played, we have a problem. The fact is that most of the universe functions outside of our awareness, direction and control, which is reason enough to go inside rather than outside for satisfaction.

The other reason is that peace and happiness have to do more with how we personally interpret and regard what happens than with what actually happens. This is why two people can ostensibly experience the same event and have such different reactions. For example, one of us might feel liberated by winning a fortune because we believe it will simplify life, while another may see it as complicating rather than simplifying life, and therefore never even play a lottery game.

Peace and happiness are lived from the inside out, which means that if they do not begin within, they do not occur at all. The occasional sense of them that happens when interpersonal and environmental conditions meet our desires is not the real thing, regardless of what we have been led to believe. Once we have gone within and found them, we forever know the difference, and we add to them by no longer hoping people or conditions will meet our needs, or trying to manipulate them to do so.

Until we do learn to take responsibility in a way that is supportive of our growth, life will not allow things outside of us to be so predictable and manageable that we orient ourselves there rather than within. We might never go within to do the work of learning to control ourselves if we did not have to. And even when we had a streak of luck in predicting the world outside, we would not like ourselves as much as we do when we become effective managers of our own emotional resources. As we advance, we prefer inner control to that of controlling others or the conditions around us. It is the only way not to feel that we are free of external forces.

Not blaming others or events for our reactions is one of the hallmarks of the individual who is on a conscious path of personal growth. This is not to say that while on this path we will not find others or conditions frustrating or irritating. We are not saints yet. And we are not to suppress or distort how we feel. We simply endeavor to no longer react impulsively or automatically, and to transform and channel the energy of our emotional reactions into thoughtful responses that resolve problems without disturbing peace and happiness. We always feel better when we do.

The Dark Side

Whether we admit it or not, there exists in all of us the markings of the dark side of the human spirit. The trolls, ogres, witches, antiheroes and villains of every myth, fairy tale and bad dream have their presence there. Most of these dark archetypes, images and figures remain locked away in the recesses of the unconscious and surface only occasionally in nightmares and the works of artists, poets and novelists. The mass of the nastiness remains below.

On occasion, a monster does materialize, usually as an infamous criminal who terrifies us with sensational crimes, a demonic leader who rules a bizarre cult, or a charismatic political figure who manipulates the minds and fortunes of his countrymen. These people terrorize us with their evil, and we hate them and want them dealt with harshly.

However, we also find them interesting. And while we may never actually identify with them because we know the trouble they wreak, we have to admit being fascinated with them in a way that really focuses our attention. Some of the worst of them catch our notice much beyond their less interesting moral betters, and they are more likely to become the subjects of the television dramas, movies and magazine articles that entertain us, and to live in memory than the others are.

Human monsters do not even have to exist to become important figures. Since they reside within, we need only access the darkness of our imaginations to erect their frightening presence. And since they are also in a similar place in the imaginings of others, we can share them through stories and conversation in a way that makes fascinated others feel just as afraid as we do. It is natural for us to do so, as our horror literature attests.

However, usually when we sense an upsurge of dark impulses in ourselves, we worry. Anxiety states are often linked to the possibility of unacceptable thoughts and desires taking form out of the disorder of our primal instincts. Even the hint that some of these impulses exist within alarms us, and we fear loss of reasonable control if they come out. Only the defenses of repression and denial keep us from having to recognize that we have a dark side to our personalities, even if we might be pretty certain that others do.

This shadow side of our self contains all of the thoughts, feelings and behaviors that we have learned or intuitively sensed are unacceptable in right living. At the same time, it also contains energy that is essential to healthy living, but that is unavailable to us through normal channels because the internal prohibition against its expression is so great that we cannot access it. What is worse, because we sense that all of that energy is of the destructive kind, we have to expend other creative energy to keep that energy locked away. We have an energy force constantly pushing down against one constantly pushing up. This is not an efficient use of the energy involved.

A condition of our healing and our development is that we be consciously aware of this primal resource, and that we tap its energy and release it for use in our waking state in amounts that are manageable. This is essential for a couple of reasons.

One reason has simply to do with our need to be aware of everything we can that might affect our feelings and behavior. Knowing what is inside helps us to understand some of what might be driving us, and allows us to take responsibility for our reactions rather than placing the blame outside of us where we have no control. Being aware of this place can also help when we feel puzzled because we do not know where the motivation for a reaction is coming from. We can look inside for an explanation because we are not afraid of what we might find there.

Another reason has to do with our being liberated from unhelpful restrictions on parts our personality that are not permitted expression because we erroneously believe that they are bad. Thus, if we believe that being selfish is bad, selfishness remains part of our shadow, which means that we may be impaired in taking proper care of ourselves because we fear that any attention to self is wrong. So, for example, if we had an overly self-centered parent, we may have decided never to be like him or her in any way; or if we were punished for not sharing, we might not know the proper balance of giving and keeping to ourselves.

In either case, without healthy selfishness as a counterweight, our caring, nurturing, protective energy may be spent on others with no fair exchange for us. We have learned to give to others but not to give to us. This is usually all unconscious, which means that our giving is not volitional, and therefore not healthy, and also that we do not see the problem for what it is. There is nothing holy about such giving; it is only saintly if we also know how not to give if we do not want to, and how to take as we have given.

This overdone self-effacement and self-denial leads to lopsided relationships in which we find ourselves taken advantage of and our love taken for granted, while perhaps refusing to admit to anyone that this is true. We may dislike the unfairness, but be so fearful of saying anything that we tolerate the conditions. Our fear is not necessarily of the reactions of others, although when we choose selfish mates, there is the threat that they will leave if we are not as giving as they require. Our fear may be of our own internal discomfort with the expression of our shadow selves. We sense that being open about our feelings would admit our scary selfish impulses to consciousness, and we do not want to have to face that monster. Therefore, we would rather chastise ourselves for being selfish and leave it at that.

Many of us know this self-sacrificial scene from our own relationships or the relationships of people close to us. The whole co-dependency literature is based on this kind of dysfunctional imbalance. Healing requires that we become familiar with our shadow self and allow it appropriate expression. We fear its power, but its power is what will affirm our right to good care and free us for healthy relationship functioning. We have to be careful not to overcorrect, because then we can become the persons we fear. But our increasing self-awareness, healthy sensitivity, and desire to be decent will serve as a correction, and we will eventually find a tenable middle ground. We just need to do a little experimenting.

This is all also true of the energy of anger. If out of fear we suppress it, it will find expression either in indirect ways, such as teasing, pouting, or purposefully inefficient passive-aggressive behavior, or not at all. We may be overly compliant and tolerant for fear of either doing harm to another or having it done to us in retribution, or we may just deny we have any angry feelings at all. In any event, we are left without he option of sharing our upset about something we do not like. Problems in our relationships then cannot be appropriately addressed.

In this case our job is not to become angry people, but to uncover and channel some of this energy into more balanced relationship behavior, such as speaking our minds. We cannot be healthy mates unless we can be honest about our feelings. Love and courage both are of the heart. We have to love from strength not weakness, otherwise what passes for love may be tainted with resentment or diluted with fear.

There are as many types of this hidden energy as there are of the obvious kind. This is because things are balanced in the universe, but also because all it takes for something to qualify for repression is that it is unacceptable to someone in power over us, so that it is buried instead of allowed into the light. Since what is or is not acceptable is at least somewhat relative, it is possible that what is right for one person is wrong for another, which means that one person's shadow could be another person's social identity. The possibilities greatly depend on what we learn from our families and cultures while under their influence.

Thus, it is possible that what many of us are absolutely certain is good behavior might be viewed as foolish elsewhere. In the world of the psychopath, kindness and compassion may be the most repressed energy because being loving is perceived as threatening to its possessor and it has to be locked away. Whole cultures differ on what is let through and what remains in shadow.

Most of the time we are not plagued by dark impulses. Our culture provides outlets for much of them through things like football rivalries, action movies, mystery and romance novels, and organized sports. This allows us to vent them without having to think about what is happening. However, this unconscious process of feeling expression is no more effective than venting in dreams if we hope to be different. Transforming this energy means becoming increasingly conscious of our feelings and motives, which requires direct observation and conscious self-expression.

Fundamental healing requires that we become familiar with what is in shadow. This means acknowledging that certain dark impulses reside within us, and accepting them as a part of us. We watch our reactions rather than playing them out or shunning them; we can just observe them quietly, without acting in one way or another, and see what happens. Usually this lessens their intensity because the pressure of having to keep them completely in the dark is relieved through conscious awareness. Afterward, they are more controllable and less fearsome. They are just impulses, after all.

When we are troubled by our impulses, such as through dreams or obsessions, we might want to discuss them with a therapist or trusted other in whose care we can look at them without fear. What we do not want to do anymore is simply judge them as bad and useless, and suppress them. Shadow is healed by light. We want to open our cellars and closets to the light as a part of transforming the energy that is there.

Healing also requires that we acknowledge darkness on a larger scale that we cannot personally control. If we know it is out in the world, and we can still be at peace within, we fashion a more conscious and healthy participation in our world. Some of this darkness is of a human variety, such as child abuse, street gangs, or repressive governments, and unjustifiable wars. Some is of the natural variety, such as killer tropical storms, epidemics, or earthquakes. These are those things that make us wonder if there is a God in heaven, or what life and we are coming to. In all of them we have to deal with horror of an impersonal kind.

We do not have to like what we see, but we do need to acknowledge it. Too little familiarity with the darker side of the world makes us naïve, weaker than we need to be, frightened, and at the mercy of occasional natural disasters and the darkness of some of the people whom we encounter. Without a balance of light and dark within us, we may feel hopelessness and despair about what we see outside.

We neither want to obsess nor repress. Locked doors, storm cellars, health insurance and savings accounts have their proper place, but if we are too fearful, we will obsess about them rather than having any balancing faith or trust. We cannot control what others or Nature do, but we can accept the unchangeable as real, and work on keeping it in balance in our perceptions of its actual effect on our personal lives.

Deep healing also includes acknowledging that what we fear or despise in others probably is somewhere within us, too, which we have learned from observing our choice of entertainment and our fascination with dark characters. We are not monsters because of what resides deep within all of us. We are all more fundamentally similar than different. Just as we hope to heal ourselves through an admission and acceptance of what is within us, we heal the world better by admitting and accepting what is there rather than denying, judging or rejecting it. It is all potentially useful. By knowing the worst of them we may also get to know the best of ourselves.

Like us, the world is both light and dark. If we can see that there is a dynamic interplay between these energies within us, we might extrapolate this to the larger world of which we are part and find a connection between it and us where before now we had feared looking for one. We are at our best when we can be fully conscious and peacefully accepting of what is unchangeable in our world. Our learning to live profitably with the truth of shadow and light is part of our mission here.

Honoring the Mystery

The supreme irony of our times may be that we have been forced by the accomplishments of our advanced science and technology to admit that we know no more about the essential nature of reality than we did hundreds of years ago. In times past, when there was no science to explain most of the phenomena that were encountered, people just had to accept the mystery of life as the province of the Unknown. They had no choice in the matter, and although they may not have been any happier than we are with the thought that some things just are, there was nothing to be done about it.

But ours has become an age in which we assume that we will eventually have explanations and information about everything. With our progress in looking far into space and deep into the structure of matter, we seem eminently capable of explaining phenomena that had previously been inaccessible to understanding. We might therefore feel fully justified in our belief that with sufficient time we will piece together all of the puzzles of life.

With the apparent gains we have made in unraveling many aspects of the unknown, it is difficult to accept that there is any part of the mystery of the universe that will not be ultimately revealed, or that will be allowed to remain in some unsullied place. But the fact is that the farther out or the deeper in we go, the more we see that in life there is always something vaster or tinier than we could have ever imagined. In a sense we have been peeling an onion that has an infinite number of layers. Answers are revealed and new secrets arise to take their place in a never-ending cycle.

It may be that our worst limitation in the process of scientific discovery is not in failing to have uncovered all of the answers to the secrets of life, but that we have not had sufficient imagination to see that we never will. If we continue to believe that it is our destiny to comprehend all of the mystery, then we will be driven to keep trying.

The rapid progress we have made in being able to observe and measure all sorts of natural phenomena will inspire efforts that can only lead to frustration, as some things will always be unmeasurable. Perhaps then we will begin to look for other ways of knowing that do not rely on always finding answers through objective means.

In a positive sense, the compulsion to know has lead to the development of many things that have been helpful to living longer and more comfortable lives, such as medicines and surgical procedures. It has also been a means by which we have exercised and expanded our intellectual capabilities, which has value whether or not the exercise actually achieves anything material. But without our acknowledging that there is something above conventional knowing, and that the most significant part of life is beyond our rational grasp, we will remain ignorant about our spiritual roots and distant from our essential selves.

As well intentioned as it might be, the perspective that we can find everything we need to know through scientific exploration can hinder our journey of healing and growth if it influences us to think that life is less than it is. If we believe that it is just a matter of time before we know how everything began and how it all works, we will have no need for an inner life, as that is where we go to address the great mysteries that surround us.

This would be a great loss since it is our inner life that makes us unique, and that provides us with a pathway to the creative source of our being. This sense of connection is not something that comes rationally through our minds, but irrationally through our hearts. What would also be a shame is to lose our sense of being part of something that is much greater than we are that we attempt to encompass with our limited science, rather than allowing ourselves to be encompassed by it in its infinite incomprehensibility.

Rather than viewing life as something to be dissected and catalogued, we might want to also consider it as something to be honored in its integrity as we study it. This perspective invites a sense of relationship based on appreciation and respect, while the other encourages a sense of separation and clinical coldness. Life is our benefactor, after all. We gain nothing examining it as a separate entity. We benefit by feeling connected as gracious parent and grateful child.

Since life is in us and we are in life, the attitude we carry about it has a bearing at a very profound level on how we feel about ourselves. In simple terms, since life and we are inseparable, our image of it and our self-image are inextricably tied together. The more we honor life, the more we honor us. The greater we believe its expanse, the better our chance to grasp the sense of the infinite within. Without an unconditional form of love for life, our love of self is diminished to a lamentable degree.

At some point in our healing journey we will have to make a conscious decision as to whether we are part of a grand mystery, or are outsiders to it. The choice we make will have a bearing on our perception of what our place in life is and will continue to be. If we understand that it is how we choose to look at life that largely defines our experience with it, from a healing and growth perspective we will want to choose to look at life in the most positive way.

If we decide to reject the possibility that there is more to life than can ever meet the conventional scientific eye, we will place a severe limit on what we can ever know about ourselves as spiritual beings. By thinking of life as completely comprehensible from a rational point of view, we effectively close the door on self-study and learning of the highest kind that comes from a non-cognitive, non-linear inner exploration that employs the heart method rather than the scientific method.

To conclude that we are less than we actually are would be too bad, as there is so much to experience when we open ourselves to the non-material, non-human dimensions of our spiritual selves. Instead of knowing life in only a physical sense, we have the potential to commune with its deeper non-physical dimensions, and to be enveloped by the indescribable sense of hope and joy that awaits us as we connect with something beyond ourselves.

And that something is surely there. It is only our fear of the incomprehensible and the restriction on imagination that that fear creates, which block our opening to it.

Unity

The more enlightened of our fellow travelers are able to see that everything in life is related and fits together perfectly. Where most of us perceive boundaries, such as between black and white, hot and cold, beautiful and ugly, and good and evil, some special and unusual souls see only continuity and unity. To them, there are no degrees of valuation from one thing to another. Nothing is better or worse than anything else is. Nothing is out of place. Nothing needs to be changed. Everything is just as it should be. No corrections, alterations, or enhancements of any kind are needed to make the world a superior place to the way it is now.

What these advanced souls do so well is completely and non-judgmentally accept things just as they are. This includes the things that horrify us, and the people who we think the world would be better without. Unlike the rest, individuals with unity consciousness are at one with the whole of life, and as a result they are at peace.

That people have the capacity for complete and unqualified acceptance of everything is almost beyond belief. Most of us share fear and revulsion toward certain aspects of life that do not seem to favor us, and we would like to see them change. It is regarding our need for guarantees of safety that the main difference between enlightened persons and us is most clear, and where they can teach us an important lesson about achieving real peace.

Where we react out of fear, ignorance and limitation, they calmly accept with appreciation, compassion and unconditional love. Where we reject what is obviously a common part of the human experience because we do not like it, they concede its place and absorb it as knowledge that is as valuable as any other in life.

The common experiences with which most of us share a nearly consensual aversion are such things as sickness, poverty, war, natural disasters, chronic unhappiness, and in the end, death. In our effort to make life tolerable, we have done about all that is humanly possible to change all of these things to one degree or another. Failing that, as a means of coping many of us for at least short periods have tried to deny their existence.

Even worse, when people have suffered, we may have attempted to blame them for their own troubles when what happened to them might happen to anyone, which frightens us. When disaster arrives, we would like to believe that there is someone to blame, or that people somehow brought disaster on themselves, as this is preferable to thinking that such disaster could befall us, too.

What usually accompanies the appearance of anything unwanted is our immediate reaction to try to avoid or get rid of it. We may demand or beg for relief, and we are often frustrated and angry when it does not come. We might hold God ultimately responsible, and when things are bad enough, we may wonder what kind of God would allow such things to happen. At that point we effectively disengage from hope and faith, we become isolated and adrift on our journey, and we feel separated from a sense of connection with the creative source. We want nothing to do with whatever would allow what has happened.

But that is in the past. Cursing our fate is not an option on a journey of healing and growth. As our conscious awareness has increased, we have become desirous of staying with what comes and trying to see it differently. Where once we might have quit adapting and despaired, we now attempt to discover what everything means and how it is connected to everything else. We are after a perspective that can bring solace and relief when problems threaten our peace.

An excellent resource at the point in our journey when we no longer follow the old course but are not settled on the new one, are persons who are at peace about conditions like ours when we are not. The grand image of these individuals is the master on a mountain peak being sought by a spiritual pilgrim for his wisdom. In truth, this image is not too different from what we seek. When trouble lays siege to our souls, we look for enlightened guides who we hope will be able to explain the meaning of it all. Many of these tend to be the sages, saints, mystics and other guides who are honored and appreciated for the lives they have lived, and the discoveries they have made and have shared in their writings.

What attracts us most to these persons is their calm acceptance of whatever enters their lives. Even if we are not quite ready to believe what they say because it seems too positive, healing has begun by our allowing the possibility of an alternative to the approaches we have used. Transformation begins with seeing things differently, and if we sense that what has worked for them just might work for us, we are on our way. In this case what has worked is their understanding that everything is as it should be.

Until we become masterful ourselves, we have to accept on faith that everything in creation has its place and its function, including the dark things. With enough motivation, and hard work, and grace, we will see that this is so. The unshakable certainty of unity among all things belongs to a select few who have done incredible work at complete openness to all possibility. For awhile we will struggle with the concept, much less the confidence that it is so. We will need to hear it over-and-over again, and to have our own experiences that reinforce the knowledge.

As a part of our daily practice of discovery, we can expand our unity consciousness by looking for its manifestation in ordinary things. We might, for example, note how all of the work that needs to be done in a society is accomplished. The different job interests and talents among its citizenry combine to make that happen.

Thus, somehow we possess abilities others do not, and we do work they would not want to do, and vice versa. In the process, we all merge our talents and efforts to take care of everyone. There appears to be no grand design in our culture to make this happen. We all just follow our natural inclinations, and without being aware of it, everyone works in unity to produce the goods and services that we need and want.

It seems logical that somewhere behind this astonishing model of social unity there is a model of which the human one is a reflection. There has to be an absolute that expresses the unity of all creation, this unconscious cooperation among human beings being only one of them.

We can also observe unity everyday in Nature. A hawk kills and devours a field mouse, which helps the natural balance by keeping the mouse population down, makes the mouse population healthier, as there are fewer of them to compete for food, and allows the hawks to survive and reproduce, too. Or a bird eats and digests a berry, excretes the seeds, which germinate and reproduce the plant with its berries.

On a grand scale, this kind of interconnectedness insures the continuation of all the other species besides those involved in the examples. For this mutually beneficial hawk-mouse, bird-berry relationship to happen there has to be a model of unity of which they are a reflection.

Other examples abound. We know that energy changes form while never actually being destroyed. Things become other things, and events relate to other events, in an ever-expanding circle of mutual influence. Thus, the stuff of ancient stars is found within us, and what is in us will be released and be found in others. All of creation has affected our creation, and our creation has to affect everything else. There is no end to the unity. Everything is related to everything else.

Of course, such examples as these cannot supply us with a complete sense of universal order. But they can be a start from which we can develop the unity concept. We can look at them as models to which we can add other examples, creating not only a reassuring chain of evidence, but also the habit of looking for connections. Eventually this will allow us to let go of the need to know and control because we will accept that it all works together in a beneficial way without our having to make it so.

The key at this point in our progression is to mimic the practice of the enlightened ones, which means to observe without reacting or making a judgment about anything, and to look for connections. Ideally this includes everything, even those things that we would normally make a judgment about in a routine way, especially things that puzzle us and make us afraid. Our habitual way of reacting is one that tends to separate events and relate them mainly to us.

Therefore, we need to try to think and say nothing for awhile, and to displace reaction with calmness. We can do this deliberately on a park bench or in our cars as we drive down the street. We are to look and not judge. The more we practice quiet non-reaction, the better the chance of gradually perceiving that what exists has equal value with everything else that exists, that everything is related, and that all of it is necessary.

This practice will help us accept that things and people are just where they need to be. We can extrapolate from the small things to big things as we go along. This is not easy work as we naturally like to discriminate, but we can do it. As we endeavor to grasp unity in small, everyday matters, we assure our eventual comprehension of unity at the level of the profound. It all works together

Practicing Peacefulness

It is fair to say that attaining inner peace is the purpose of being in life. The desire for peace has been the motivation for our change from our previous way of looking at things to how we perceive them now. Becoming peaceful is the culmination of all of our work of healing and growth. The more peaceful we are, the more appreciative we are of life and the better we can love others and ourselves.

It is probably true that, had we been at peace in our marriages, we probably would have remained in them; and if we had been completely at peace with ourselves, we might not have been in those marriages in the first place. If we have entered new relationships without having learned to be peaceful, we have other relationship changes ahead of us. If we do not yet cherish inner peace above all other achievements in life, we will not attract relationships with peaceful others, which means the hard work will continue.

We get the level of peace in relationships that reflects our own. In other words, we get what we have earned through our hard work, and what we are capable of sharing and reciprocating. This is as it should be. It is an arrangement that will motivate us to improve. If we want it with someone else, we have to have it within.

Stacked against us is the historical evidence that peacefulness is the most difficult state to reach and to maintain. This is true on an international as well as a personal level. Nations struggle to find peace and so do we. But this bleak situation fits well with our concept of what makes something precious. In our world that which is most desirable is also hardest to find. Peace, then, is a rare gem. On our journey its discovery is both our greatest challenge and our highest goal.

We obviously do not live in a peaceful world, and it is unusual to meet a truly peaceful person. In these lie the problem and the solution. The world is not peaceful because its inhabitants are not peaceful. Therefore, our best hope for world peace is to first be peaceful ourselves. This is the only way it works. In fact, if we are not peaceful within, it will not matter that there is peacefulness around us because we will not appreciate it.

Instead of practicing inner peacefulness, what most of us do is avoid even the preliminary and prerequisite states that would encourage it. In truth, we are mostly unaware of what being at peace actually means, as many of us have had only a rudimentary experience with it, and we do not know an effective way to go about finding more. The cause of this is ignorance and fear.

Our work is to ultimately experience peace and the goodness it holds. Our need for peace together with our growing tired of the unpeaceful way we have lived will encourage us to finally choose to do what is necessary to have it. As with any significant change for the better, we usually have to get to a place where what we were doing is no longer tolerable before we get started. All of us will eventually start because it is in our nature to want peace, and once we have been touched by it to any degree, we will seek more. Therefore, our first order of business is to reorder our lives so that it may touch us, which will in turn make us more likely to pursue and find it.

The first step in an effective reordering is to practice mindfulness, which we already understand as paying attention. Our job is to focus our attention on our inner state and to connect this with the conditions that affect it. We need to recognize the helpful or harmful effects of our style of participation in the world immediately around us if we are going to change that pattern.

The conventional view of peace is that it is the absence of strife. This means that to achieve it we have to focus more on external conditions, and try to control them to keep conflict down, while adjusting our behavior to help make that happen. But since from a transformational perspective peace means feeling at one with our minds, hearts, souls, and bodies and then with everything around us, we have to shift our attention to what we experience within ourselves in relation to our outer lives, and to change the internal first. We then will work to modify our environments to reflect the internal rather than the reverse.

This means constantly monitoring our physical and emotional responses to events and people, and calming our responses according to our inner standards of peaceful living, but not changing our responses to accommodate someone's requirements in order to get along, or trying to force them to accommodate ours. The latter is the basis of conventional relationships, and why the emotion in them is referred to as drama. It is not the authentic feelings of peaceful people, but the manufactured and manipulated stuff of people struggling to adjust to each other's demands in a mutually dependent relationship. When we are centered within this does not happen because we always go to ourselves to find peace rather than to the other person.

The second step supports the first. It involves removing distraction so that we can pay attention to the inner us without undue interference or intrusion. This means trading stimulation and excitement for tranquillity and repose. Peaceful people prefer silence to noise, placidity to activity, and harmony to conflict. Therefore, we have to deliberately filter the tumult of the environment, or remove ourselves from it, in order to do the work of becoming peaceful within. This means deliberately and voluntarily restricting external stimulation in all of its forms.

This step has to emerge as a fundamental daily practice. This is necessary because peacefulness is not a static state, and so it requires that we learn to filter distraction continuously. Like everything else in Creation, the feeling of peace has a natural rhythm and flow, and therefore it is more accurate to say that we constantly practice being peaceful than it is that we remain constantly in peace. Thus, we have to continuously monitor the forces that compete for our attention, and that intrude on the state of peace we wish to experience.

These steps address our ignorance of how we might begin the path to peaceful living by helping us break the habit of excitement seeking and chronic over-stimulation. Next we have to address our fear of entering a state of peace, as it is fear, above all else, that keeps us from relaxing in a way that would foster peacefulness.

It is part of our animal heritage that we remain vigilant against danger. We can see this vigilance in birds at our feeders, or rabbits and squirrels eating on the lawn, as they constantly scan the environment for predators. Our animal brains are programmed to do the same thing, and if there are no real dangers about, we will imagine them. The evening news and frightening movies help keep us alert if the immediate environment does not.

Until they get used to the feeling, our brains interpret peacefulness as vulnerability, which is why they will send out an alarm when we first attempt to practice a withdrawal from stimulation. We can panic merely from experimenting with being quiet and still. This is why once having removed external stimulation we discover that the disruption continues within. We find thoughts, feelings and images that present us with an internal version of the noisiness, hyperactivity and disharmony that were outside. We escape one level of distraction only to encounter another. Our brains need to believe that it is safe to relax, which can only come from the experience of actually letting down our guard and finding that nothing bad happens.

We might believe that our typical leisure activities promote our letting down our guard, but they are usually filled with activity and noise. We can only provide the corrective experience that our brains require by further and further reductions in levels of stimulation until we arrive at a place of quiet stillness. If we doubt that we use stimulating activity to avoid the fear of letting down our guard, all we have to do is try a period of true silent inactivity to encounter the truth. The quieter we are, the greater our feeling of uneasiness.

The fact is that we unconsciously misuse many leisure opportunities to reassure our vigilant brains that we are safe. The presence of stereos, televisions, books and other entertainment see to this. We are so conditioned to their presence that we do not realize the ongoing contribution they make to our problem. A daily practice of being quiet and still will break this pattern, as it slowly introduces peacefulness in non-threatening increments.

A fine-tuning of this practice involves not reacting to stimulation of any kind, including that which we would normally think of as harmless, and perhaps even helpful, to feeling peaceful. Examples of this are our reactions to sunrises and sunsets, spectacular autumn scenes, rainbows, fireflies, or deer appearing on a trail we are walking. We are not trying to filter out beauty and joy, but are practicing a peaceful response to everything, including things and events that we normally seek to make us feel good. What we want is to not allow the one experience to affect us more than another because we judge it as more important, wonderful or beautiful. We want to feel content from within and not be reliant on external experiences to generate it.

This practice was describes previously, and it has application now. The ideal is to find all things the same, and to enjoy life with equanimity in all circumstances. This is serenity, and such a state is not beyond our ability at all. If we do not do it perfectly, we can accomplish an approximation that will bring a sense of deep joy and enthusiasm that is superior to what usually passes as happiness. We seek to be happy to just be.

This does not mean that we are not to enjoy things of natural or human-made beauty. They are gifts placed here for our use. We are merely considering a model from which to work at achieving inner calm that we can apply to life in interesting ways.

Everyone needs a break from too much quiet and to much stillness also, and the great variety of natural and other recreations provide this. We are just looking for a middle road. We will find with time that we prefer being quietly in nature to other forms of entertainment, and that we will not need to go looking for recreation as frequently as we did.

It is important to keep in mind that our culture does not support becoming peaceful in the way we need, so we have to be additionally concerned with developing settings that promote becoming quiet and still, and not allowing ourselves to be seduced into conventional ways of finding it.

Our internal nature will work against us, too, if we do not know how to settle our hyperactive brain and central nervous system. Because we secrete adrenaline when stimulated, especially by things that make us afraid, we frequently go from chronic vigilance to flight-or-fight activity as this hormone initiates a protective reaction. Then we settle back to vigilance, awaiting another round of excitement. This becomes habitual, or worse, addicting, so that we actually crave it, and miss it if it has not been initiated for awhile. This vicious cycle obviously does not promote rest.

We can counter this cycle and change our activation level by introducing therapeutic breath work in our lives. This breathing style is called diaphragmatic breathing or belly breathing because inhalation causes an expansion in our abdomen when it is done properly. We want no movement in our chests when we inhale; we want it all below the rib cage, which can monitored by placing one hand above the solar plexus and one hand below it. The lower hand should elevate with an in-drawn breath, and the upper hand should remain still. When we exhale, we need to let the whole body relax as if it were a rag doll or slowly melting wax. This is to be repeated until we can notice where the expansion is without using our hands as monitors. Then we are to pay attention to it as often as we remember.

As simple as this might sound, it can be frustrating work because most of us breathe incorrectly with no awareness that this is the case. Our normal breathing involves the upper portion of our lungs and chest when we inhale. As we attempt to change, we may notice that our body seems to fight us, that we feel awkward and uncoordinated, and that we even feel lightheaded. This is all the more apparent if we have been under stress.

Sleeping pets and children will show us how it is naturally done. Their normal breathing is natural. Our normal breathing is unnatural. We are constantly over-stimulated, our shallow breathing is a result, and our inability to relax completely is the effect.

The good news in this is that a simple correction in breathing can dramatically change our lives. There is nothing more important that we can learn than this technique. It is central to all relaxation and meditation practices, to yoga and La Maze, and is essential to becoming peaceful. It will quiet and reassure our brains by providing an appropriate balance between carbon dioxide and oxygen, keeping the sympathetic nervous system from coming on-line to deal with what it perceives as an emergency.

This breath work should be practiced frequently and consciously so that it becomes our normal way of breathing. We can be mindful of it as we walk, drive, sit quietly, or any other time. It should also be consciously applied as first aid when we are beginning to get upset, so as to settle the feelings before they get a foothold. With time, less deliberation is required, although truly peaceful people use awareness of breathing as a sort of metronome to pace them in life.

A bonus for breathing this way is that it tends to have a calming effect on those around us, too. Others may unconsciously imitate what we are doing. This is one of the primary ways our individual practice spreads peace. In effect, we not only breathe for ourselves; we breathe for the world.

A complementary practice is that of paying attention to our feet against the ground. We do this best by going outside barefoot, if possible, and focusing on the interface between the soles of our feet and the ground. Like conscious breathing, this is a little harder than it sounds because we typically never think about our actual physical connection with the Earth. We may at first not even feel the sensation. Certainly as we try to pay attention, we will find that we are distracted. Our brains do not want the peace that this simple procedure can bring.

Make no mistake, this practice actually does ground us in an energy sense, and lends the peace and stability of the Earth to our personal energy field. This is not a metaphor but a reality. The Earth has a low frequency to its energy, which is similar to that in which we meditate. Because of its immense mass, its energy field is incredibly powerful, and our energy fields respond to its energy field by alignment and imitation, and she slows us down. This is one of the reasons peace practitioners spend so much time in Nature. There is a natural affinity between the Earth and us. She is our mother, after all. As we become adept at feeling our feet against the ground we will be able to consciously promote peace within. It is an illuminating experience.

What further insures inner peace is the decision to place being peaceful above our other interests. This allows us not to have to think about what our first response should be in any circumstance. It will always be the same: to remain peaceful. This includes anything that excites or stimulates us in any way. Instead of reacting as we used to, we can draw an abdominal breath, deliberately calm ourselves, and then respond from that peaceful place.

If we perceive everything as essentially the same, there is no need to respond differently to one than another, and there is absolutely no reason to become unstable or unsteady. Again, this is an ideal, but we use it as a model and achieve reasonable approximations of it that will change us forever. It starts with always centering our breathing and practicing being calm at all times.

What naturally follows from this practice of becoming quiet and still, and finding our true relationship with the Earth is our awareness of the eventuality of death. It becomes quite apparent that this is the ultimate fear from which we have sought distraction. When we become peaceful, we will think about death with a degree of clarity that was not possible before. There is no avoiding this, but in time we will not wish to avoid it any longer. As we come to peace, we embrace death; and as we embrace death, we come to peace.

It is no coincidence that the foremost practitioners of the conscious path of peace work deliberately at being at peace with death. It is viewed as one more expression of our being. With peace comes an awareness of our spiritual nature, and death is a part of the journey of our spiritual selves, just as life is. Of all of the separation experiences we face, death is the most frightening. Until we can embrace the possibility of no longer being in our bodies, we will never be at peace while we are still in them.

It is also no coincidence that a culture that denies death is also one that promotes noise and activity over quiet and stillness. Since the latter are prerequisites to finding peace, and finding peace promotes the awareness of death, we disallow them as an means of keeping mortality distant from our thoughts.

In our quiet moments, thoughts of death will come forward, and over time will become increasingly real. This is necessary. We invite the reality of death long before actually dying both as a way of preparing for it, and as a way of becoming familiar with its presence so that it is less frightening.

This is where we begin to discover a hidden gift from our marital separations as we chose the path of healing and growth. By having approached that tremendous change with love, compassion, courage and faith, we have lived through a death to find that life not only goes on but it improves. We are the beneficiaries of the gift of certainty that we are in an unending process of being, with nothing to fear about the future. We are here for a reason.

With our gift of knowledge we can conclude that all separations are beginnings as well as endings, and that the essence of life never really ends it just changes. We are indeed on a journey and when the end of this particular expression of it comes, there will undoubtedly be another. We have been provided with everything that we need to make this journey worthwhile, and if we continue to walk in faith we will always be on the high road, and we will be at peace.

Reflections

Sit quietly, breathe slowly, and relax your mind.

Silently read the following:

- My life is a journey. Each day is a paving stone on a worthwhile path. I will look for the meaning, lesson and value in all of my experiences.

- I am in continuous movement. I came from somewhere and am going somewhere. Feeling stuck is merely a misperception.

- I am beginning to recognize that everyone is on a journey similar to mine. This knowledge encourages feelings of empathy, compassion and camaraderie.

- I choose gratitude over pessimism and scarcity thinking. I will look for the manifestations of abundance in all of life.

- It is important to differentiate between what I really need and what I think I need. I am aware that I have been provided with everything that I need to make this journey worthwhile.

- Everything in life is related and fits together perfectly, including the dark things. I will learn to observe without judging.

- Peace and happiness come from within. I will look for them there.

- Inner peace will be the reward for my hard work on the journey of healing and growth. I choose the peaceful path.

Repeat what you have just read, concentrating on what is really new to you so that it begins to become familiar.

Write all of the phrases down with great attention to them.

Say them aloud, and repeat.

Imagine a life of peace and abundance for yourself. Let your thoughts run wild. Rather than dreading how far you might have to go, think about how far you have already come. Take this affirmation with you as you continue your travels.

Printed in the United States
821800001B